P9-CMX-641

"Describes the impact of childhood loss with painful accuracy . . . a wise guide for coping with loss and asserting a powerful will to live."
—Jill Ker Conway, author of
The Road to Coorain and *True North*

"A wonderful book which will be very helpful because it is intellectually sound as well as warm and caring."
—Eda LeShan, author of
Learning to Say Goodbye: When a Parent Dies

"Maxine Harris sensitively recounts the deeply moving individual life stories of adults who suffered a parental bereavement during childhood. Their accounts will be a comfort to the many who share their fate and will widen the horizons of feeling and understanding for those who relegate death to the infinite future."
—Erna Furman, author of
A Child's Parent Dies

"A 39-year-old woman remembers feeling embarrassed when her father died 31 years ago. She thinks she is alone in this experience. This book will help her know she is not. Dr. Harris provides the reader with moving stories of people with whom they can relate, identify, and connect."
—Lois Akner, C.S.W., author of
How to Survive the Loss of a Parent

MAXINE HARRIS, Ph.D., is a clinical psychologist and the codirector and cofounder of Community Connections, a full-service community mental health agency in Washington, D.C.

Also by Maxine Harris

Sisters of the Shadow
Down from the Pedestal
Women of the Asylum (with Jeffrey Geller)

THE LOSS THAT IS FOREVER

The Lifelong Impact of the Early
Death of a Mother or Father

MAXINE HARRIS, PH.D.

A PLUME BOOK

PLUME
Published by the Penguin Group
Penguin Group (USA) Inc., 375 Hudson Street, New York, New York 10014, U.S.A.
Penguin Group (Canada), 90 Eglinton Avenue East, Suite 700, Toronto,
Ontario, Canada M4P 2Y3 (a division of Pearson Penguin Canada Inc.)
Penguin Books Ltd., 80 Strand, London WC2R 0RL, England
Penguin Ireland, 25 St. Stephen's Green, Dublin 2, Ireland (a division of Penguin Books Ltd.)
Penguin Group (Australia), 250 Camberwell Road, Camberwell,
Victoria 3124, Australia (a division of Pearson Australia Group Pty. Ltd.)
Penguin Books India Pvt. Ltd., 11 Community Centre, Panchsheel Park,
New Delhi – 110 017, India
Penguin Group (NZ), 67 Apollo Drive, Rosedale, North Shore 0632, New Zealand
(a division of Pearson New Zealand Ltd.)
Penguin Books (South Africa) (Pty.) Ltd., 24 Sturdee Avenue, Rosebank, Johannesburg
2196, South Africa

Penguin Books Ltd., Registered Offices: 80 Strand, London WC2R 0RL, England

Published by Plume, a member of Penguin Group (USA) Inc. Previously published in a
Dutton edition.

First Plume Printing, September 1996
30 29 28 27 26 25 24 23 22 21 20

Copyright © Maxine Harris, 1995
All rights reserved

Excerpts from "Self Portrait 1" and "Self Portrait 2" by Tove Ditlevsen. © Gyldendalske
Boghandel. Nordisk Forlag A/S, 1969. Reprinted by permission.

Excerpts from numbers 101 and 310 from *The Dream Songs* by John Berryman. Copyright
© 1969 by John Berryman. Reprinted by permission of Farrar, Straus & Giroux, Inc.

Ⓟ REGISTERED TRADEMARK—MARCA REGISTRADA

The Library of Congress has catalogued the Dutton edition as follows:

Harris, Maxine
    The loss that is forever: the lifelong impact of the early death of a mother
or father / Maxine Harris.
        p.   cm.
    Includes bibliographical references.
    ISBN 0-525-93869-9 (hc.)
    ISBN 978-0-452-27268-2 (pbk.)
    1. Maternal deprivation.   2. Maternal deprivation—Case studies.
3. Paternal deprivation.   4. Paternal deprivation—Case studies.   5. Death—
Psychological aspects.   6. Bereavement in children.   7. Parent and child.
I. Title.
BF723.M53H37   1995
155.9'37'085—dc20
                                                                    95–10336
                                                                    CIP

Printed in the United States of America
Original hardcover design by Leonard Telesca

Without limiting the rights under copyright reserved above, no part of this publication may
be reproduced, stored in or introduced into a retrieval system, or transmitted, in any form,
or by any means (electronic, mechanical, photocopying, recording, or otherwise), without
the prior written permission of both the copyright owner and the above publisher of this
book.

PUBLISHER'S NOTE
The scanning, uploading, and distribution of this book via the Internet or via any other
means without the permission of the publisher is illegal and punishable by law. Please purchase
only authorized electronic editions, and do not participate in or encourage electronic
piracy of copyrighted materials. Your support of the author's rights is appreciated.

BOOKS ARE AVAILABLE AT QUANTITY DISCOUNTS WHEN USED TO PROMOTE PRODUCTS OR SERVICES. FOR
INFORMATION PLEASE WRITE TO PREMIUM MARKETING DIVISION, PENGUIN GROUP (USA) INC., 375 HUDSON
STREET, NEW YORK, NEW YORK 10014.

*For my mother, Sara Harris, and
for my husband, Mark Smith, and
for the fathers they lost so long ago.*

*For my father, Bernard Harris, and
for Alex Adams, a young mother
whose early death left behind two small children.*

Acknowledgments

This book could not have been written without the sixty-six men and women who gave their time and shared their stories with me. They were my inspiration throughout this project, and I hope they are pleased with the result.

My agent and friend Leslie Breed has supported and nurtured this project for several years now, and I thank her for her continued encouragement. Deb Brody, my editor at Dutton, has been both helpful and enthusiastic.

Helen Bergman helped with the references, and Sybil Trader and Laura Farrah carefully transcribed the interview tapes and typed the manuscript.

My family and friends gave me love and support throughout the project. My husband, Mark Smith, deserves more than just a thank-you. This book is as much his as it is mine. He was there with his experience, his ideas, and his support from beginning to end. He lovingly and carefully edited the manuscript and helped me write the best book I could.

Contents

The Stories

Preface

FIVE YEARS AGO, IF SOMEONE had asked me to make a list of all the topics I might want to research for a possible book, the early death of a mother or father would not have made the top ten. I did not set out to write this book; in many ways this book chose me.

In the summer of 1991, I was interviewing women about their lives for what would eventually become a previous book of mine, *Down from the Pedestal: Moving Beyond Idealized Images of Womanhood*. The seventy women with whom I spoke shared many common experiences and many similar perceptions about the forces that had helped to shape their lives. Despite the unifying life themes that were shared by these women from diverse backgrounds and varied circumstances, one life event emerged in the stories of a small group of women that seemed so powerful as to overshadow all other events and to dominate the story itself. These women told of the death, occurring while they were still children, of a mother or father. The death, whether it was sudden or came at the end of a long illness, divided childhood into a clear "before and after." All subsequent development, all further happinesses or disappointments, began with the reality of death and loss, a reality that always seemed to be there no matter how much time had passed.

Since I was writing a book about female development and

not about early loss, I took these powerful and moving stories and stored them somewhere at the back of my mind, not quite sure that I would ever be able to find a way to make them public. I continued to believe that "loss" was not something I would ever write about.

Then I received a call from a young woman who had been my student years before. She was a charming and bright woman who by anyone's account had it all: a loving husband, two healthy children, a successful career, classic good looks, and a trust fund that freed her from financial worries for the rest of her life. Yet on the phone she sounded frightened. She wanted to see me; she needed to talk. She had found a lump in her breast and was going for a biopsy. Over the next fifteen months I listened to her fears and her hopes, her anger and her bargains with God, her eventual acceptance, and her overwhelming weariness. Throughout her ordeal and her dying she had only one concern: her children—a young son and an infant daughter. She ached and wept as she thought of their growing up without a mother. She loved her life and she did not want to die, she adored her husband and did not want to leave him, but it was for her children that she begged God to let her live just a little longer.

As I sat in the church and listened to the minister eulogize a loving mother and a devoted wife, I could not take my eyes from her four-year-old son: a boy, dressed like a man, for an occasion he did not understand, but one that would change the terms of his life forever. He may not have known it then, but he had just been struck by a lightning bolt. As I left the church, I felt desperate to make some sense of this untimely and tragic loss. Her death would become my mission; if she could face death, I could certainly face thinking and writing about the trauma of early loss.

Once I decided to write *The Loss That Is Forever,* I could allow myself to acknowledge that I had lived in the shadow of early loss my entire life. My mother lost her father when she was six. His death, a sudden event from which she has probably never recovered, changed her life then and shaped who she became. I always knew that parents could die young; I had only to think of the faceless grandfather who was known by his absence. Throughout my childhood, I was forever calculating how many years of parenting I would need before I would be old enough to survive on my own and then pleading with God to let my parents live long enough to launch me into adulthood safely.

As a grown woman, my childhood fears seem quite far away, yet I have not escaped the reach of early loss. My husband of almost twenty years lost his father when he was only three. My husband almost never mentions his father; he barely knew the man who gave him life. Yet, his father's death was probably the single event that determined who he has become, what he fears, and what he treasures. My husband is a wonderful man, and I know that some of what I love most about him grew not from his strengths but from his vulnerabilities—vulnerabilities that were etched deep when his father died.

Some events are so big and so powerful that they cannot help but change everything they touch. When we think about change, we often ask ourselves whether the change was for the good or for the bad. Politicians ask us every election day, "Are you better off now than you were four years ago?" And when we fail to reach some longed-for goal, we often rationalize that it was "for the best." Change without judgment is something we find hard to make sense of. Yet the change in a child's life following the death of a parent is the change that "just is." A girl who lost her father learns how to be independent and self-reliant—Is that good or bad? Another girl develops compassion for people in pain and in need—Is that good or bad? A boy becomes more cautious in his relationships, waiting before he commits himself—Is that good or bad? Early loss sets a child on a particular path, and like all roads it has detours and potholes and smooth patches. It is the road that will lead that child to become a certain man or a particular woman. Would another road have been better? Who knows. All we can say is that it would have been different.

When a tree is struck by lightning, if it survives, its growth is altered. A knot may form where the lightning hit. The growth on one side of the tree may be more vigorous than on another side. The shape of the tree may change. An interesting twist or a curious split has replaced what might have otherwise been a straight line. The tree flourishes; it bears fruit, provides shade, becomes a home to birds and squirrels. It is not the same tree it would have been if there had not been a lightning storm; some say it is more interesting this way; few can even remember the event that changed its shape forever.

Just over 5 percent of children under the age of eighteen grow to adulthood needing to make sense of profound loss. They are the survivors of the early death of a mother or father. Most, because men tend to die young at higher rates than women, have lost fathers. A tragic few have lost both parents.

Despite the greater prevalence of father loss, more has been written about the impact of losing a mother. Mother loss seems more tragic, or so we imagine. Fairy-tale characters from Bambi and Babar to Cinderella and Snow White are all survivors of the early death of a mother. The recent bestseller *Motherless Daughters* tells the moving stories of scores of women who grew up without the guidance and secure love of a mother.

Yet, what about all the men and women who longed for a loving father, a strong protector, a trusted mentor? Disney's *The Lion King* tells the story of young Simba, who witnesses the violent death of his father and must grow up with only a few fleeting memories of his powerful father to guide him. One does not need a modern fairy tale, or the groundbreaking work of the women's movement, or the rallying cry of the men's movement, to tell us how important fathers are. One only has to listen to the stories of those who lost fathers to know how important they are and how much their loss hurts.

When a child loses a parent—a father or a mother—that child grows up feeling different and alone. A story is written in a secret place in that child's mind—a story of loss and pain and the triumph over that pain. Because there is no place to share that story, it remains intensely private, hidden sometimes even from the child. *The Loss That Is Forever* recounts the stories of sixty-six men and women who had the desire and the courage to share their stories of loss and its lifelong legacy.

The Sample

Sixty-six men and women—thirty men and thirty-six women—were each interviewed for up to three hours. All of the interviewees were self-selected and responded to an open letter that described the project and invited interested men and women to call for an interview. While this was in no way a scientific sampling, some attempt was made to balance the number of men and women. The interviewees resided in one of six large urban areas at the time of the interview. As is often the case with people who settle in big cities, many had migrated from smaller towns and rural settings.

Twenty-five of those interviewed had lost mothers, while forty-one had experienced the death of a father. The age at which the interviewees had been orphaned varied from a few months to almost 18 years of age: 24 were from 0 to 5 years, 22 from 6 to 12 years, and 20 from 13 to 18 years. At the time of the interview, the sample ranged in age from 24 to 66 years. I was most interested in men and women who had reached early midlife or beyond, since it was the lifelong impact of early loss that I wanted to understand.

Eighty percent of the sample were of European American descent, with 20 percent being of African, Caribbean, or Asian American origins. Of this latter group, 80 percent were African American. Fifteen percent of the sample were gay or lesbian.

One hundred percent of those interviewed had taken at least one college course. However, even of those who completed college, many did so by stretching their college careers over many years, often combining college with some work experience. At the time of the interview, 55 percent were either married or living in a relationship of at least one year's duration. Forty-five percent currently had children, although many more intended to become parents.

In recounting the demographics of the men and women I interviewed, I do not pretend to wrap my work in the garb of scientific sampling. Rather, I would like the reader—as much as is possible without compromising confidentiality—to know who these men and women are. So often, when we listen to a story, we must be able to feel that that story speaks directly to us, is about someone like us, before we can really hear what the story has to say. It is my hope that every reader can find a kindred spirit among the many stories presented here.

The stories are presented using pseudonyms to protect the privacy of the interviewees. At times, identifying details have been altered. All of the material is from the sixty-six people who consented to be interviewed, even when, in a short vignette, the speaker is referred to in the third person as "one man" or "one woman."

The Interview

All of the interviews were audiotaped. They took place either at my home or office, in the interviewee's home or office, or, when I was interviewing out of town, in a hotel room. The site and time of the interview were selected to accommodate the interviewee's schedule and level of comfort. The interview was a modified clinical interview that was loosely structured chronologically. In general, I let people tell their stories, asking questions and providing direction where appropriate.

People came to the interviews with mixed expectations. Some were looking for answers; they wanted me to help make sense of feelings and reactions that they usually did not feel free to share. Others came armed with a box of tissues, ready for a good cry. Many came hoping to help someone else; despite what I told them about my own goals for the book, they imagined that I was working with some newly orphaned boy or girl who would be helped by what they had to tell me. Only a few began the interview by telling me that the death of a parent had really not affected their lives, but they would be glad to do the interview in order to help me.

All of the people I interviewed found the interview moving and meaningful. Some jokingly called it free therapy, others just felt that telling the story was something they needed to do periodically. Most people cried: some were surprised by the depth of the feelings they still had for a parent who had been dead for so long.

As a clinical psychologist and a writer, I spend my professional life listening as other people tell their stories. I have been told, and I have come to believe, that I am a good interviewer. People feel safe and comfortable telling me their stories. But no experience I have had, in over twenty years as a psychologist and therapist, can compare to doing the interviews for this book. I often felt that people were letting me enter a space so personal and so sacred that I should lower my voice to a whisper. Many times I cried as people spoke of their loss; there are some stories I still cannot tell without crying. My tears were rarely tears of sadness; most of the time I cried in awe of the incredible strength and courage I heard described.

Each person came to me with only one story; by the time I completed the interviews I had sixty-six stories, sixty-six journeys through tragedy and loss to resolution and in some cases even triumph. The stories seeped into my core, I dreamed about them, thought about them at the oddest times. Not only the interviewees, but the phantoms of lost parents became my mental companions. At one point, I felt so drawn into the stories I was retelling that I feared I would die while writing this book. One night I had a dream. I was sitting at my desk, thinking, and an idea for a new book occurred to me. I became excited and animated. The dream became a swirl of creative activity as I grabbed books from the shelves and began making notes. I kept thinking, This is such a good idea, I have to remember it when I wake up. When I awoke I was relieved. I took the dream as a sign that my life was not over. The dream meant I could think about death, feel the pain of accumulated loss, and still live. In the dream I was committing myself to new ideas, to creativity, to life. I did not have to be swept away by the awesome power of death.

Eventually, I came to see my dream as a metaphor for the healing that so many survivors of early loss must undergo. At some point, one makes a commitment to life, to love, to creativity, to joy, and to continued personal growth. To live does not mean that we forget the dead. It does mean that we embrace life and move forward. I hope this book will help survivors on that journey.

PART I

~

In the Beginning

CHAPTER 1

~

The Language of Loss

IMAGINE FOR A MOMENT THAT you are able to gather all the people you know in one large meeting hall. Assembled are not only family, friends, and loved ones, but all the different people who help your world to run smoothly—your dentist, the mail carrier, the mechanic who services your car—your whole world of connections and relationships. Now imagine that in a single flash one half of the people fall dead, lost forever. You are so overwhelmed by the magnitude of the loss that you cannot even begin to absorb what it means. In your panic, you focus on some minor detail—who will drive you to work tomorrow—ignoring the fact that your son and your best friend now lie dead at your side.

Now imagine that you and two friends are embarking on a trek up the side of an unexplored mountain. You have as your guide a seasoned climber, someone who knows the mountain well and, as importantly, someone who understands what it means to embark on such an adventure. You are nervous, yet exhilarated; you and your companions feel secure because your guide understands the technical aspects of the mission as well as sensing more personally what it means for each of you to undertake this climb. Now imagine that as you round a bend in a particularly confusing part of the ascent, the guide disappears. You and your companions look at one another. There is no one to lead you, no one to help you complete this most difficult and arduous climb. You feel yourself gripped by a feeling of complete terror and aloneness.

With these two examples, we begin to enter the emotional space of a child whose world has been ripped apart—a child whose parent has just died.

When an adult encounters death for the first time, he or she is someone able to care for him- or herself; someone who knows who he or she is at the core; someone with friends, colleagues, loved ones; someone capable of surviving. When death enters the world of a child, the story is quite different. A child is unable to sustain him- or herself alone. A child is not yet clear as to who he or she is. A child is totally dependent on family first and only peripherally on friends and schoolmates. A child is incapable of surviving alone.

At no time in our lives as adults do we experience such total dependency on another person as we did in childhood. As adults we may love deeply, completely, and passionately, but we love as separate and independent people. We may feel bereft and empty when someone we care deeply about dies, but we know that we will survive. Our own existence is not completely bound to the life and existence of another.

Virginia Woolf, in talking about her mother, who died when Woolf was thirteen, says, "Certainly there she was, in the very centre of that great Cathedral space which was childhood; there she was from the very first"[1] ... "the creator of that crowded merry world which spun so gaily in the centre of my childhood."[2] Woolf is not talking here about someone she merely loves. She is talking about someone who is at the very center of her own being; someone whose existence makes possible all that she knows and everything on which she depends.

We make a fundamental error when we liken the experience of loss known by a child whose parent dies to the experience of loss felt by an adult. The concepts and the very language of adult loss are inadequate to capture the panic, pain, terror, and confusion of a grieving child.

As adults, we generally assume that we have the narrative tools both to explain how we feel to others and to make personal sense of life's many experiences. As our vocabularies grow, we have not only the words but also the explanatory concepts to help us make meaning out of what would otherwise seem to be random events. We share only a limited number of scripts or stories that we use to understand our world. When we leave home to find our own way, we recognize the text of the heroic quest just as the romantic plot guides us through our first love affair. When we face loss, death, or failure, we have the text of tragedy to help us make sense of our sorrow and despair. Without these shared stories, these structures for understanding, we would find ourselves both literally and psychologically "at a loss for words."

When children experience the death of a mother or father, they are in every sense "at a loss for words." If they are young enough, they literally have no words to help them understand what has happened. Even if they have the vocabulary to talk about their loss, the flood of feelings, likened by one woman to a tidal wave, is powerful enough to overwhelm any conceptual abilities that do exist. Most important, children have no story, no organizing text, with which to process their loss. Abraham Lincoln, whose mother died when he was nine, wrote that sorrow comes "with bitterest agony" to the young because it "takes them unawares."[3] A child does not have the language to begin to make sense of a parent's death.

In modern history, adults who survived the devastation of the Holocaust or the annihilation of the bombings of Hiroshima and Nagasaki had the rare and unwelcomed opportunity to live through horrors that were beyond words. Survivors literally had no way to understand what had happened because the events were so beyond our language's ability to describe, much less explain, them. Here were adults, faced with realities for which they had no words, no concepts, and no stories, adults who felt as helpless as children to make sense of the catastrophes that had changed their lives forever.[4]

In searching for a word to name what English-speaking people call the Holocaust, French intellectuals chose instead the Hebrew word *Shoah,* which means "catastrophe."[5] A catastrophe is a great and sudden calamity, a violent and abrupt change.[6] Adult survivors of the early death of a parent use just such language to describe their loss. The event is known by its enormity; nothing in the child's life remains untouched; the *catastrophe is absolute*. A child must make his or her way in a changed world after catastrophe occurs. The new world order is marked by *total discontinuity* with what went before. Everything feels different even though certain external realities—house, school, playmates—may look the same. While a child may have been naively unaware of all the comforts and supports that lent a sense of security to childhood, he or she is all too aware of the *terrifying insecurity* that marks life after the catastrophe of early death intrudes. If a loved and needed parent can disappear forever, then nothing is safe, predictable, or secure anymore. Beyond the immediacy of their personal loss, bereaved children must now make their way in a world itself marked by *profound emptiness*. The loss felt inside seeps out and engulfs everything.

When adults recall the early and premature death of a parent, they may or may not recall a last good-bye, the smell of illness, a funeral, or a period of mourning. What they do recall are feelings born in the wake of catastrophe—feelings of total discontinuity, terrifying insecurity, and profound emptiness. These feelings often find their way into images, images of war, disaster, destruction, and desolation; and those images form the rudimentary language of early loss.

Absolute Catastrophe

Catastrophe occurs when the world as we know it and understand it ceases to exist. Robert Lifton suggests that the atomic bombings in Japan during World War II left survivors with an overwhelming encounter with death. The natural order of life had been replaced by an unnatural order of "death-dominated life."[7] The Nagasaki and Hiroshima of prewar Japan ceased to exist as physical and social entities. No aspect of life was untouched by the devastation.

Virginia Woolf had known, even as a child, that her mother was not only the center of her own world but the hub of family life as well. The world as Woolf knew it ceased with her mother's death. She recalled many years later, "For after that day

[May 5, 1895] there was nothing left of it. I leant out the nursery window the morning she died. It was about six, I suppose. I saw Dr. Seton walk away up the street with his head bent and his hands clasped behind his back. I saw the pigeons floating and settling. I got a feeling of calm, sadness, and finality. It was a beautiful blue spring morning, and very still. That brings back the feeling that everything had come to an end."[8]

One woman whose father died when she was seventeen describes a similar feeling as she was being told of her father's death in the hospital emergency room: "I think we all felt we would not be able to overcome it. I remember feeling like the world had ended. In the emergency room I was sitting at this desk. It was like a school desk with a little chair. I just sat there and put my head down on the desk, and I thought, 'I will never get over this. I don't even know how I am going to get out of this chair.' " At the moment of catastrophe, this woman experienced her world as being shattered and she herself felt like a small child who could barely control her own movements, let alone comprehend the enormity of the event that had just occurred.

Catastrophe is a fundamental assault on the order of our lives. Daily routine is disrupted, the rules governing how we live and behave are violated, our beliefs about the world are attacked. The orderly progress of our lives is forever disrupted when absolute catastrophe occurs.

One woman recorded the sense of a world upside down with one simple recollection: "We ate cake for breakfast instead of cereal and we were allowed to play Monopoly all day." In a child's world, these are powerful markers that order and routine are gone. Another woman whose father died when she was five remembers sitting, like a war refugee, in her abandoned house on the day of her father's funeral: "I remember the funeral day because it was just incredibly quiet. I remember the silence the most. It was very, very quiet. I was home alone with my aunt, and I remember a big basket of fruit sitting on the dining room table and me sitting alone on the floor under the table." One senses the emotional numbness of a lost and bewildered little girl, huddling for comfort underneath the dining room table, as acceptable behavior is suspended in the wake of death.

For those who live in a country ravaged by war, catastrophe disrupts the normal order of life in obvious ways. The rules for how to behave, what is safe, and who is to be trusted are totally altered. Journalistic reports from cities in the throes of fighting often depict people running helter-skelter. Confusion permeates the normal routine of city life. Instead of going about their business in an orderly fashion, people are consumed by a frenzied madness in which the normal order no longer exists.

In addition to daily routine and ordinary rules of behavior, fundamental world order is shattered when a parent dies young. A child no longer believes that the world is a safe place. Principles of fairness, predictability, and reliability are toppled, and chaos now governs the unfolding of life events. In his memoirs, writer Alexandre Dumas, whose father died when he was only four, recounts his own reactions following his father's death. First, Dumas wanted to know where his father was and who had killed his father. When a relative told him that his father was in heaven with God and that it was God's will, the child became angry at God. No longer believing God to be a benevolent protector, he grabbed a gun that had belonged to his father and ran into the attic of his house, trying to get to the sky so that he could kill God for having taken his father away.[9] In that moment and in that act a young boy's sense of the world order altered dramatically.

Given that the catastrophe of a parent's early death disrupts a child's world in every imaginable way, it is not surprising that people use images of physical devastation to describe it. Natural disasters such as storms, floods, and hurricanes, and human disasters such as wars, bombings, and mass murders are common images of psychic catastrophe.

From the moment that catastrophe happens, a child's world actually looks different. That difference is often experienced as a profound change in the atmosphere. A dark cloud descends on what had been a normal and happy family life. Of her mother, Virginia Woolf said, "her death was the greatest disaster that could happen; it was as though on some brilliant day of spring the racing clouds of a sudden stood still, grew dark, and masked themselves; the wind flagged, and all creatures on the earth moaned or wandered seeking aimlessly."[10] Woolf's loss not only affected her and her immediate family, but it was as if the entire world had altered. A dark storm cloud had descended on her reality and had changed the way the entire world now appeared.

Toward the end of her life, Charlotte Brontë, who lost her own mother in girlhood, wrote a novel about a woman who was the sole survivor of a shipwreck in which everyone she knew and loved had died. An angry sea had battered the ship, leaving behind devastation and desolation.

For some people, the experience of having one's world shattered by early death is remembered in the imagery of war and holocaust. One woman who was five years old when her mother died recounts feeling as if she herself were the sole survivor of a community that had been wiped out by a terrible battle. This woman was not told that her mother had died. She was merely told that her mother was going on a trip from which she would never return.

The young girl, an only child, was then sent to live with six different relatives over the next six months, a different home for each month of her bereavement. At the end of six months' time, she was reunited with her father, who had also inexplicably disappeared. Her father returned, bringing with him a new wife, a strange woman whom the little girl was instructed to call mother. Her own mother was never mentioned, and within a short time, relatives from her mother's side of the family, shocked and upset by her father's quick remarriage, also disappeared. The world continued to shrink, as not only her mother, but her cousins, aunts, and uncles as well were all eliminated from her life. By the time she was nine years old, she could not even remember the name of the woman she had once called mother. "I had nothing consistent in my life. I wasn't in school. I didn't have my own home or my own room. I didn't have a brother or a sister. There was literally nothing to carry me along that was the same. The world as I knew it had ceased to exist. Part of the horror was that I couldn't make any sense of it." It was as if a bomb had fallen on her world and she was the only survivor. There was no one to share the horror of her loss, no one to help her hold on to her memories of the past. After a while she came to doubt those very memories. "I know this sounds ridiculous, but it was as if there was a conspiracy to blot out my mother and my relationship to her." Conspiracy, treachery, and devastation are the language of war; they are also the images held by some survivors of early loss.

For one man whose father died when he was fifteen, the Holocaust has become the standard against which all other tragedies are measured. When friends tell him about problems they are having at work or difficulties with lovers, he thinks to himself, Well, it isn't as bad as the Holocaust. As an adult he has often wondered why the Holocaust has such a strong reference for him, since no one in his own family was touched by its devastation. It has become a very personal image, an image of total loss and total catastrophe against which all other events must now be judged, an image that resonates with his own experience of the premature death of his father.

Total Discontinuity

> The world became eternally
> divided into a before
> and after.
> I was five years old
> since then everything
> has changed. [11]
>
> —*Tove Ditlevsen*
> (Danish poet who lost both
> parents in childhood)

Most people who suffered an early loss remember the day the world changed. Personal time became marked in terms of a "before" and "after." And not only was there a difference in the world, but the self was different as well. Many people have memories of closing the book on childhood and becoming a different person following the death of a loved parent.

More than anything else, the death of a parent marks the

end of childhood. For many, there is some particular event, some discrete happening that occurs around the time of the death itself, which becomes remembered as the time when things changed or when they first became aware things were different. One woman remembered the evening of the day her mother died, when her father took her and her sister to a restaurant for dinner. The restaurant was a place where the family had gone often—mother, father, and two daughters—a place where they had shared not only food but many good memories as well. When the food came, this girl, who was only twelve at the time, remembers putting a forkful in her mouth and being acutely aware that the food did not taste right. "I think this was the first time, but it happened many times after that, that I realized life was never going to be the same. It was like shedding the skin of my childhood."

Her feeling that things were different initially stayed with her only a short time. She went back to school, back to her life, and attempted to pick up where she had left off. As the Easter holiday approached, she felt excited and full of anticipation. She had been raised in a traditional Catholic home and Easter was, after all, the time of resurrection. When Easter came and went and her mother was not returned to her and to life, she felt once again the weight of her loss. Life was not going to be the same; her world had been changed now in a way that could never be repaired. On the first Christmas following her mother's death, she felt the change again: "It was like somebody let the air out of a balloon. My father tried to make a nice Christmas, but it was another one of those situations where it was so plain and so obvious that life had changed forever."

Some survivors of early loss become aware that something is fundamentally different by watching the behavior of the surviving parent. One man whose mother died when he was seven vividly recalls seeing his father for the first time after having just been told by a family friend that his mother had died: "I remember walking down the hall to where he was sitting with family and friends and having to face him for the first time in front of everybody and being upset because it was in a group and because he didn't get up and hug me and I had to walk to him. At that moment, I knew I was all alone." His father's lack of response, coupled with the loss of his mother, told him not only that the world was different, but that he himself was now a solo traveler, a boy alone in the world.

For another woman, whose father died when she was eleven, it was her mother's treating her for the first time like an adult that caused her to realize things were different. Her father had been ill for many months. On one particular afternoon, though, she recalled playing in the backyard with a pet mouse, which had been given to her by her science teacher. She was excited about her mouse and had just given him a new name. She ran eagerly to tell her mother a story about the cute new mouse. She can still recall the way her mother responded to her call: "She walked down the stairs and just looked at me. Then she said, 'Heather, your father has to be taken to the hospital in an ambulance now. We can't talk about the mouse.' All of a sudden, the whole thing was in front of me and I understood everything. I realized what was happening, and I knew my father was dying. I needed to become an adult."

Following her father's death, she began thinking that she would now need to live her life on her own. Despite the fact that she had a close and secure relationship with her mother, she felt adrift and cut loose, and that she needed to adopt adult behaviors in order to survive in the world. "I changed the way I related to everyone. I learned how to get along with people. I became very popular, was even elected class president. It was a matter of necessity. I needed it for survival."

For others, the sense of change is tied less to a loss of childhood or loss of innocence than it is to a general sense that one has been altered and marked in some permanent way. One woman recounts, "I was twelve when my father died. It was a Sunday and I had been at the movies with my friends. My mother took me into the living room, which was very unusual, sat me down, and told me that my father had died. I remember sitting on that couch in the living room, which was kind of a cold place, and feeling like a soft tidal wave had hit me. I wasn't completely stunned and undone, but I had been marked and overshadowed by something."

Her father had been a successful man whose career and whose personality formed the core of family life; his death marked the abrupt and premature end of a particular chapter in her own life. The big house was gone. The social prominence had come to an end. She found herself "quite unprotected, going out into a new community to live and going to a new school." From the time of her father's death, the realization that anything and everything could be swept away in an instant was "bred into her bone." The world had changed from being a place where things were secure and predictable to being a place where anything could and did happen.

Author Russell Baker talks about becoming a skeptic at age five, following the death of his father. "After that (my father's death) I never cried again with any real conviction, nor expected much of anyone's God except indifference, nor loved deeply without fear that it would cost me dearly in pain."[12] The child Russell Baker died as "an icicle slid into his heart"[13] with the death of his father. The skeptic Russell Baker was born from that event.

Engraved on the wall of the Holocaust Museum in Washington, D.C., is such an acknowledgment of profound disruption by Holocaust survivor Elie Wiesel: *Never shall I forget those flames which consumed my faith forever. Never shall I forget that nocturnal silence which deprived me for all eternity of the desire to live. Never shall I forget those moments which murdered my god and my soul and turned my dreams to dust.*

The death of a parent in childhood does not merely mark time for a survivor, becoming one of many important life events. It is the psychological Great Divide, separating the world into a permanent "before and after." Thirty, forty, or fifty years after the death occurred, men and women still refer to the early death of a parent as the defining event of their lives.

Terrifying Insecurity

> . . . a sense of total loss
> afflicted me thereof:
> an absolute disappearance of continuity & love.[14]

> —*John Berryman*
> (Berryman's father committed
> suicide when Berryman was a boy.)

For most, the loss of a parent registers as a ten on an emotional Richter scale. The solid ground beneath one's feet no longer exists, and that which held things together and made them solid and secure is gone.

C. S. Lewis, whose mother died when he was nine, says, "With my mother's death all settled happiness, all that was tranquil and reliable, disappeared from my life. There was to be much fun, many pleasures, many stabs at Joy; but no more of the old security. It was sea and islands now; the great continent had sunk like Atlantis."[15] Solid ground was forever gone from Lewis's life, and while he could experience moments when he felt secure and stable, often his life felt as if he were being tossed about in an unsteady sea.

One man, whose mother died suddenly when he was thirteen, shared Lewis's sense of being adrift. His mother had been the center of family life. She had structured their time and organized their activities; he referred to his mother as the glue that held the family together. With her death, the entire family dispersed. Older siblings went away to college, younger siblings were placed in boarding school. He remained at home with his father, but the home he now inhabited was a different place from the home that had been anchored by his mother's stable presence. There was no longer someone to guide him in living his own life: "I would go to school in the morning and come home to an empty house. The house had been still. It was just still. The air was still. Every aspect of it was still. You would walk into it like a summer house where the furniture is all covered." At night, when his father would come home, the two of them would float around the house like two lost souls.

The day-to-day structure and routine that held the family together was no longer present. He describes his father during this time as being lost and adrift; a man who would cry out at night like a tormented soul in hell.

When he went off to college, this man felt even less anchored than when he had been at home. He recalls feeling so unlike the other freshmen: "I could not relate to their experiences, having structured families and parents and going home on weekends. I felt completely lost and at loose ends. I came home feeling suicidal, in terrible deep despair."

This feeling of being rootless, of having no solid ground, of being without an anchor, is shared by many who have lost parents in childhood. Another man talked about losing his own secure foundation, his very core sense of self, when he lost his father at age fifteen: "When he died, something was absolutely ripped out of me that cannot be replaced. It's as if we are all made up of a series of building blocks that mount over time, new experiences with families and friends. When someone dies, it is like ripping the base out. There is something completely missing for the rest of your life and it affects, to some degree, every decision you make." As a young man who needed his father's guidance and mentoring as much as he needed his father's love, the loss of a father was the equivalent of losing the foundation on which his own self was being constructed. He experienced a crumbling of his personal identity, and spent his college years haphazardly sifting through the rubble until he felt strong enough to rebuild the structure that was his self.

Profound Emptiness

The aftershock of early loss leaves a void in the world and an emptiness in the self. One woman referred to the "hole in her heart" that had been there ever since her father died when she was five years old. Actress Liv Ullmann, whose father died when she was six, says, "My father . . . was in my life for six years and did not leave me with one real memory of him. Just a great lack. That cut into me so deeply that many of life's experiences relate to it. The void Papa's death left in me became a kind of cavity, into which later experiences were to be laid."[16] Ullmann asserts in her autobiography that the void has become a central part of who she is. It exists as an emptiness that remains, regardless of any happiness or any success she might achieve.

One woman whose father committed suicide when she was a girl fantasized that if she had more things, she could somehow fill the emptiness inside of her. Yet, when she imagines winning the lottery and going on an extended shopping spree, she knows that nothing is going to fill the hole inside of her. She said somewhat wistfully, though at the end of our interview, "It would be nice [for the hole to be filled]."

Many survivors of early loss speak of an internal emptiness that can never be filled. Some feel the void as a constant presence; for others it seems to wax and wane in intensity. Some try repeatedly and unsuccessfully to fill the emptiness; others accept the void as part of who they have become because of their experience of early loss. Tennis star Arthur Ashe, who lost his own mother when he was seven, wrote in his posthumous autobiography, "For a long time now, I have understood that this quality of emotional distance in me, my aloofness or coldness—whatever the name I or others give to it—may well have something to do with the early loss of my mother. I have never thought of myself as having been cheated by her death, but I am terribly, insistently, aware of an emptiness in my soul that only she could have filled. As I considered the new beginnings I was facing, I felt the emptiness acutely. I also guessed that only my mother's return to me, which was an impossibility, could have filled the emptiness."[17]

For others, the emptiness lies not in the self, but in the world. The death of the parent landed like a bomb on the earth and left a crater, which author Richard Rhodes called "a hole in the world."[18] When Rhodes was still an infant, his mother killed herself. "At the beginning of my life the world acquired a hole. That's what I knew, that there was a hole in the world. For me there still is."[19] At times in his life, the hole has grown smaller. He has nurtured himself through relationships and through his own imagination and his unending desire for knowledge and mastery. At those times, when he has felt nurtured, "the hole has shrunk to the size of a window."[20] At other times when he has felt most alone the hole has grown. Yet the world is never as it would have been if his mother had not died. "If she hadn't killed herself she'd probably still be alive. Her older sisters are. Fifty years of her I can't imagine. I am sorry for her pain, but what pain she inflicted on us all with her selfish suicide."[21]

One man, whose mother died when he was seventeen, not only carried a sense of emptiness but also felt unable to prevent that same feeling from coloring his ideas about his future. When he looked ahead to a life without his mother, he was unable to see anything in front of him. He said of himself just before her death from cancer, "I would go to work and feel the emptiness, the void, the numbness. My brain would turn to stone. It became ceramic, nonhuman. There was no electrical activity happening up there and I couldn't think. The first person I had loved was dying. When she died I became reconciled to a gray, dreary, loveless life. If I tried to project the future, it was blank, gray, and dismal. The future was not a safe, wonderful place full of hope. Without my mother in it, the future was empty. I had no concept of how I could ever love again." To him, a world without his mother seemed not only like an empty world, but a loveless world, and he spent many years after her death unable to plan for his own future and to take the steps required to accomplish certain adult goals. He felt frozen because when he looked ahead, all he saw was emptiness.

Loss versus Absence

People whose parents died when they were still infants or toddlers feel not loss but absence. The void "coils around absence."[22] Because the parent was never known, the surviving child does not have the experience of being torn away from a parent who was loved and cherished. The survivor knows only absence. Like the mysterious dog that is important because he does *not* bark, the dead parent is known by his or her nonexistence. The narrator of a novel about the Holocaust described this as "the whitened pages whose letters were suddenly, angrily erased in the monstrous catastrophe that preceded his birth."[23] The survivor's only reality is the "whitened page." One knows that a text exists, because one has been told so, not because one possesses any personal memories. Survivors of such very early losses must contend with what has been called, paradoxically, the absent memory.[24] The survivor is haunted by the story of a mother or father whose face *does not* appear in the family album.

One man whose father died when he was three said, "There is a hole there when I think of my father. It is marked by absence, not just for my own father, but for the role of father as well. I don't know what 'father' means. When I started school, I remember feeling different from other kids who had a mother and a father. All I had was a mother. I had no father; that was my life. I didn't know anything else. I didn't know anything about a father. It's not like a reverse image or even a shadow. There was no image, just me, my brother, and my mother; that was my family." When he moved beyond the orbit of his immediate family, he encountered other children, other families, and knew that something was missing in his own life. Father became that which was absent, and his ideas about his own father and the more general image of "father" were built up around this absent image.

Another woman, whose mother died when she was an infant, said, "I grew up knowing that I had no one but myself. I didn't have anybody to miss. I've never lost a mother. My oldest brother was thirteen when she died, and all he can talk about is what life would have been like if Mom had lived because he knows what life was like with her, so he can really miss her. I never had her, so I don't feel the loss. I experience the absence of a mother. There is a hole where Mother should have been, a blank space. That's very different from loving someone and losing them. I have no memories. I had no attachment." She went on to say, "My brother has a beautiful portrait of my mother, and I see this image of her and I see that I look just like her. It's her; it's me; that's me there. I can see it. I look at my little baby picture and, yes, I can see that face but I don't know her. I don't really know who she was." For this woman, her mother was "the woman who did not exist."

Loss requires some prior relationship. One can experience emptiness, however, when one has known only absence. For the survivors of the very early death of a parent, emptiness and void are inextricably tied with the enigmatic image of a parent they never knew.

The language that adults use to describe their experience of losing a parent in childhood is the language of catastrophe, devastation, and emptiness. There are no less dramatic images that accurately convey the experience of having one's world invaded by death. The words must be powerful, severe, and absolute because the experience is such. It is an experience recorded in the mind and the memory of a child, someone not yet able to conceptualize or intellectualize as an adult.

Recently, I attended a High Holiday memorial service to remember and honor the dead relatives of members of the congregation. As the rabbi began the service, those who had not lost a loved one filed out of the temple. Only the mourners remained. Seated next to me was a father and his young daughter. She sat still as the ancient chanting began. At one point, she got up and walked into the foyer of the sanctuary. She looked very determined and sure of herself. Moments later she returned and took her seat. As she sat down, I caught a glimpse of her face—no words, only silence, and a look of unbearable longing.

CHAPTER 2

The Event That Shatters Childhood

The Bustle in a House
The Morning after Death
Is solemnest of industries
Enacted upon Earth—

The Sweeping up the Heart
And putting Love away
We shall not want to use again
Until Eternity.

—*Emily Dickinson*[1]

ALL DEATHS ARE NOT CREATED EQUAL. Some are sudden, violent, and unexpected. Those who are left behind have no time to prepare, either practically or psychologically. Other deaths are slow and tortured, lasting for months, or even years, and filled with a series of lesser losses and painful withdrawals. Some deaths, resulting from war or natural disaster, are shared with a larger community. Others, like suicide, are very private family affairs.

Regardless of the cause, no death of a young parent is what might be called a "good death" or a "pretty death."[2] When asked to describe a "good death," most people picture a peaceful end to a long and satisfying life.[3] The soon-to-be-deceased is usually at home, surrounded by loved ones and in full control of his or her physical and mental faculties. After a brief statement thanking those assembled for their love and support and reminiscing about a good and well-lived life, the individual closes his or her eyes and is peacefully transported into the next world. Despite the fact that few if any of us have experienced such a parting, we often envision such a scene when we are asked how we might like to die.

If this is a "good death," then the death of a young man or woman in the middle of his or her life with many as yet unlived possibilities is certainly a "bad death." When death comes to a young parent, it comes as an unwanted intruder. The person has much life to live, pleasures to enjoy, responsibilities to fulfill. Death here is often painful, sometimes violent, and never welcomed.

Untimely death shatters our assumptions about how the world works. We never believe that someone will die in the middle of his or her life. Death is supposed to be the particular province of the last stage of life. When death happens out of order, "out of time," it jars our sense of what is right in the world.

For a child, the death of a parent shatters assumptions even more basic than the order of how a life should proceed. It shatters core beliefs about the world itself. A child believes in *a safe and secure world,* a world in which events are predictable and orderly, a world that can be understood. When death is sudden and unexpected, the world and everything in it seem less safe and more precarious. If a loved mother or father can disappear overnight, then who knows what other disasters lie ahead.

A child believes in the power and invincibility of his or her parents. In adolescence some of our idealizations about our parents begin to crumble, yet we hold on to the idea that they are *stronger and more powerful* than we are. When chronic illness slowly and inevitably weakens a parent, beliefs about parental power are shattered.

Children take it as an absolute given that they are *loved by their parents.* This belief is so necessary for secure development that children hold to it even when the realities of physical, sexual, or emotional abuse contradict that perception. In order to feel safe in the world, a child must believe that he or she is loved by a mother and father. One type of death—suicide—assaults a child's core belief that he or she is loved. The child asks, If my mother or father really loved me, how could she or he *choose* to die? Finally, a child grows up needing to believe that *what he or she sees and hears is true and real.* In order to make accurate judgments, in order to learn from his or her experience, a child must trust that the experience is an accurate reflection of the reality in the world. When well-meaning relatives deny or lie about the circumstances surrounding a parent's death, they shatter a child's belief in his or her accurate perception of reality.

Early death shatters core beliefs about *safety, parental power, lovability, and reality itself.*

Sudden Death/The World Is a Safe and Secure Place

Sudden death, whether it results from murder, accident, or an unexpected medical crisis, shatters a child's sense of security in the world. The suddenness is both jarring and terrifying. As one woman whose mother was killed in a car accident said, "One minute we were a perfectly happy family and the next minute . . ." She had no words for what they became in the next minute. What she knew, however, was that the happy family they had been ceased to exist.

Children are so unable to make sense of the dramatic change in their lives brought on by untimely parental death they often find themselves asking what later seem like silly questions: "Who will take me to school tomorrow?" "Will I still be able to go to camp this summer?" These are questions that reflect the overwhelming need to live in a predictable world. "Who will take care of me?" "What are we going to do now?" As adults, many individuals who asked these relatively naive questions now fault themselves for having been unable to appreciate the seriousness and finality of death. Yet, as young children, it was impossible for them to make sense of a world so drastically altered in such a short time.

Ron, now in his fifties, remembers clearly the day his mother died. It was the summer of eighth grade, a perfect sunny day, and he recalls the house being peaceful and cool. His mother was upstairs lying down because she had a headache. He left home to join some friends for the daily game of baseball, thinking little about his mother and feeling good about what a lovely day it was. When he returned home, he discovered that his mother had been taken to the hospital. His uncle was there to take care of him and his brother and sisters. After a somewhat strained dinner, he recalls going to bed. Sometime after midnight, he was awakened by his father, who told him and his siblings that their mother was dead. She had died suddenly and unexpectedly of a cerebral hemorrhage.

The next time that Ron saw his mother, she was lying perfectly still in a pink-lined casket. He recalls that he did not cry at her funeral. He was "just unprepared. It was all too sudden." The world changed dramatically after Ron's mother's death. His father's grief was overwhelming, and Ron's father was unable to care for his youngest child, a daughter. Consequently, she was sent to boarding school. Ron's two older siblings moved out of the house to apartments of their own. From being one child in a family of six, Ron became the companion of his bereaved father, the only child in a now empty and lifeless home.

One cannot feel safe or secure in a world that changes so much, so quickly. A child cannot trust that today's happy home will endure for even a few more hours. Regrettably, it only takes one shattering event of sufficient magnitude to change one's core beliefs about life. Ron recalls becoming numb, almost like a sleepwalker going through the motions of his life, unable to comprehend what had happened to him.

For Janice, the suddenness of her father's death was compounded by the trauma of actually witnessing the moment he died. Janice's father was a much-loved physician—popular, competent, successful, at the height of his career. He came home early the day before Thanksgiving because the family was hosting a large gathering of friends and relatives. Janice recalls that her father took his brother on a ride on their new snowmobile. He was proud of his new toy and wanted to show it off to his younger brother. The two got stuck in the snow and had to pull the snowmobile back toward the house. Janice recalls that when her father came in the house he complained of chest pain. He looked somewhat pale and was not his usual outgoing and cheerful self. After about an hour, Janice's mother, who was a nurse, became concerned and called for an ambulance. Janice recalls that initially the ambulance did not go to the right house. She and her brothers watched anxiously out the window as they saw the ambulance turn down another street. They went running out of the house and chased after the ambulance, crying and screaming as they tried to get the ambulance, which was now stuck in the snow, to come to their house, where their father was in great pain.

When the medics arrived, Janice and her brothers were told to wait in another room. Janice, however, sneaked to the side of the door and peered into the room where her father lay dying. She watched as the paramedics performed CPR and as her father's body convulsed for the last time. Janice, who was only eleven, turned from the door with the authority of someone who had witnessed death and announced to her two brothers that their father was dead. She says, "The suddenness of it shocked everyone." One minute the family was joyful and happy, preparing for a holiday feast; the next minute, they were preparing for a funeral. In that short time, Janice recalls going from being a carefree, playful girl to a "serious, wiser, older woman."

At one point during the funeral preparations, Janice was invited by a neighborhood friend to come over and play. For a few hours she felt able to reenter the secure world of childhood, and she recalls what a treat it was to feel free of the burden and responsibility of her father's death. Her return to childhood was short-lived, however, and Janice went home to her family and to a world that had changed so dramatically.

Often, sudden death is the result of some violent act: lightning strikes, a car fails to slam on its brakes, a trigger is pulled. The world holds unexpected dangers and a child may grow up feeling tentative and frightened, never trusting that random violence will not happen again.

Thirteen-year-old Felicia went to bed as her mother and father drove off to take her sister to the airport for a return flight to college. Felicia's mother never returned home. After they dropped her sister at the airport, Felicia's mother and father met some friends and went out for a late snack. As they were driving home, a police officer ran a red light without his sirens on and slammed into their car. Felicia's mother was killed almost instantly. Her father was bruised but not seriously injured. However, he was detained for several hours by the police, who wanted to make sure that he had not been driving while intoxicated.

When Felicia woke the next morning, she was greeted by an older brother who had moved out of the family home two years earlier. She was surprised to see him sitting in the living room, and when she asked him what he was doing there, he remarked casually that he had come over to read the newspaper. Felicia remembers thinking that this seemed "kind of ridiculous," but since she had usually deferred to her older brother, she walked off into the kitchen to prepare her breakfast. Within a half an hour Felicia's father arrived home and told her that her mother was dead. She recalls thinking, This is totally unreal. This cannot really be happening. It cannot be happening to me.

At first Felicia, like many survivors of violent death, thought there must have been some mistake; it was not her mother who had been killed, but some other woman, and she insisted on seeing her mother's body. At the time her insistence grew out of her own sense of disbelief and chaos. Yet, in retrospect, she is glad that she asked for this tangible, visible proof that her mother was dead. She says now that otherwise she would have continued to believe that somehow, somewhere, her mother was still alive. When she saw the body, Felicia says, "I knew it was final."

Another woman, whose father died in a car accident when she was seventeen, actually shook his body as he lay in the casket, crying and pleading with him "not to be dead." Despite seeing and feeling her father's dead body, this woman continued for several years to believe that there had been some mistake and that the man in the casket just looked like her father, that her real father, suffering from amnesia following the accident, was wandering and lost somewhere out there in the world.

Sudden death shatters a child's core belief that the world is a safe and predictable place. When terrible things can happen without warning, a child is left feeling vulnerable and insecure.

Slow Death/My Parents Are Strong and Powerful

To young children, mothers and fathers seem like invincible giants, kings and queens who rule the kingdom of the family with perfect knowledge. The conversations of preadolescent children in particular are often peppered with anecdotes about some accomplishment of a mother or father. When a young boy says, "My father knows how to fix everything," he is not just referring to the home repair skills of his father. He is referring to his sense that his father makes the world run right, that his father is powerful and competent, and that he himself can feel secure and safe knowing that he is protected by this powerful man. When a girl says, "My mother knows the most things of anybody," she is not just referring to her mother's practical knowledge but also to her sense that she can go to her mother to find the answers to all of life's questions. Her mother is the source of knowledge and once again she can feel secure knowing that that knowledge will be available to her when she needs it.

When a child witnesses the slow deterioration of a parent, he or she sees not only impending death but the collapse and destruction of a powerful protector as well. C. S. Lewis writes of his mother's death, "For us boys the real bereavement happened before our mother died. We lost her gradually as she was gradually withdrawn from our life into the hands of nurses and delirium and morphia, and as our whole existence changed into something alien and menacing, as the house became full of strange smells and midnight noises and sinister whispered conversations."[4] One woman recalled standing at her father's bedroom door and peering in at his weakened and emaciated body. She was filled with horror as she saw what had become of this once strong man.

For some children, a parent's invalidism causes the normal

roles within the family to be reversed. Generally, children expect that parents will be caretakers and that they will receive care. When a parent is sick and debilitated, a child is often asked to become a caretaker. For some, this new role feels empowering and important. For most, however, it is daunting and overwhelming. "How can I, a child, take care of her?"

Were it not for a chain of family tragedies preceding his mother's death, Troy would never have been asked to become his mother's primary caretaker. Three months before his mother was scheduled for open heart surgery, Troy's father's parents were involved in a serious, and in his grandfather's case, fatal accident. Troy's father and his only sibling left home and went to be near Troy's grandparents to help his grandmother through her convalescence and to handle his grandfather's funeral arrangements and business affairs. For three months, Troy was alone with his mother. He was privy to her fear, her pain, and her overwhelming need for support. If Troy's father had not been taken away because of another family tragedy, he would have been there to attend to Troy's mother. Instead, Troy became his mother's confidant and her nurse. He was sixteen years old, and he remembers vividly his awareness of mortality, in particular his mother's mortality, as he took care of her.

What he saw again and again was how sick and frail his mother was. On one occasion he remembers being in her room, sitting next to her in the dark, and holding her hand as she cried in pain and fear. Days before her husband and his ailing mother were to return home, Troy's mother begged him to help her clean the house so that the family home would look presentable to her mother-in-law. Troy was no longer a dependent child, and he recalls growing up overnight, becoming wise before his time. In those three months he had ceased to be his mother's son and he had become her caretaker.

Many adults who lose their parents in adulthood talk with pride and gratitude at being able to provide care in the last months of a parent's life. The reversal of roles seems natural and perhaps even fitting when death comes at the end of a long life and the caretaking child is now an adult him- or herself. When the roles are reversed in childhood, the fundamental order and structure of a family is violated. Children do not grow up believing that they will ever have to take care of their parents, and although they may rise to the occasion, the image of their parents as powerful and strong is shattered forever.

Several people recounted, with a sense of relief, stories in which parents had remained caretakers despite being ravaged by debilitating and incapacitating illness. A parent's ability or willingness to remain a parent, even in death, was seen as reassuring and comforting by the children who were left behind.

When Lee's father found out that he was dying from a rare blood disease, he called his sixteen-year-old son into the library of their large home. He told him in a calm and reassuring voice that he was suffering from an illness that would be fatal. He said, "I will receive treatment. I will return to work for a time and we will all continue on." When he left the library, Lee broke down and sobbed. Yet he felt secure knowing that his father was in charge even in death. The image of his father's stoicism and strength is something that has stayed with Lee throughout his life and continues to be not only a source of comfort for him, but also a model for how he himself should face adversity.

Arthur Ashe concludes his autobiography with a very moving letter to his daughter, Camera. Ashe knows that he is dying as he writes the letter and knows that he will not live to see his daughter grow into a woman. His letter is filled with fatherly advice, advice he knows he will not be able to give her in person. Nonetheless, he wants to pass on to his only child his experience and his wisdom about the world. He gives her very practical advice about how to manage her money, how to respect her growing sexuality, how to understand issues of racism and sexism, and how to respect the roles that family, education, and sports play in the life of an individual.

He concludes his letter, "I may not be walking with you all the way, or even much of the way, as I walk with you now. Don't be angry with me if I am not there in person, alive and well, when you need me. I would like nothing more than to be with you always. Do not feel sorry for me if I am gone. When we were together, I loved you deeply and you gave me so much happiness I can never repay you. Camera, wherever I am when you feel sick at heart and weary of life, or when you stumble and fall and don't know if you can get up again, think of me. I will be watching and smiling and cheering you on."[5] In his last months of life, Ashe remained a caretaking parent for his daughter. His final thoughts were of how he could continue to be a presence in her life even after death had taken him away.

Suicide/Of Course My Parents Love Me

The suicide of a parent shatters a child's belief that he or she is lovable and worthy of being loved. Poet John Berryman, whose father committed suicide, wrote that suicide "dangles a trail."[6] Alice James wrote in her diary in 1889 of suicide, "It's bad that it is so untidy, there is no denying that, for it bespatters one's friends morally as well as physically."[7] When death happens suddenly or violently or after a long illness, a child must contend with the uncertainty of the world and with a parent's inability to prevent disaster. Yet that child knows that his or her parent did not want to die. Given a choice, he or she would prefer, like Arthur Ashe, to be there forever.

When a parent commits suicide, a child must contend with the fact that the parent died willingly, that he or she sought death and knowingly, thoughtlessly, and selfishly left the child behind. The refrain of "If my mother or father loved me, how could they have left me?" haunts the lives of the survivors of suicide. Children may come to doubt their own worthiness and inherent goodness. Perhaps it was because they were not good enough that the parent chose to leave them.

JANE'S STORY

Jane was only six years old when she was awakened by the lights of an ambulance flashing on her bedroom ceiling. She went downstairs to find her mother and three older sisters crying and holding on to each other. At first she was only told that her father had died. She learned the truth that he had hung himself in their basement two years later when a boy in her class began teasing her on the school playground. He kept singing, "I know how your father died. I know how your father died," and she ran from the playground with the sound ringing in her ears. It was only then that her mother told Jane that her father had killed himself. Jane's mother, who had lost her own mother when she was a girl, was completely undone by the loss of her husband. She was bereft and overwhelmed, and she took much of her grief and anger out on her youngest child. Although she had been a caring mother before her husband died, Jane's mother became a tyrant in widowhood. She began hitting Jane, beating her until she was black and blue, and screaming at Jane that she hated her and wished that she had never been born. Jane says she lived much of her childhood in a fog: "I was like the walking wounded. I don't remember much of anything. I was completely unhappy my whole childhood. The first time I remember feeling any joy was when I was twenty years old."

When Jane was twenty-two, she was touched by suicide once again. A troubled young man who had been her boyfriend asked her if he might come and spend some time at her apartment, hoping perhaps that they could rekindle what had been a passionate but unhappy romance for both of them. Jane told this young man that she did not think it was a good idea for him to come and stay with her. Six months later, Jane discovered that this same man had killed himself two months after her rejection. "I blamed myself. I had a mini nervous breakdown when I found out. I couldn't stop crying and I was in bed for four months." With the help of a therapist, Jane came to realize that some of her grief was not only for this young man, but also for her father, and that she was crying now perhaps for the first time for the father who had abandoned her years ago. As an adult, Jane says that she has made "suicide" a part of her own vocabulary. For her, suicide exists as a real option in a way that it does not for those who have never seen it touch someone they love.

Once in her late twenties, Jane made a serious suicide attempt. The attempt was precipitated by a man she loved rejecting her. Although she knows rationally that this must have been connected in some way to the death of her father when she was a girl, Jane remains unable to control her overwhelming sense of unlovability whenever she feels rejection. When she made her own suicide attempt, not only was Jane feeling abandoned, but she was also aware that she wanted to rejoin her father. She had a strong sense that if she died, she would at last be reunited with the father who had left her. Not only would she be with him, but this time she would get a chance to know him, to understand him, and perhaps to understand what had motivated him to leave his family without any warning.

In order to avoid the intolerable blow to self-esteem that comes from believing a parent chose to die, some children construct explanations for the suicide that allow them to continue to believe they were loved.

Harry's mother killed herself when he was eight years old. Her successful attempt had been preceded by years of failed attempts. Harry remembers coming home from school on more than one occasion to find that his mother had been taken to the hospital because of an overdose, or that all of the windows and doors were closed because she had attempted to turn on the gas and kill herself.

When Harry was only six years old, his father left the family. He took his two sons for a ride in the country and told them that he could no longer live at home with their mother. The boys continued to see their father, but they were now the sole witnesses to their mother's self-destruction. She drank heavily, invited a series of men into her bedroom, and was frequently depressed. Despite her behavior and her eventual suicide, Harry has managed to continue to believe that his mother loved him. He points to two things in particular: first, that she frequently hugged him. If she had not loved him she would not have embraced him as she did. Second, he remembers her saying to him, "Where I am going I will always see you and I will always be connected to you." As an adult, he has sometimes wondered whether her promise of continued love and connection was just the alcohol talking. Yet he continues to believe that despite her personal anguish, his mother loved him. As I was concluding the interview with Harry, he asked me if I had ever read a story by Raymond Carver entitled "What We Talk about When We Talk about Love." I told him that I had not, and he recommended it to me highly, saying he thought it was very relevant to the book I was writing about early loss.

Shortly after the interview I obtained a copy of Carver's story. It is about four friends who are sitting around a table, drinking and talking about the meaning of love. One of the women recounts the story of her ex-husband who killed himself. When their marriage ended, her husband had become threatening and abusive. He bought a gun, which he used to threaten her, yet ultimately he put the gun in his own mouth and used it on himself. His ex-wife says, "I was in the room with him when he died. . . . He never came out of it. But I sat with him. He didn't have anyone else." Her current husband responds, "If you call that love, you can have it." "It was love," she said. "Sure it's abnormal in most people's eyes, but he was willing to die for it. He did die for it."[8] As the story continues, the four friends continue their emotional, somewhat drunken discussion of what this thing we call "love" really is. It seemed an apt story for a man who continued to believe in the love of a mother who had killed herself.

Denial/I Can Believe What I See, Can't I?

The circumstances surrounding early death often give a child the confusing message that reality is not as he or she sees it. Early and unexpected death is overwhelming not only for children, but for surviving adults as well. In their own grief and confusion, these adults sometimes reason that it is better for children if the reality of illness, death, and painful feelings is denied. Regrettably, these would-be helpers compound the trauma of loss by telling children, over and over again, that things are not as they see or believe them to be. Even in the face of tangible, physical evidence, some family members insist that children ignore or deny that a parent is seriously ill, that a death has actually occurred, or that the child has any feelings about illness and death that must be acknowledged and expressed. This triad of denial may create an atmosphere of unreality in a bereaved family. If a child speaks the truth about what he or she sees and feels, then the child breaks the conspiracy of denial. If, on the other hand, the child accepts the shared distortion, then the child must deny the validity of what he or she sees, hears, and feels, creating an assault on the child's belief in a rational and knowable world.

Denial of Illness

From the time when someone first noticed a lump on her father's neck to his eventual death six years later when she was sixteen, Tanya thinks her family mentioned the word *cancer* only once. Her father's illness was not only not spoken about within the family, its very existence was denied. In recent years, Tanya has been told that her father had cobalt treatments, which severely burned the skin on his neck, yet she has no recollection of seeing burns on her father. She has also been told that the initial lump was followed by several others and that her father's disfigurement increased toward the end of his life. At the very end of his life, her father's voice changed, and his ability to breathe was compromised. Yet despite these obvious changes, Tanya has no recollection of ever seeing the physical changes taking place in her father or of having the opportunity to talk about the changes with members of her family.

Once when she was in the sixth grade, Tanya remembers a boy in school taunting her by saying, "Your father has the 'big C.' " She remembers being ashamed and mortified and running home crying, vowing that she would hate this cruel little boy forever. His act was clearly an insensitive one, but it served at least temporarily to break the almost total denial surrounding her father's illness. She and her siblings were not only prohibited from saying what was real, they were also denied the right to see what was obvious to all of them.

Shortly before her father died, Tanya's mother assembled the entire family for a final group portrait. Once again, however, Tanya's mother was unable to acknowledge to her children that she wanted this portrait because she thought it was the last time the family might all be together. Instead, she used the occasion of a relatively minor school event to gather her family for this last photographic memory of their life together.

It is not merely that Tanya's family prohibited talking about her father's illness. The veil of silence that fell over her childhood prohibited her from seeing what was going on. The denial assaulted her sense of what was real. Her memories of the time from age ten to age sixteen, the period of her father's illness, are either distorted or nonexistent. Because she was not allowed to see what was going on, it was impossible for her to remember what happened.

Denial of the Death

In some families, where death happens suddenly and unexpectedly, there is a collusion to deny that the death has occurred at all. Rebecca, the woman described in the previous chapter whose mother's disappearance was never mentioned, remembers being six years old and standing outside the hospital, being told by her father that her mother had gone on a long trip. Rebecca recalls looking up and seeing the subway and thinking perhaps her mother was on that subway beginning her journey. Since Rebecca had not been to many places, she thought that perhaps her mother had gone to Florida, one of the only places to which Rebecca herself had actually traveled.

When her father reappeared after six months and presented her with a new mother, her own mother and the imagined trip to Florida were never mentioned again. There was an attempt on the part of her father to deny that a death had happened at all. As an adult woman, Rebecca has made serious attempts to reconnect with her mother's surviving relatives. This reunion has not only linked Rebecca to living family members, but it has validated her experience, confirming for her that what she knew at the time was in fact true. Her mother had not gone on a long trip; her mother had died.

One day when Tony was five years old, he and his sister were picked up at school and brought to the home of a neighbor. They were told that their mother had gone shopping. There was no mention of their father at all. After three days Tony and his sister began to become suspicious. They knew that their mother liked to shop, but this made no sense. At the end of three days, their mother reappeared. They never saw their father again and no mention was made of what had happened to him. The events surrounding his death were completely obscured. The children were expected to believe that somehow their father had vanished and their mother had just been on an extended shopping spree. Several months later, Tony, his mother, and sister were taking a trip, and he remembers hearing the porter yell, "We are holding the train for a new widow and her two children." At that moment, Tony realized that his father had died.

The suppression of information and the denial of reality is one of the aspects of early death that adults who lost parents in childhood report was most traumatic and most damaging. Although it may be hindsight and the voice of an adult talking, many people told me that they would have much preferred to know the facts of what was happening rather than to be "protected by the silence of denial."

Denial of Feelings

In some cases, families acknowledge that there is an illness, acknowledge that there is death, but deny any reactions to or feelings about the trauma that has occurred. If the child expresses any emotion, he or she is quickly told that either those feelings are not real or that those feelings are not acceptable.

Tracy grew up in a family where looking good and appearing cool and calm were highly valued, so it is no surprise that her family worked hard to deny its feelings when her mother died. Tracy was fifteen years old and completing tenth grade when her mother went into the hospital. Tracy herself was to leave for a cross-country camping trip a few days later, and the family reassured her that there was no cause for concern and that she should continue with her summer plans. In early July, Tracy received a call saying, "Your mother isn't expected to live." At that moment she guessed that her mother had probably died. When she arrived home her brother met her at the airport and told her that in fact her mother had finally succumbed to the cancer that had been compromising her life for many years.

During her mother's funeral, Tracy remembers that the entire family placed a premium on being stoic. Her older brother advised her that if she felt at all inclined to cry she should say something ridiculous like "bananas, bananas" to herself and that silly refrain would temporarily distract her and prevent the tears from coming. After the funeral, Tracy was put back on a plane and sent to complete her summer adventure. There was no mention that the grief she was feeling over the loss of her mother might prevent her from enjoying her summer vacation or that perhaps she needed to be near her family. On the plane, Tracy remembers crying to a stranger about the loss of her mother. It was safer to cry on the plane than it was to mourn among her own family members who were so intent on denying that they had any feelings at all. Back at camp, Tracy bonded with a girl who had lost her own father several years earlier. They shared stories about life without a parent, and Tracy remembers feeling somewhat comforted by hearing of this girl's experience.

When she returned home, her feelings were ignored and her mother's death went unmentioned. Tracy's brother was away at college and she and her father resumed life, two boarders sharing the same space, but in no way two mourners comforting one another. Tracy knew she would need to get on with her own life, but she was very aware that she could not feel anything that might be upsetting to her father or that might break the family's injunction to remain aloof and detached in the face of powerful feelings. Tracy now realizes that she dulled her own feelings during those years with precocious sex and marijuana, two powerful drugs used to numb a hurting child.

Lucy, whose mother died when she was seventeen, told me about a custom in her Caribbean homeland designed to prevent mourners from denying their feelings. The funeral begins in the family home with the body laid out in familiar surroundings. Family and friends are joined by a group of professional mourners whose sole responsibility is to make sure that family members feel their feelings at each appropriate moment.

When Lucy first saw her mother stretched out in the coffin, she remembers trying to distract herself by examining the coffin itself. She looked at the hinges, the metalwork, the way the wood was polished. One of the professional mourners, realizing that Lucy was avoiding her feelings, came up to the casket and began to wail. She called out Lucy's mother's name and said, "Why oh why did you leave me?" At that moment, Lucy began to cry. The mourner had accomplished her task.

As the funeral procession continued to the gravesite, the professional mourners again and again made sure that family members were not allowed to deny their loss. At the gravesite, Lucy began to walk away, and one of the professionals grabbed her arm and brought her back. Lucy would not be allowed to leave the gravesite of her mother until she had cried. At the time she remembers thinking, What a nuisance these intrusive mourners are. As an adult she has realized how important it was for her to cry and weep and feel her pain at the loss of her mother.

A Triad of Unacceptable Feelings

Much has been written about both the sadness and anger that accompany early loss. The pain of loss is heart-wrenching, and a child is often filled with anger and disappointment at the abandonment by a trusted parent. Although these feelings are powerful, they have become "understandable" and form part of our standard lexicon of grief reactions. There are other feelings, however, that are more difficult to acknowledge and easier to deny because they challenge what we think we "should" feel when a loved one dies. These "forbidden" feelings include shame, guilt, and relief. Again and again, adult survivors talked about these less acceptable feelings and about their struggles in adulthood to acknowledge and to accept the powerful feelings that had accompanied early loss.

Shame

At first it seems almost as if it must be a mistake to say that someone feels ashamed because a parent has died. Yet shame is one of the most common experiences of children who lose parents. Russell Baker recounts that when he first heard that his father died, the words "Your father is dead" sounded like an accusation, as if someone were telling him that his father was a criminal, and he felt the need to defend his father by saying, "He is not. He is not either."[9]

The shame that a child feels can come from a variety of sources. In some cases, just being associated with death and the taint of death feels shameful and embarrassing to a young child. Sam's father had always been sickly, suffering from diabetes since he himself was a child. He was hospitalized often, and Sam remembers trips to the hospital parking lot where he would stand outside, look up at his father's window, and wave. The last time his father went into the hospital, some of the residents in the small town where the family lived began to gossip that Sam's father suffered from tuberculosis. As a result, the school took action to keep Sam out of school. For several months he was not allowed to join his classmates or to participate in the normal activities of being a seven-year-old. There was no truth to the accusation that Sam's father or anyone in their family had tuberculosis, yet once the rumors began, Sam himself felt overshadowed by the stigma of his father's illness.

For Cynthia, the shame she felt when her father was killed in a plane crash when she was only eleven years old came from her own experience of vulnerability. Cynthia remembers being pulled out of class by the school principal. She went with him to his office, to be greeted by one of her father's business associates, who told her that her father had just died. Cynthia was to go and wait for her sister in the hallway. She remembers that the wait seemed interminable as she tried to control herself, telling herself that if she could only hold on until she got home then she would be fine. Unfortunately, the wait was too long. Cynthia's sister was kept in class longer than expected, and Cynthia began weeping. She was taken out to a car and asked to wait, and she remembers sitting alone in the backseat of a strange car, crying. People would look at her as they went by, and she was overcome not only by her grief, but by her shame as well.

When she got home, Cynthia, her sister, and the rest of her family cried together in a private space where at least the tears seemed more acceptable. Cynthia remembers, however, going numb for the rest of the week as the family prepared for her father's funeral. Her father had been a prominent businessman and the circumstances surrounding his death drew much attention from the local media. Cynthia remembers that during that week at home all the rules and routines were suspended. She spent the week playing Monopoly and eating cake, living in a world that seemed less than real. When the week ended, Cynthia was expected to return to school and to act "normal." In school she remembers that she was unable to control her feelings. She would sit in class and just start crying. The teacher would have her removed and she would be required to stand in the hallway alone. One can just imagine Cynthia's shame as she stood there alone, weeping with her head down. She says, "I lost all my friends because I became the weird one." The school doctor prescribed tranquilizers for Cynthia, and whenever her unacceptable feelings came out, Cynthia was given medication to calm her down.

The strong message that Cynthia learned was that it is not okay to cry or to be upset. One must pretend always that everything is fine, since to do otherwise is shameful and humiliating. During that time, Cynthia began to idolize the fictional character Spock on *Star Trek*. "He had no emotions" she said, "only logic and rationality," and it seemed to her that the answer to her problems would be to become like Spock and never have to feel anything again.

In some cases, shame is brought on by the circumstances of the parent's death. In particular, suicide is seen as an unacceptable death. In many religious traditions, suicide is a sin, and the successful suicide is not allowed to lie in hallowed ground. There was a time in the history of the United States when suicide was considered a crime. If one survived a suicide attempt, one actually could be punished for the crime of attempted suicide.[10]

MARGIE'S STORY

Margie's lifelong struggle with shame began when she was ten years old and saw the police cars drive to the front of her house. She had been playing outside with a group of friends and remembers being excited by the sound and sight of these cars coming down the street. She was curious, however, as to why police cars would be coming to her house in the middle of the day. After the police finished their business and the cars drove away, Margie went home to ask her mother what had happened. Her mother told her that the officers had come to announce that Margie's father had shot himself. He had gone out in his car, pulled to the side of the road, and shot himself in the head.

Margie's mother had no explanation for such a death nor did she know what the "appropriate" response for a widow might be when the cause of death was suicide. Margie knew even as a young child that her mother was ashamed about her husband's death. Her mother never talked about it, and she distanced herself from her own family, embarrassed to talk with them about the source of her humiliation. Margie's father was treated as if he had just disappeared from their lives.

Margie remembers a neighborhood boy teasing her about her father's death and can recall some of the news stories that appeared shortly after his suicide. Her family's shame seemed so public, and consequently all the more painful.

When she was in junior high school, Margie remembers that her school bus used to drive by the bridge where her father had pulled his car over and shot himself. Every once in a while on the ride to school, someone would say, "Do you remember the story about the man who killed himself over there?" Margie would bow her head and not admit that she knew anything about the story at all.

Throughout high school, Margie remembers feeling different from the other children, different because she did not have a father. She says, "I felt like I did not measure up, in part because I had no father but also because the father I had had wasn't what he should have been."

Margie was eager to leave her hometown to go away to college, hoping that at college she could leave the past behind her. At college it would not matter if you had a father or not, since no one had their mother or father close by. She says, "I could finally be judged for me." Yet Margie could not escape the shame of her father's death, and she remembers feeling tentative and shy as father/daughter weekend approached and she knew she would have to explain to her friends why she was not going to attend.

When she returned home to family gatherings, especially occasions that included her father's family, Margie would have to hear stories about what a disappointment her father was. Occasionally, one of her father's brothers would say out loud, "Boy, I hope my children don't turn out like him."

Although she was unaware at the time that shame and her desperate longing to fit in were operative factors in her choice of a husband, Margie now believes that these were part of the subtle mix that drew her to the man she eventually married. Her husband was handsome, charming, and from a very good family. There were no skeletons in his family closet, and Margie felt that as his wife she could escape the taint of her father's suicide.

Throughout her adult life, Margie has tried hard to do everything "just right," conscious of not wanting to draw any attention to herself and of wanting to be acceptable and appropriate at all times. One of her unstated goals was not to bring any shame on herself or on her family. While Margie has enjoyed being a mother and has raised three children who have grown into successful and competent adults, she recalls that her children's adolescence was an especially trying time for her. During adolescence, it is not uncommon for teenagers to rebel against their parents and to rebel in very visible ways. Margie's children, not unlike their peers, grew their hair long, wore tattered jeans, and engaged in occasional public pranks. While most parents might be annoyed by some of these behaviors, Margie was mortified. She felt her children were shaming her in front of the community. To her credit, Margie knew that hers was an overreaction, and with the help of a counselor she came to realize that her fear of being shamed had little to do with her children and had much to do with the legacy of her father's suicide and her own incredible humiliation at being the daughter of a man who had shot himself.

Guilt

Psychoanalytic writers have suggested that children feel guilt at the death of a parent because it is normal for children when they are angry or upset with their parents to wish them dead. While there were some interviewees who did indeed experience guilt after a parent died, no one I interviewed felt guilty because they had actually wished the death. Instead, guilt seemed to come from feeling that they had somehow failed the parent and were thus, at least in part, responsible for the parent's death.

Brent had always known he would lose a parent before he reached adulthood. His mother had been sick with cancer since he was a boy. He felt close to his outgoing, gregarious father and assumed that when the inevitable happened and his mother died that he and his father and two younger brothers would manage together.

One day, when he was twelve years old and in the middle of seventh grade, Brent decided to skip school with some friends. He remembers feeling guilty but also proud of his daring and his risk-taking. As he came home at the end of his adventure, he was surprised to find the police at his house. Of course, he assumed that the police were there for him and that his boyish escapade had been discovered and he was about to be punished. However, the police were at his house to tell his mother that his father had collapsed at work and died of a heart attack. Brent remembers not only feeling shocked at the unexpected death of his father, but also feeling tremendously guilty, guilty because he believed that somehow his own truant behavior might have been involved in his father's unexpected and sudden death.

Brent was studying for his bar mitzvah at the time of his father's collapse, and he remembers hearing the Hebrew schoolteacher say that until a boy becomes thirteen, all of his sins are visited on his father, that God holds a boy's father responsible for any crimes or misdemeanors. Brent found himself unable to stop feeling guilty that somehow his own behavior had killed his father.

As he grew into adolescence, Brent again felt guilty because he believed that he used his status as an orphan to gain pity from other children. When he would meet a young girl, he would reveal his vulnerability and talk about his loss. It never occurred to him that his popularity derived from his outgoing and warm personality, rather he assumed that his sly manipulation, his use of his loss in order to gain sympathy, was the cause of his success with those other boys and girls. Throughout his young adulthood, Brent continued to feel guilty whenever he was treated warmly or lovingly. He attributed his particular success with women to his brazenly and openly displaying what he came to call "his irresistible vulnerability."

Other than his one attempt at playing hooky, Brent was never able to be more specific about exactly what crime had cost his father his life.

In Clare's case, her immediate sense of guilt came from the way she treated her father on the last day of his life. It was a Sunday afternoon and she was going to the movies with some friends. Her father leaned down to give her a kiss as she was leaving the house and she pulled her face away from him and gave him a dirty look. Clare's father was a weekend alcoholic and he had been drinking earlier that day. She was angry at him because of what he was doing to himself and what he was doing to their family with his weekend binges. When he went to kiss her, Clare remembers feeling disgusted by the smell of alcohol on his breath. She also wanted to punish him for failing to give up the habit that seemed to be destroying her family.

When Clare returned home from the movies and learned that her father had died of a heart attack, she remembers being overcome by a sense of guilt. She had been her father's special child, the one he would seek out on a Saturday morning to do special projects, and she had rejected him. Earlier in the week she had asked him when he was going to stop drinking and he had made her a promise that he would stop after the family returned from its yearly vacation. Clare spent many years feeling guilty and bad about herself because she had been unable to forgive her father and to show him some love in the last hours of his life.

Almost forty years after her father's death, Clare reexperienced her guilt. She learned from a family member that her father had not died of a heart attack but in fact had committed suicide. The guilt she thought she had laid to rest through years of therapy and self-reflection came back and hit her like a wave. As an adult woman, she once again had to confront the role that her behavior might have played in the suicide of her father. She finally came to accept that her rejection may in fact have been one of the factors that pushed her father to take his own life. It was not, however, the only factor, and it was probably not the main reason. She is now strong enough, however, and wise enough, to know that any action is the result of a complicated set of circumstances, and she is willing to accept whatever responsibility is legitimately hers for the way she behaved as a child.

Relief

While it is rarely mentioned because it seems so unacceptable, some people experience a sense of relief when a parent dies. The most obvious examples are when the parent has been an abuser. For one woman, the death of her verbally abusive alcoholic father when she was seventeen years old came as a relief. At last the fighting, screaming, and pleading ended and her home acquired some semblance of quiet and normalcy. For another woman, the abuse that ended with her mother's death was less obvious but no less real.

DONNA'S STORY

When Donna was five years old she learned that her mother was sick. The family was traveling to a local resort for a brief vacation, and while they were riding in the car, her father announced that her mother was suffering from a progressive, chronic illness that would eventually affect her mother's ability to function. Donna remembers her older siblings crying in the car. She herself was somewhat numbed. As a young girl, she did not know how to understand the information her father was giving her. She also had no way of imagining just how much her mother would change or how overwhelmed and frightened she would feel at having to care for her disabled and demented mother. When her mother died thirteen years later, Donna experienced an overwhelming sense of relief and the end of a childhood that can only be described as a nightmare.

Although Donna's mother's health did indeed decline progressively over time as had been predicted, her initial decline was rapid. Her vision became impaired. She had difficulty walking. She could not think clearly and she became emotionally volatile. More than anything, Donna remembers her mother's anger, her midnight outbursts and rageful complaints about her life.

Frequently Donna's mother would get up in the middle of the night and attempt to perform some household chore. She would go to empty the dishwasher or fold the towels and because she could not walk well she would make a strange shuffling sound as she moved around the house. Donna says, "I can never forget that sound. I always hear it in my mind."

Donna's mother became obsessed with cleanliness, and she would follow Donna around the house, cleaning up after her. She would wait for her when Donna went to take a bath so that she could clean out the tub and immediately wash the towels. When Donna got older, she was given permission to lock her bedroom door so her mother could not break in and intrude, but her mother found ways to break the lock with a knife or a screwdriver and to invade any private space Donna tried to make for herself.

As she was growing up, Donna remembers thinking, This woman will never die. She is going to torture me forever, and in fact her mother's behavior seemed to Donna, both during her childhood and her early adolescence, as manipulative torture designed to drive Donna crazy by making life as miserable as possible.

Not only did Donna grow up with an incapacitated mother, but she also assumed many of the homemaking and nurturing responsibilities that might have been performed by a functioning mother. When she was six years old, Donna remembers being dropped off by her father at a department store and told to buy her own clothes. By the time she was twelve, she was shopping not only for herself but for her mother as well, and she was given a note to accompany the charge card she carried in her purse. The note said, *Please allow my daughter to buy clothes.*

By the time she was ten years old, Donna was cooking for the family. When I asked her who taught her how to cook, she stopped and said, "I must have taught myself. I guess I just opened a book and read recipes." She recalls with much sadness a picture of herself, aged eleven, standing at the stove preparing dinner. She looks bedraggled and haggard, not like a little girl, but like a kitchen maid.

When she was thirteen, Donna's father actually began paying her for cooking and cleaning. It seemed to him that since she was already doing the job, she might as well earn the salary. Her role in the family thus went from daughter to employee. If dinner was not prepared just the way her father liked it she remembers that she would "catch hell." Her father, it seems, was not the kindliest of employers.

As her mother's health continued to decline, Donna's father began to consider that perhaps her mother would be better cared for in a nursing home. Donna's mother objected vehemently. But finally over her objections the family secured a placement that seemed humane and reasonable. Donna's mother, however, immediately began calling Donna on the phone and begged to be allowed to come home. Donna's father, once again abdicating parental responsibility, said to Donna, "It's up to you." Donna was unable to resist the pleas and entreaties of her mother so finally she consented, and after just a short respite Donna's mother returned to the family home where she continued her bizarre behavior and where Donna continued to be her primary caretaker.

By the time she was seventeen, Donna could no longer tolerate the pressure of living at home. She announced to her father that she was going to move out and live with her boyfriend. At this point, she was numbing herself with marijuana and other street drugs. Her father did not object to her plan, and Donna packed her bags and moved out of the family home. One month later, Donna received a call from her father announcing that her mother was dead; she had choked to death on a piece of food. Donna's first reaction was one of panic and overwhelming guilt. She could not stop herself from thinking, If only I had been there. If only I had not moved out my mother would not be dead.

Gradually she began to accept the fact that she was not responsible for her mother's death, that she did not move out in order to kill her mother, but that she had moved out in order to save herself. Donna continued to live with her boyfriend for another month and then returned home to her father's house. Now, with only a few months before she left home for good to go to college, Donna recalls feeling lost. Much of her childhood had been spent mothering her irrational, sick mother. She had received little of the guidance and nurturance a girl needs in order to grow into a woman. Although she had many feelings about the death of her mother and about her own experience growing up, Donna remembers more than anything her overwhelming sense of relief. "My thirteen-year nightmare had come to an end. Maybe at last I could get my life back."

Regardless of the form that it takes, the early death of a parent leaves an indelible mark on a child. A child comes to have a very personal image of what death looks like, an image colored by feelings that are powerful and overwhelming.

Jean-Paul Sartre, who often denied that his father's early death affected his life, writes of his own encounter with death: "I saw death. When I was five it lay in wait for me. In the evening, it would prowl on the balcony, press its nose against the window. I saw it but I dared not say anything. Once we met it on the Quai Voltaire—It was an old lady, tall and mad, dressed in black . . . she muttered as I passed. . . . Another time, it assumed the form of an excavation . . . [We] were visiting Madame Dupont and her son Gabriel, the composer. I was playing in the garden of the cottage, frightened because I had been told that Gabriel was sick and was going to die. I was playing at horses half-heartedly, galloping around the house. Suddenly I noticed a shadowy hole: the cellar had been opened. I do not quite know what manifestation of loneliness and horror blinded me: I turned around, and singing at the top of my voice, I fled. At that time I had an assignation every night with it in my bed. It was a ritual. I had to sleep on my left side, my face to the wall. I would wait, trembling all over, and it would appear, a very conventional skeleton with a scythe. I was then allowed to turn on my right side. It would go away. I could sleep in peace."[11]

When a parent dies young, children have a meeting with death that influences the way they see the world for the rest of their lives.

CHAPTER 3

~

The Surviving Parent

IN THE EYES OF A CHILD, the surviving parent undergoes a transformation almost as dramatic as death. Like the fairy-tale character who swallows a magic potion, the parent left behind grows enormously in size. He or she is no longer one of two parents or one part of a large extended family, he or she is now the only parent. In that new role, the surviving parent assumes enormous power and influence in a developing child's life. As the only parent, he or she bears the weight of all of the child's expectations and fantasies. No longer free to be just a parent, the survivor must be the "perfect" parent.

Richard Rhodes says that "he fixed his father up" because his father was the only parent he had.[1] A child often cannot afford to see the weaknesses and deficiencies in an only parent. One's very survival, after all, depends on the competence and strength of that parent. Children may find themselves selectively denying certain aspects of a parent's behavior, and embellishing or even inventing characteristics that cast the surviving parent as a safe and trusted caretaker.

The "fixing up" of a surviving parent is often no small task, however. When a spouse dies, the surviving parent is not merely a man or woman with normal weaknesses and foibles, he or she is an adult in the throes of profound and personal grief. The survivor has also lost someone important, someone loved and trusted. Not only has the survivor felt the devastation of having love and dreams ripped away, but he or she is now faced with an overwhelming task: raising children and guiding a family alone.

Not all surviving parents wear their grief the same way. Some mourn openly and freely; others mourn privately; some appear not to mourn at all. A child cannot help but be affected by what he or she sees reflected in the face of this now all-important caretaker. Children watch the responses of the surviving parent for clues as to how they themselves are "supposed" to mourn. "It's okay to cry" or "Be strong and tough" are often unspoken directives adopted without question by a vigilant and confused child. Children also learn what their new role in the family will be by watching the surviving parent. Although he could not articulate it then, one man whose father died when he was three now believes that his overwhelming sense of responsibility was born as he watched his mother cry uncontrollably on the day of his father's funeral.

When two parents raise children together, they serve as checks and balances for each other. The opinions of one parent are modulated by the advice and guidance of the other. When a child has only one parent, that parent's behavior goes unchecked. His or her influence is often the only influence a child feels. In a divorce, a child loses the family structure of a two-parent household, but does not usually lose the influence of two parents. The child continues to have two separate adults from whom to learn and grow.

Several problems arise because grieving families often become closed systems.[2] Family members and friends do not know how to deal with the pain of death and the emptiness of loss. At times out of respect, but more frequently from awkwardness, friends and family members stay away from a grieving family, depriving a child once again of alternatives to the influence of the surviving parent. In the closed system of a grieving family, a child can only hope the powerful surviving parent is benevolent since he or she will most certainly wield total and absolute control.

As they recalled their experiences with surviving parents, interviewees described several parenting styles. The most painful memories were of surviving parents who failed to parent well. Some remembered incapacitated parents whose own emotional response to the loss overwhelmed the child. These parents were felt to be depressed, angry, or incompetent. Others remembered a neglectful parent who became emotionally distant and unavailable. For some, the surviving parent, unchecked by another adult, became abusive.

Others recalled a close bond that developed with the surviving parent. In some cases, the bond grew as the child assumed the role of a companion or a friend. While the child relished the closeness and was initially glad to comfort the parent, these relationships often placed excessive demands on the child. Others recalled with gratitude, and some relief, a competent parent who managed to raise the family with a sense of purpose and determination.

The Incapacitated Parent

More than anything else, a child needs the surviving parent to appear strong and competent. In many cases, however, this is impossible. The survivor is so distraught over his or her personal loss that he or she is unable to be strong and competent for a child. When a parent is unable to function, a child becomes frightened and overwhelmed. Once again a child's basic assumptions about the world are shattered. Parents are supposed to be strong and competent. It is children who are allowed to be weak and vulnerable. When the surviving parent appears incapacitated, a child must contend doubly with the shattering of a secure and safe world order.

Incapacity in surviving parents takes a number of forms. Generally, the parent is so overwhelmed by his or own response to the loss that no energy remains to parent a family. The surviving parent's obvious depression, anger, or helpless incompetence become the focus of family life. By far the most frequent form of incapacity is depression.

Depression

When Virginia Woolf's mother died, she left behind not only dependent children, but also a grieving and inconsolable husband who frequently shared with his children his own wish to die. Not only were Woolf and her siblings burdened by their father's pain, even worse, they were implicitly charged with the task of making his life bearable. "The silence was stifling. A finger was laid on our lips. One had always to think whether what one was about to say was the right thing to say. It ought to be a help. But how could one help?"[3] Children who themselves needed care were left with the task of having to care for a parent whose grief was overwhelming.

Children have many reactions to parental grief, not the least of which is shame. Parents are not supposed to be weak and vulnerable, much less to cry like children. More than anything, C. S. Lewis recalls his own embarrassment when confronted with his father's grief following the death of Lewis's mother. Lewis wanted to turn away, to change the subject, not to have to look upon the face of his now weakened father.[4]

For Ron, whose mother's sudden death left his family in shock, his father's grief was frightening and incomprehensible. Ron recalls, "I could not feel my own loss because I was so overwhelmed by his grief." At night, Ron's father would roam the house unable to sleep, wailing in pain. His fourteen-year-old son would lie in bed, cover his ears, and wait for the night to end. Ron's father was inconsolable, not merely because he had lost his wife, but because he felt that he had failed in his marriage and her untimely death robbed him of the chance to repair what had been a troubled relationship. For Ron, his father's grief was mixed with self-loathing and recrimination. Frequently his father would cry out how all he wanted was to die. Until he left home to go to college, Ron shared a life of despair with his father. Several years later when he was dying of cancer, Ron's father requested that Ron not come to the hospital to see him one last time. Ron believed that this final act was his father's way of saying, "It is time for this pain to end."

Troy's response to his father's depression was somewhat different. He felt burdened but also angry that his father gave up on life after Troy's mother died. The family had been socially active and prominent in their community. However, once his mother died, Troy's father "hermetically sealed off our house." Visitors were no longer welcome, and Troy and his father rarely went out to socialize. When things in the home broke, Troy's father refused to repair them. "At one point it got so bad that we had to bail water out of the bathtub. It was like we were living in a cave." Without his wife, Troy's father only went through the motions of living; Troy remembers feeling angry at his father for not caring enough either about Troy or about himself to continue to engage life like the robust man he had been.

Ted, whose father died when he was an infant, only knew a depressed mother. He has heard stories about his mother before his father died, stories that describe a vivacious, lively, and funny woman, but that has never been his experience of her. His mother has always been withdrawn, depressed, and very serious. A Holocaust survivor herself, Ted's mother lost most of her extended family during the war. When she lost her new husband, she shut down emotionally. Ted describes her as being numbed, a woman who was unable and unwilling to engage too intimately with anyone, perhaps knowing that she could not bear the impact of another loss. Her muted response to life had a powerful impact on Ted and how he subsequently felt about himself. Living with a mother who was unable to be very loving, Ted grew up feeling not very lovable. Not until he finally married in his early forties did Ted begin to feel that he might be a person who could inspire joy and love in someone else.

Anger

When a surviving parent's grief manifests itself as sadness or despair, a child may be unable to ease the pain, but at least the emotional climate seems to fit what we expect when one has lost a loved one. In other families, a parent's grief manifests itself not as sadness, but as anger and rage at the world. This parent feels cheated, deprived, and resentful. Sometimes the anger is directed at the surviving children, sometimes it is directed at the deceased spouse. Almost always, anger is accompanied by a sense of stinginess and pessimism. The surviving parent may feel that the world is a bad and unfair place and may be unable to share any of his or her limited resources even with frightened and dependent children.

Kitty's mother felt burdened even before her husband died. She and her husband lived in a depressed and dying industrial town where they both needed to work two jobs in order to support their nine children. When her husband died of complications resulting from his lifelong addiction to cigarettes, Kitty's mother was filled with rage. She would rail against her husband, screaming, "You got out first and left me behind with this lousy life." As the youngest of this large family, Kitty felt acutely that she was a burden to her mother. Her mother hated her life and seemed not to have the interest or the strength to raise one more child. Kitty recalls an incident shortly after her father's death when the family was trying to decide for whom it would make most sense to take Kitty as a deduction on their income tax. Several brothers argued that it did not make sense for them to assume even nominal responsibility for her. Kitty remembers feeling like a child no one wanted.

Shortly after her husband died, Kitty's mother began drinking; not surprisingly, she was an angry and hostile drunk. Her drinking escalated to the point where she began having blackouts, leaving Kitty feeling very alone and very frightened. In order to save herself during high school, Kitty began to spend less and less time at home. She joined school activities, church groups, and community organizations and tried to limit the time she was subject to her mother's anger. After Kitty had left home to go to college, her mother finally received treatment for her alcoholism. However, she has not been able to tame the anger and resentment that have filled her since the death of her husband.

While Kitty's mother's anger seemed rageful and out of control, the anger Tony's mother felt was cold, controlled, and mean-spirited. It was as if Tony's mother went on strike following the death of her husband. Whenever Tony or his sister asked to do anything, his mother's response was, "We would've been able to do that if your father had lived, but. . . ." Life had deprived her of what she considered to be her only success, her marriage to a competent and well-respected man. Given her loss, she was not about to provide any real care or support for her children. She was deprived and they would be deprived as well.

Once when he was a young boy and was being teased by some classmates, Tony came home to tell his mother of his problems at school. "She just lit into me. 'Don't bother me with your problems. You are not entitled to have problems. I am the one with problems in this family.' " Tony quickly learned that his mother was not a source of support or guidance. She was too angry about her own loss to be able to give to anyone else.

Tony remembers that Christmas was the worst time of year for his mother. Christmas was "enforced institutionalized giving," and his mother could not bear to have to be generous with her family and with her children.

Throughout high school, Tony was never allowed to participate in any activity that required parental cooperation or involvement. Tony's mother was very clear that she wanted to give nothing and had nothing to give. On the day of his senior prom, Tony asked his mother if she would cosign a lease agreement that would allow him and some friends to rent a car for the prom. Although her signature obligated her financially in no way, Tony's mother flatly refused, saying, "How dare you bother me. I have already given you some of my time today." Tony's mother was stingy with her time, with her energy, and with her emotional and financial resources.

Surviving parents who are crippled by an incapacitating anger not only deprive their children of love and support, they also frighten their children. The world is not a safe place when one's only parent seems like an angry, irritable tyrant. Both Tony and Kitty had to battle the sense that they were burdensome and unwanted. The surviving parent seemed so troubled and resentful of life itself that it was almost impossible for these children to feel valued and good about themselves as they grew into adulthood.

Helpless Incompetence

Finally, for other surviving parents, incapacity takes the form of incompetence, or what the grieving child experiences as incompetence. It may be that the surviving "real" parent is unable to compete with the gone and now idealized parent. Nonetheless, the child grows up believing the parent to be helpless and inept. After his mother's death, Abraham Lincoln could see his bumbling father only as an incompetent fool. Lincoln desired to distance himself from his father and felt contempt for the man who was left as his primary caretaker. Lincoln went so far as to imagine that his mother was really the illegitimate daughter of aristocrats and that his maternal bloodline went back to some very prominent people. This fantasy allowed Lincoln to gain as much distance as he could from the legacy of his father's family.[5] Lincoln felt so little compassion and warmth for the man who was his father that many years later when Lincoln's father was dying, Lincoln chose not to go to his bedside.

Following the plane crash that killed her father, Cynthia's mother became the dependent child of the family. Cynthia recalls that whenever she cried, her mother would cry louder. It was as if the two were in competition to see whose loss was greater and whose pain was deeper. Cynthia felt that her mother was intent on establishing her greater incapacity so that she, the mother, would receive more care and attention from other people.

Throughout married life, Cynthia's mother had never learned to drive. When her husband died, it would have seemed natural for his newly widowed wife to obtain a driver's license so that she could take care of her family. Instead, Cynthia's mother petitioned the court so that her underage son might be able to get a driver's license and chauffeur her around. Now in her seventies, Cynthia's mother has still not learned to drive and continues to be dependent on her adult children for transportation.

Throughout Cynthia's adolescence, she recalls, her mother was conspicuously absent whenever there was difficulty or trouble. At one point her mother said to her directly, "Don't tell me anything that might upset me." Her mother gave all of her children the explicit message that she was a vulnerable and dependent woman. They could not rely on her for practical support, nor could they count on her for emotional guidance and nurturing.

Cynthia felt no compassion or tenderness toward her mother. Instead, she grew up filled with contempt for this woman who was unable to care for herself. Watching her mother, Cynthia vowed to herself that she would become an independent woman. As an adult, she is now financially and professionally quite successful and quite able to take care of herself. She regrets, however, that her reaction to her mother's dependency has been so extreme. Cynthia so hates the thought of being dependent on anyone that she has difficulty allowing her husband to share in some of the routine household tasks. She has often found herself unable to take even limited support from her husband for fear that she will either become too dependent or will appear to be too dependent.

Although she has not yet made up her mind about whether or not to have children, Cynthia is fearful of being responsible for a dependent child. She says, "Children are all dependency; I don't know if I could handle that. I might want to make a child into a little adult." While she knows that her anxiety and contempt for dependency stem from her reaction to her mother's vulnerability, Cynthia is still not sure that she can overcome those feelings enough to be able to mother children of her own successfully.

Cynthia's mother's incompetent parenting also forced Cynthia to become an adult long before she was emotionally ready to assume adult responsibilities. Cynthia was working and buying her own clothes before she was sixteen years old, and as soon as she received her driver's license, she shared driving responsibilities for the family with her older brother. Although Cynthia has some relationship with her mother now that she is an adult and has moved away from home, she admits that of all of her siblings, she probably has the most troubled relationship with her mother. She is still unable to forgive her mother for failing to be a competent parent.

When a parent is incapacitated by depression, by anger, or by incompetence, the child is confronted with a world that does not behave the way it is supposed to behave. The parent stops being a caretaker, sometimes temporarily, sometimes permanently, and the child is left in a world where loss is intermixed with fear and uncertainty.

The Negligent Parent

Some parents feel so overwhelmed by the task of having to raise children alone that they become unavailable, either emotionally or literally. In some cases a child is temporarily placed with other relatives. While this may make sense for the surviving parent, it serves as a double loss to the child, who has lost not only the parent who died, but, for reasons that are incomprehensible, has lost the other parent as well.

Movie idol James Dean described his double despair at losing his mother to an early death and then losing his father to incompetence. His father felt overwhelmed by the task of having to raise a nine-year-old boy alone. So, shortly after his wife's death, Dean's father sent the boy home to his family to be raised by an aunt and uncle. For the rest of his life, Dean rarely saw his father.[6]

One man remembers being sent to live with a grandmother after the death of his father. He was told very little about his mother, only that several times a year he would receive gifts and postcards from a woman who lived far away and was called "Mommy." When he was reunited with his mother several years after his father's death, it was as if he was being introduced to a stranger, a woman who existed only in his imagination and who was no more real than the father who had died.

As Charlotte Brontë's mother lay dying, she repeatedly said, "Oh, my poor children, my poor children."[7] She knew that the stern and temperamental husband she was leaving behind would be unable to raise her four daughters and her one son. Brontë's father became angry and inconsolable following his wife's death. He retreated into his work, and friends recall that his children roamed the hillsides like ragamuffins.[8] Eventually, unable to care for his daughters, Brontë placed the oldest girls in a boarding school. Knowing little about the needs of young girls, he found a school that was harsh, unnurturing, and unsanitary. Within months his two oldest daughters were dead from tuberculosis. Charlotte Brontë quickly learned that the world was a harsh and cruel place and that any care and nurturing she would get in her life she would have to find for herself.

Throughout her childhood, Brontë and her brother, Branwell, invented a magical world about which they wrote stories, poems, and adventures. In this make-believe universe, they felt in control, nurtured, and loved. The two created a world quite different from the one in which they grew up and had felt so neglected and abandoned.

Many children first feel neglect and abandonment when a surviving parent remarries. By remarrying, the parent seems to be embarking on a new life, forming a different family, and leaving the surviving child behind. One woman commented quite directly, "We lost my father to this other family. He chose them and just left us out." Once her father remarried, all of the pictures of her mother were removed from the home and the life the family had enjoyed before her mother died was never spoken of again. Often the child is not included in the plans for remarriage, so that the announcement that the surviving parent is going to take another spouse seems as precipitous and unanticipated as the announcement of death.

Tracy learned of her father's remarriage when she was visiting cousins over the summer. Her father called and said that he had met a woman from another town, they had married, and when Tracy returned home this woman and her two daughters would be waiting to greet her. Tracy felt abandoned by her father, who now had a new family, a family with which he could be more spontaneous and more loving, a family in no way associated with the grief he still felt over the loss of his wife.

Although Tracy does not remember feeling neglected or abandoned by her father at the time of his remarriage, she remembers keenly her response to his death twenty-five years later. Tracy's brothers decided to sit vigil in their father's hospital bedroom so that they could be present at the moment of death. Tracy decided to stay away, and she remembers thinking, What difference would it make? "The man in bed didn't even look like my father. To me he was already dead, so what did it matter if I was there or not for the actual moment he died? I realized then how he had really abandoned me when my mother had died a long time ago."

Because of the close bond he and his father developed in the three years following his mother's death, Victor felt terribly abandoned when his father chose to remarry. Although he was only eleven years old when his mother died, Victor became the primary caretaker for his alcoholic and diabetic father during the three years they lived alone together. Every morning Victor would give his father medication to make sure his father did not drink. He would watch his father's diet, monitor his blood sugar, and function like his mother before him as a nurse-companion to his surviving parent.

When Victor's father decided to remarry, Victor's first thoughts were that at last he would have someone with whom he could share the responsibility of caring for his father. His stepmother, however, did not see the arrangements in quite the same way. To her, Victor was an intruder, a competitor for the affections of her new husband. Victor's stepmother was also much less solicitous of his father's drinking than he had been. Within a short time Victor's father and stepmother began to fight, and Victor's father would leave the home and stay in a rooming house where he was free to drink as much as he wanted. This arrangement left Victor alone in a big house with a stepmother who saw him as a troublemaker and a spy for his father.

Victor remembers feeling totally abandoned by the father he had loved and for whom he had cared so diligently. Often when coming home from school, Victor would see his father's car parked in front of the rooming house and would know that his father was continuing his drunken binge away from home. Victor was excluded from the rooming house, and in his own home he felt unloved and unwanted. Victor decided that the only way he could survive in this alien environment was to numb his own feelings, to act the part of the perfect good little boy, and to try desperately to fit in.

Three years after this mismatched marriage began, it ended

with Victor's father's death. Victor was now totally abandoned. He was at home in a big house with a family that did not love and want him and with no parents of his own. Ironically, however, he was also the man of the house. His father had chosen to leave all of his substantial wealth to Victor, so while he was an emotional burden for his new family, he was their financial lifeline. Eventually Victor moved out of the family home to an apartment of his own. He remembers feeling as hurt and abandoned by the neglect of his father as he had been by the death of his mother years before.

The usual causes of neglect and abandonment on the part of a surviving parent are emotional unavailability or remarriage. Occasionally the death of a spouse opens up new possibilities in the life of a surviving parent, possibilities that do not include raising a dependent child. Regrettably, when this happens, a child may be perceived as unwanted baggage.

RACHEL'S STORY

Rachel's father was a prominent, successful businessman and the mayor of his small town. Everyone knew him and everyone loved him. From the time Rachel was born she was told that she was special because she was her father's daughter. Her mother was several years younger than her successful husband and took her lead from his direction. She became a supportive and loyal wife, dedicated to furthering her husband's already successful career. When, three years after she married, her husband died leaving her with a sizable fortune, an enhanced reputation, and a two-year-old daughter, Rachel's mother saw the world opening before her in a way she had never even imagined. She had always wanted a career in business, yet never imagined that opportunities would be open to her. Her husband's death, although at one level a sad event, gave her possibilities and options she was not prepared to deny. The life she now envisioned for herself was no longer the life of a supportive wife and a nurturing mother; it was the life of a career woman, and a child seemed only to be an unnecessary burden.

Rachel remembers that throughout her childhood her mother was always busy with one project or another. She invested in small businesses, became a property owner and a landlord, and gave generously to a variety of charities. She hated being a homemaker and a mother. Rachel recalls that her mother rarely cooked and never cleaned their large house. In the small town where Rachel lived, Friday was a traditional cleaning day. Many of her friends would spend Friday afternoon after school cleaning with their mothers. Not Rachel. Her mother never cleaned the house, so there was no shared activity, and Rachel remembers being ashamed to bring friends to this large house that was in such disarray. Her mother also rarely cooked dinner, and often Rachel would come home to find some money and a note saying: *Go buy yourself something to eat.*

As soon as she was able to go off by herself, Rachel would leave home for the day, never leaving a message telling her mother where she was and not returning until after dark. Her mother never asked her where she had gone and Rachel assumed that her mother really did not care. As long as she was out from under foot, her mother was satisfied. When she would try to approach her mother to ask for some guidance or advice, her mother would respond with, "You had a wonderful father and you are a special child. What else do you need to know?"

If school activities required the participation of a parent, Rachel was unable to attend. She remembers vividly a Girl Scout tea when all of the girls prepared a lovely luncheon for their mothers. Only one mother failed to attend—Rachel's. When she would bring her report card home from school, Rachel would need to show her mother where to sign. If she asked her mother what she thought of the report card her mother would often respond, "I didn't read it. I just assumed you're doing well."

Birthdays were a burden for Rachel's mother, so she chose to forget them. Throughout her childhood Rachel never remembers a birthday celebration, not a card, not a cake, not a gift. This neglect happened despite the fact that Rachel would repeatedly remind her mother of her birthday the week before, prompting her mother and encouraging her to do something special. Her mother always failed to meet Rachel's hopes and expectations.

Rachel spent much of her time alone, during which she developed a rich and elaborate fantasy world, a world in which she was the special child of her wonderful father. As soon as Rachel was old enough to ride a bicycle, she asked for one and began to take long rides. When she was moving through the air, the wind against her face, she would feel free of this barren home life. Part of what was so difficult for Rachel is that she saw her mother's energy and enthusiasm being directed toward friends and business ventures. Rachel's mother was not depressed, she was not angry; she was simply a woman who had moved on from the role of wife and mother and had no use for a little girl.

When Rachel was older, her mother decided to rent part of their large house as a rooming house. Rachel remembers socializing with some of the rooming-house tenants who used to enjoy sitting on the large balcony that surrounded the house. As a child, Rachel had always been forbidden to go up on the balcony because her mother told her it was likely to collapse. When Rachel saw the boarders sitting out on the balcony, she asked her mother if it was now safe for her to go there as well. Her mother laughed and said, "The balcony has always been safe. I just didn't want you out there because I didn't want to have to look after you."

When she finally went to college, Rachel remembers her mother driving the station wagon to the dorm, taking the luggage out, waving good-bye, and driving off. The other girls in the dorm had their mothers there to help them unpack and set up their new rooms. Not Rachel; her mother couldn't wait to be rid of her.

Despite the fact that she herself has had a successful career, a long marriage, and has raised three children, Rachel continues to be haunted by a basic sense of insecurity, a sense of not being wanted that she says "has never healed over." Not surprisingly, Rachel finds it difficult to share herself and her feelings even with those who are closest to her. She cannot shake the feeling that other people just are not interested.

Abandonment and neglect on the part of a surviving parent are especially difficult for a child to comprehend. It is painful enough to be abandoned by a parent who dies, a parent who leaves unwillingly. It is doubly painful to be abandoned by a parent who seems to choose to leave you behind.

The Abusive Parent

Richard Rhodes, who was the victim of a brutal and sadistic stepmother for years, continued to believe that his father was not in any way responsible for the abuse that occurred. To be honest with himself and to acknowledge that his father had abandoned him to the care of a heartless stepmother would have been to admit that he really had no one. He writes, "Then and for many years afterward, I refused to acknowledge Dad's complicity in what had happened to us; to do so would have meant also to acknowledge that the hole in my childhood could never be filled. I see that now. I couldn't then. I craved a loving, protective father."[9]

Occasionally the stress of loss turns an otherwise benign parent into an abuser. What happens more often is that the loss of the parent who functioned as mediator and protector unleashes the tyranny of the abusive parent. Without the intervention and the oversight of the now deceased parent, the abusive parent is free to do as he or she wishes. There are no checks, no balances, no controls.

When Jonah's mother died, he remembers, he thought, "Oh, my God, I have no one to protect me now." His father had always been critical and abusive, but Jonah's mother had routinely interceded on her son's behalf. She had calmed her irritated and irritable husband and had found a way to deflect his anger away from his only son. Jonah recalls, "I always knew that my father did not love me. I just thought that I didn't need his love because I was so sure of my mother." Once he was left alone with his father, Jonah felt panicked that he would now have to earn at least the respect if not the love of his tyrannical father.

Although he was physically abusive and would routinely beat Jonah and his sister, Jonah's father's worst crimes were the psychological abuse he perpetrated against his children. Jonah recalls, "He destroyed my image of myself as a brave and truthful person." Repeatedly Jonah's father would accuse him of some offense that Jonah had not committed. His father would rage and scream, calling Jonah a liar and beating him across the shoulders and the back. Eventually Jonah would "tell the truth." However, since he had not been lying in the first place, "telling the truth" actually meant telling a lie. Jonah would have to betray himself in order to stop his father's abuse. He likens his experience to the kind of torture that prisoners in a POW camp experience. Not only are they beaten, but they must deny their reality in order to appease the aggressor.

Jonah's father was unable to tolerate any competition from his son. As his son grew and matured, Jonah's father repeatedly called him weak, stupid, and cowardly. Whenever Jonah would find some quiet time to study, his father would purposely interrupt him. Jonah was convinced that his father did not want him to succeed because he could not tolerate the competition of a successful son. When he was sixteen, Jonah remembers beating his father at handball for the first time. His father was so enraged that he refused to speak to Jonah for a week and when he finally started talking, he ranted and raved at Jonah for his many character flaws.

Having known the love of a nurturing and supportive mother, Jonah could not comprehend how a father did not want his own son to become competent and strong. Until he finally left home at the age of sixteen to go to college, Jonah continued to be the object of his father's anger and abuse. Although he was freed from day-to-day contact when he moved away to go to college, Jonah continued to return home during vacations, each time hoping it would be better and hoping he would find some way not only to appease his father, but to win his father's affection and love.

After graduating from college Jonah entered law school. He was excited about pursuing law and about entering the profession that his father also practiced. Once again, though, his decision met with his father's disapproval. His father told him that law was a terrible profession and that anyone with any brains would seek another career.

In his second year of graduate studies Jonah came home and

announced to his father that he planned to get married. His father, without even meeting the young woman in question, immediately objected. He told his son, "You are clearly crazy, and this tells me that you will never make a good lawyer. I am going to call your dean and have you thrown out of school." Once again Jonah's father was attempting to crush his efforts to find love and happiness. Jonah returned to law school dejected and almost beaten. He approached the dean, however, and found that even if his father withdrew financial support he would not need to leave school. Jonah applied for a series of loans and scholarships, continued with his plans to marry, and severed all contact with his father.

Although he has felt a sense of loss and emptiness over the death of his mother, Jonah's greatest pain comes from the abuse he experienced at the hands of his father. As a man who has now successfully raised three children, Jonah cannot comprehend how a father could be so intent on destroying his own child. At several important occasions throughout his life, Jonah has regretted that he never reconciled with his father and that his father was not the kind of man who could have shared in his joy and his happiness.

Jonah knows that he would not have had a loving father even if his mother had lived. However, he is quite sure that his mother would have been able to continue to exert her calming influence and would have saved him from some of the worst abuses his father committed. At the very least, he would have continued to feel her love and approval, which would have stood as a counterweight to his father's damaging criticism.

In other cases, the parent who becomes abusive following the death of a spouse was not always an abuser. For some, the pressures of being a solo parent and a sole provider are overwhelming. Often these parents feel panicked and anxious, unable to control the world in which they must now be competent. Regrettably, anxiety and panic lead some to lose control and to vent their own frustrations on dependent children. Often when life settles down, these abusers return to being benign parents, only to be filled with tremendous remorse and guilt for their behavior.

Many years after her daughter had left home, one mother

who had become abusive following the death of her husband recoiled in horror while watching a daytime talk show about mothers who had abused their daughters. She looked at her daughter pleadingly and said, "Tell me I wasn't that bad." Although it is always damaging for a child when a surviving parent becomes abusive, it is doubly confusing when a parent who has been loving or even passive ceases to be so and becomes a tyrant. The child must then contend not only with the loss of one parent and the abuse of another but also with the perplexing reality that nothing is as it appears to be.

SAM'S STORY

Before his father's death, Sam and his younger brother had lived in what appeared to be a very traditional and typical American home: two children, a father who went out to work, and a mother who stayed home and tended the children and the house. When Sam's father died suddenly, the world changed for everyone in the family. All of a sudden Sam's mother was confronted with the need to support her family. She was determined to get a job and, says Sam, "to gain control of her life." Unfortunately she had few skills for earning a living and became a waitress, working the evening shift. Her job was difficult. She earned little money, and always felt tired.

Soon she needed to move her mother and aunt into her home in order to provide some help with child care, rent, and the support of the family. Both her mother and aunt began treating her once again like a dependent child. Sam's mother had been a wife and mother, the woman of the house, and now she was being told by her own mother how she should do things and how she should run her home.

Although she managed to function marginally for a few years, Sam's mother became increasingly stressed and increasingly distraught. She was often irritable and angry with her sons and frequently would remind them of how much she was doing for them and how much she was sacrificing on their behalf.

After four years of living without a husband, Sam's mother met a man she thought she might be able to marry. Unfortunately, before marriage plans could be finalized, Sam's mother became pregnant. Within nine months she had given birth to twins, quit her job, and moved her unemployed boyfriend into the family home. At this point, her life seemed completely out of control. Sam's mother's tenuous hold on maintaining the structure of her family life began to slip. She became irrational and abusive, and her twin babies were the object of her abuse. As they grew and became more willful and unmanageable, she would hit them, scream at them, tell them how bad they were, force them to sit for long periods of time in a chair with their hands tied behind their backs, and humiliate them when they failed to toilet train easily.

The torture and torment for Sam came in having to witness the abuse of these young children. He likened himself to a Jewish guard at Auschwitz. He himself was not in danger, yet he was a collaborator in the torture and degradation of others. Part of Sam's assignment as a young adolescent was to assist in the care of the twins. At times he would try to be nice, and kind, at other times he found himself being as harsh as his mother. When this would happen he would hate himself and feel even worse. Sam recalls that he knew something was very wrong in his home, yet he did not know what to do. He felt too young himself at age thirteen to deal with the problem. He tried to tell his aunt and grandmother, but they told him to be quiet. He did not know that he could tell people at school and perhaps gain some relief for his family. He remembers feeling as if he were dying inside when on one occasion he witnessed his mother break the arm of one of the children.

As he grew into adolescence, Sam describes himself "as one dismal individual." He rarely bathed, never combed his hair, and scowled all the time. He looked like a monster because he felt monstrous on the inside. He says, "I was one tough, mean misfit at school; very strong, very scary, yet totally afraid on the inside." Sam struggled with issues of power and abuse. He was so afraid of hurting anyone because he had seen terrible abuse of vulnerable children on the part of his mother.

Repeatedly Sam thought about his father and lamented that he had no one to teach him right from wrong. As he entered high school, Sam began reading voraciously books on all of the world's great religions. He felt desperate for moral guidance. His experience of growing up with a mother who was out of control made him feel a desperate need for order in the world. After months of reading, Sam came away with one maxim by which he would judge his own and others' behavior: Good begets good; evil begets evil. If he acted as a good person, good things would come to him. Throughout his life, Sam has tried to live with that morality as a guiding principle. In the absence of a living father, Sam sought a heavenly father who might instruct him in how to live a moral and good life.

As the twins grew and his mother gained some sense of control over her life, her abusive behavior subsided. By that time, Sam was already at the point of leaving home to go off to college. The damage for him had been done, however. He felt as if he had indeed been a guard at the death camp, a man who watched the torture and torment of others, and it took him many years to forgive himself for his inability to stop his mother's abuse. Over the years, his mother has been able to repair her relationship with the twins, who stayed under her care for many more years. It has been harder for her to repair her relationship with Sam and the damage that her abuse did to him.

The Parent Who Looks to a Child for Friendship and Love

The death of a parent and a spouse is such an overwhelming event that all the usual rules of family life are temporarily suspended. Parents do not behave like parents; they are confused, depressed, irritable. Families do not seem like safe places and the world is out of balance. At times, what emerges from that chaos is a newly defined family structure, a new order in which a child is no longer a child, but rather a peer and a companion.

Subtle and unspoken demands conspire to elevate a child to adult status. At times the surviving parent lets it be known that he or she would be much happier if the child could function as a friend or even as a surrogate spouse. Occasionally, members of the extended family let it be known that family life would be restored to normalcy much more quickly if the child could be "a big help." Well-meaning but misguided statements such as "Now you are the man of the family" encourage a child to believe that it is his or her role to assume adult status.

At times, the memory of the deceased parent serves as an impetus for a child to assume a new role. The child either believes that Mom or Dad would like it that way or else the child tries to identify with the functions and behaviors of the loved but gone parent. At first, a child may be exhilarated by assuming a new and more important role in the family. But invariably children feel overwhelmed because they are finally only children and do not have the emotional or mental capacities to function as adults for very long.

The child may be forced into one of two roles. When a same-sexed parent survives, the pressure to become a friend may be very strong. When it is an opposite-sexed parent who remains, an adolescent or latency-aged child may be pushed into the position of being a surrogate spouse. Both roles are fraught with peril for an immature child who does not yet know the rules of adulthood.

Friends

The friendship that develops between a surviving parent and a child is best called a pseudofriendship. It is not based on mutuality or reciprocity or shared interests, rather it is based on the child's implicit knowledge that his or her survival depends exclusively on the remaining parent. With so much riding on this parent's well-being, the child cannot risk an unhappy caretaker. The young child feels bound to care for a surviving parent any way he or she can.

After Janice's father died, she became "my mother's best friend." Shortly after her husband's sudden death, Janice's mother tried to go out with a group of adults. Her first foray into the singles world was not successful. She got drunk, came stumbling home, and needed to be put to bed by her twelve-year-old daughter. Janice remembers her mother saying, "I don't know what I would do without you. You are so comforting to me. It's a couples' world out there, and there is no place for me alone." Janice remembers her sense of shock as she felt herself being transformed from her mother's daughter to her mother's friend. "I wasn't prepared," she says. Yet Janice felt determined to be the very best friend she could to her grieving mother. She included her mother in all of her own activities and felt that it was her personal assignment to keep her mother happy. "I tried to keep her busy because I knew that if she wasn't busy she would get depressed and be very sad."

The first Christmas after her father died, Janice remembers being preoccupied with her mother's mood. Every time a favorite carol was sung or a special present opened, Janice would lean toward her mother and ask, "Are you happy now?"

In addition to being a good friend, including her mother in all of her activities and her social outings, Janice tried to be a "problem-free" friend. She reasoned that her mother had already had enough anguish over losing a husband, and she did not want to cause her mother any more distress. Obviously this evolved into a very unnatural friendship. Friends bring each other their problems and share their sorrows as well as their joys with one another. But Janice was so committed to her mother's happiness that she could not share the normal ups and downs of friendship, much less the struggles of her own adolescence. As a girl, whenever she felt like crying, Janice would go up to her room, put on a sad record, and start to cry. If her mother asked her what was bothering her, Janice would say, "Oh it's nothing. It's just the lyrics of the song."

At times, the model of friendship evolves into one of lifelong companionship. Some daughters feel they can never leave their mothers because their mothers have made no other friends and will be lonely and bereft if they move away. One woman described living with her mother until she herself was well past thirty. This was despite the fact that she had married, had a child, divorced, and was engaged to another man. She continued to be her mother's daughter. She says quite thoughtfully, "My mother's only identity after my father died was as a mother. I felt that I could not take that away from her." This woman was willing to sacrifice her own independent life in order to continue the mother/daughter companionship that allowed her mother to feel she was a valuable and worthwhile person.

Regrettably, these pseudofriendships are often filled with guilt and resentment. Whenever a daughter moves out on her own, she experiences a sense of guilt at leaving her mother behind. A number of women who had developed these dependent relationships with their mothers felt guilty if they did not call their mothers every day. Some of these women lived a great distance from their mothers, yet they each felt obligated to make the daily call in order to continue the illusion of close connection with a mother they imagined to be bereft and lonely.

Some adult children who have developed these companionate relationships feel angry and resentful. One woman, who is now in her forties and has not missed a day of talking to her mother in her entire life, feels burdened by the responsibility she has assumed for her mother's happiness. The calls to her mother invariably include some complaint on her mother's part, which the daughter feels obliged to try to fix. "My main function is to entertain her and make her happy. I fight against that constantly because I don't think it's natural or healthy." Another woman felt resentful at having to share the stories of her life with her mother. It seemed as if she was living for two, that she needed to have an abundance of adventures because her lonely mother lived vicariously through her daughter's escapades in the world.

Although it is certainly possible for companion relationships to develop between fathers and sons just as they evolve between mothers and daughters, most of the people in my sample who participated in these pseudofriendships were mothers and daughters. There may be two unrelated explanations for this, one arithmetic, the other cultural. Women are more likely than men to be widowed; consequently more mothers are left alone, and these women are also less likely than men to remarry.

Secondly, mothers and daughters, as women, both participate in the mythology of the dutiful daughter. The dutiful daughter is a cultural icon of idealized womanhood.[10] She is the daughter who sacrifices her own life willingly and lovingly for the happiness of her parents. It is almost impossible for a woman to be raised in this society and not to have been introduced through folklore, mythology, or popular culture to the image of the self-sacrificing, dutiful daughter. This mythological image is certainly one of the factors that guides a daughter's choice as she decides to assume the role of friend and to make herself the keeper of her mother's happiness.

Surrogate Spouses

If a child over the age of ten is left with a surviving parent of the opposite sex, the temptation is strong to engage in a pseudocouplehood.

For Brent, a series of circumstances conspired to make him the designated replacement for his father. His father died just a few weeks before Brent's bar mitzvah, the official time in Jewish culture when a boy becomes a man, at age thirteen. Brent was already beginning to think of himself as a boy about to move into a new and different phase of his life. He had also been identified as the son who was "just like his father." In fact when guests greeted him at his bar mitzvah, many commented on how much Brent looked like his father and how lucky his mother was to have him as a son.

Given those subtle and not so subtle suggestions, it was easy for Brent to start to think of himself as a replacement husband for his mother. He began to worry about the family's finances, and he soon assumed responsibility for paying the bills. He orchestrated the shopping for the family meals, while his mother continued to cook, clean, and care for the home. Brent remembers consciously thinking to himself that he was fathering his brothers and husbanding his mother. At first he felt proud of himself, almost arrogant that he had been able to step into the shoes of a man, and when people praised him for his competent behavior, he enjoyed being recognized and applauded by his relatives. Soon, however, he became overwhelmed and very aware that he was a boy doing a man's job.

The praise of his relatives also eventually gave way to criticism. Brent was told repeatedly how he did not measure up to the responsible and competent behavior of his father. One incident in particular became symbolic of Brent's failure. Brent was away on a camping trip and unreachable when his mother fell ill. The recriminations from his family were overwhelming. In every way Brent felt that he was a failed man. His own internal sense of inadequacy told him that he did not know how to provide the support and love his mother needed.

Yet Brent continued to play-act the part of "adult male" and became expert at what he called "the whore's game," the ability to fake passion when one really feels nothing at all. Brent was intent on faking manhood when he felt very much like a scared and inadequate boy.

Regrettably, the sense of being a fraud followed Brent into adulthood, and it was only in his late thirties when he had a child of his own that Brent finally began to experience himself as a real man with real strengths and real competencies. He was no longer pretending to be the father, he really was the father.

Brent felt damaged because he failed to live up to his father's role in the family. For Rose, succeeding too well at replacing her mother posed problems.

ROSE'S STORY

Rose's mother had been ill for many years before she finally died. During that time, Rose was her constant companion. She and her mother would sit for hours talking, and her mother would share with Rose her own hopes for the future, her regrets about her own marriage and her life, and her aspirations for her young daughter.

Rose's father was a stern and critical man who was verbally and physically abusive to Rose's older siblings. Rose always felt that her father left her alone because of the special relationship she shared with her mother.

In the last years of her life, Rose's mother suspected that her husband was being unfaithful. She took her youngest daughter into her confidence and asked Rose to become her ally and her spy. Rose and her mother would talk for hours about her father's indiscretions, and Rose became her mother's eyes and ears around the house.

Although her mother had been sick for years, Rose never be-

lieved her mother would actually die. She shared the myth held
by many children whose parents have chronic illnesses, namely
"Mother will be sick forever but she will never die." When
Rose's mother actually did die, Rose, a girl of seventeen, found
herself living alone with a man who felt like a stranger. As
Rose and her father rode to the hospital to see her mother's
body for the last time, they began to cry and share their sadness with one another. Rose confessed her past indiscretions
and mistakes to her father, begging his forgiveness and telling
him that she wanted to be his good daughter.

The night of her mother's death, Rose had accompanied her
father to have dinner at the home of a woman he was dating.
By sharing in her father's secret, Rose felt as if she were be-
traying her mother; she had already begun her new alliance
with her father. In the months following her mother's death,
Rose assumed all of the responsibilities of "woman of the
house." She cleaned, cooked, shopped, and attended to her
father's emotional needs. At night she would crawl into
her father's bed and sleep in her mother's spot. Rose felt
comforted by being near her father and also felt close to
her mother, snuggling into the pillow where her mother had
once slept.

Rose and her father became constant companions. They
would talk late into the night, make weekly pilgrimages to the
cemetery, and cry about their mutual loss. Rose, however, did
not forget that her father was a frightening and critical man,
and she lived in fear of displeasing him. Every night at dinner
she would worry that the meal would not be to his satisfaction
and that he would fly into a rage.

One year after her mother died, Rose's father remarried, but
the marriage did not last long. When he divorced his second
wife, Rose's father told her and his other children that his loy-
alties were to them and that he had been unable to make a
marriage work because "first and foremost" he was their father. Over the next several years, Rose's father married twice
more and had several live-in girlfriends. Each time his children,
now adults themselves, would give him their blessing, but each
time they would nod knowingly at one another, secure in the
belief that their father's attempt to build a new life for himself

would fail because as he had told them "they were all more connected to one another than they would ever be to anyone else." Repeatedly Rose's father would say to her, "No matter where you go or what happens to you, remember there is no one like your family."

When she was a senior in college, Rose and her father had their first difficult fight. At the end of a screaming match, Rose's father hung up the telephone and refused to speak to her for three months. Rose was devastated and likens her feelings at the time to those of a lover having had a tempestuous quarrel. She always knew that she and her father would reconcile, but she felt an angry determination not to be the one to give in first.

Throughout her twenties, Rose and her father remained close. She moved to a city on the other side of the country, established a career of her own, yet her father remained her primary confidant. They would speak almost daily, and she would share with him not only her business successes, but also her latest romances. Not surprisingly, none of her relationships ever developed into anything other than casual flings. For Rose, her heart literally belonged to Daddy, and it was impossible for anyone else to compete with the powerful image of her father.

Rose remembers being told by friends that her conversation was so filled with references to her father that it almost seemed as if she was talking about a husband. She would frequently quote her father and relay amusing anecdotes about him as if he were a constant part of her everyday life. Rose never felt a lack at not having a partner of her own. She always felt satisfied by the closeness and connection she shared with her father.

When Rose was thirty-five years old, her father died suddenly. She remembers being absolutely bereft. Now she was without a parent, completely on her own, and for the first time Rose began to consider the nature of her connection to her father. She had lost not only a father but a substitute husband as well, and she felt completely unable to move on with her life. Her own mourning lasted for several years, and it was not until her late thirties that Rose finally felt that she could bury her father and begin to consider a relationship with a man her own age who might be her real husband.

The Competent Parent

Although many of the stories in this chapter describe parents whose own grief and confusion prevented them from parenting their children at least for a time, there are also stories of parents whose competence and ongoing nurturing were a source of inspiration and support for their children. For the most part, these parents do not share their own mourning with their children. First and foremost, they remain parents and find other adults with whom they can mourn and from whom they can get the support they need. They may be withdrawn for a period of time, but they quickly resume the roles of being mothers and fathers and provide a constant, steady support to their children.

Repeatedly, the adult children of such surviving parents recall that their parents took parenting seriously and made raising their children their number one job. It is not surprising that children see this as the height of a parent's competence and worthiness. These were parents who felt they had a job to do and set about doing it well.

In the sample of people with whom I spoke, these parents were by and large mothers who assumed a competent role within the family and who allowed the family to continue with as little disruption as possible. In most cases they were models of courage and determination, women who did not initially have the skills to support and raise their families alone, but who acquired those skills and did so with a minimum amount of disruption to their families. They assumed new roles and grew into a competence that served as an inspiration and a model for their children.

When Luke's father was killed suddenly in a car accident, his mother was an unemployed schoolteacher whose teaching certificate had long ago expired. The summer after her husband died, Luke's mother packed up her three children, took them to a state university, pitched a tent where the family lived for the summer, and got the credentials she needed in order to return home and teach in the fall. She tried to turn their trip to state college into an adventure, and enlisted her children in catching butterflies and helping her with her biology assignments. Luke remembers feeling that his mother saw her mission as raising her children. It was a job she wanted to do well. Luke's mother did not marry again until she was in her early sixties and all of her children were successfully launched in their own lives. Although he never asked her, he assumes that this was purposeful, that his mother felt that she could not turn her attention to her own life until the mission of raising her children was accomplished.

When Jason's father was killed in Vietnam, his mother was only twenty-one. Her husband had been her high school sweetheart, the only boy she had ever loved. When he died, he left her with one small son and a baby on the way. Although she lived near her large family all of her life, Jason's mother became determined to raise her two children on her own. She never dated, saying she wanted no distractions in bringing up her children, and she used the money she received from the Veterans Administration to take her children on trips and provide special treats and entertainments so they would not feel deprived.

When Jason's younger sister graduated from college, he remembers that the family had a big outdoor barbecue. At one point a delivery truck drove up with a huge bouquet of flowers. Jason assumed that the flowers were for his sister, probably from one of her many boyfriends. Instead, the flowers were for Jason's mother, a token of recognition from her own parents with a card that said, *You've done just fine. We're very proud of you.*

Jason is filled with tremendous respect for his mother. Just as he feels that his father served his country, he believes that his mother served her family with the same level of integrity and honor. Jason senses that he has a great deal of respect for all women because of the example that his mother set.

Patrick thinks that his mother also took care of her family. She chose a more traditional route. After Patrick's father died, his mother began to look for a new husband. She had a young son and she herself was a young woman, and she wanted a man who would make her family whole. When she remarried, she chose a man who willingly accepted Patrick as his son. Throughout her loss and her remarriage, Patrick recalls that his mother remained loving, warm, and supportive, always there for him. Within two years, however, Patrick's mother's second husband also died, leaving her once again widowed, this time with two children. After a period of several years, Patrick's mother again began to search for a husband who would complete her family, and again she chose a man who welcomed Patrick and his sister with open arms. Patrick remembers feeling well cared for by his mother and believing that she was doing all she could to create a loving family for all of them. Patrick's mother's third marriage has been a long and successful one, and Patrick feels that throughout all of her ordeals, she has remained a steady and loving force. She has always been there for him and has remained his biggest fan and booster. Patrick has seen his mother's optimism and hope for the future as her most powerful quality. She never lets circumstances get her down, and that is what Patrick has learned from her and taken into his own life.

For Jack, it was not only his mother's competence, but her love, attention, and guidance that allowed him to get through the trauma of his father's death. Jack was a teenager when his father died and felt acutely the loss of a man who would have been a model and mentor for him. Jack says, "My mother became the sun around which we all orbited. She became so much more important because she was all we had."

In the first year following her husband's death, Jack's mother spent her time caring for her children, doing volunteer work, and reestablishing her life as a single woman. After a year, however, she returned to work, not out of financial necessity, but because she wanted to have a career and an independent life away from her children. Jack said he saw his mother grow strong and confident, and he felt he could lean on her throughout his own turbulent adolescence.

For many years following his father's death, Jack floundered. He did not know how to direct his own energy and attention. School seemed too unstructured, and he took a variety of courses, never really focusing on anything he liked or to which he could make a commitment. His mother stood by him throughout his difficult times. As he says, "She gave me the freedom I needed to experiment. She prodded me when I needed it, and finally she gave me the big boot when that was warranted. When I think back on what life would have been like if my father had lived, I wonder if he would have been able to handle me quite as well."

Jack also realizes that he would never have gotten to know his mother as he has if his father had lived. His primary relationship probably would have been with his father, and he and his mother would have developed a more distant connection.

Jack is grateful for the close relationship he and his mother share, and he says, "I will be indebted to her for the rest of my life. I feel very lucky to have had her as my mother. She is not only a loving woman but she has been in my corner one hundred percent, always reassuring me and standing by me."

What is particularly striking is that all of the adult children who recalled their surviving parent as being competent are sons remembering mothers. It may be that mothers feel that they must be strong for their sons who have lost the role model of a competent father. These mothers present their sons with an image of competence so necessary for their own development into adult men. Surviving mothers may feel freer to reveal their vulnerabilities to their daughters, who then assume a caretaking, companion role.

Some of what sons look for from fathers is a sense of accomplishment in the world, a belief that one can bring order and control to external events. Sons fear that when fathers die, competence and a sense of control die with them. Consequently, when mothers are able to function competently, sons are both awed and reassured by their mother's performance.

Parents always seem like giants to their children. Parents are our protectors and our guides. When a child has two parents, two people share in that awesome responsibility. When there is only one parent, that parent truly looms larger than life. He or she becomes all important to survival, both practical and emotional. A child becomes not only acutely aware of that parent's feelings and vulnerabilities, but also acutely sensitive to those feelings. When there are two parents, a parent's temporary withdrawal or depression might go unnoticed. When there is only one parent, the unhappiness a child witnesses seems intolerable.

In telling their stories of early loss, many people focused on the role of the surviving parent. As important as the loss was, equally important was the person who now became not the primary caretaker, but the only caretaker. The child came to know and experience the world through a single set of lenses.

CHAPTER 4

∿

Personal Mythologies

WHENEVER A CATACLYSMIC DISASTER OCCURS, the individual, whether a child or an adult, needs to make sense of what has happened. Sometimes the event is so shattering that one's beliefs and assumptions about the world are permanently rent. Sometimes those beliefs are so well grounded and so well integrated into one's life that after a period of mourning, they can be reaffirmed. Whether it is indeed possible to reaffirm or repair one's core beliefs following a public or private disaster depends on both the scope and impact of the disaster and the strength and depth of those beliefs.

On Palm Sunday in 1994, a tornado destroyed a small church in rural Alabama, killing almost a fifth of the parishioners, including several children. The congregation consisted of almost all the members of a small and close-knit community, people whose faith had been sustained over many years. The horror and magnitude of the event might have destroyed a less well anchored community. Instead, this congregation grew together and reaffirmed, at least publicly, its faith and its belief in God.

Sometimes an event is disastrous and calamitous, but it exists within a context that has a precedent for what has occurred, making it easier to understand and process the event. The state of California has been repeatedly struck by natural disasters—floods, earthquakes, fires. Residents of that state find it possible to affirm their belief that they will survive. "After all, this is California and we survive disasters here," they say. Californians have developed a worldview that includes natural disaster, a view that asserts that life in California is well worth the risk of some natural calamity. Moreover, this worldview incorporates the idea that people survive disaster; life goes on and through strong will and determination, people pick up and continue with their lives.

When faith is not fully established, when a worldview has not been solidified and integrated into one's life, or when there is no precedent for disaster, a calamitous event—like the death of a parent—will shake the order of things in a fundamental way. When a parent dies, a child is faced with a monumental task. The unthinkable has happened, yet the child must find a way to think about it, to understand the disaster. Children often invent stories—naive stories told in the language of childhood—to help them make sense of what has happened. These stories or childhood myths sometimes later form the core of an adult's view of the world or personal philosophy.

After his father's death when he was only six, Russell Baker says that he no longer fully trusted God. A God who could take his father away was not a God on whom Baker wanted to depend.[1] Despite his devoutly Christian upbringing, Friedrich Nietzsche, whose father died when Nietzsche was only a boy, evolved an elaborate philosophical system, which became identified with the statement "God is dead."[2] Nietzsche, not known for his sense of humor, was fond of an existentialist joke that began, "God's only excuse is that he does not exist."[3] For a child whose world was disrupted by early death and loss, the idea of a benevolent God became at best irrelevant and at worst a cruel joke.

The stories that children construct following the early death of a parent do several things. They often suggest a rudimentary understanding of the world and of how events happen. On a more personal level, these mythologies inevitably create an idealized image of the parent who has been lost, the self that might have been, and the relationship these two would have shared.

Many of these mythologies have an "if only" quality: If only my parent had lived I would have had a different life, I would have been a different person, my pain would have been less. If only death had not disrupted our family, my parent and I would have had a special relationship, a wonderful connection. Some of these idealizations are based on real information about the parent who has died. Some are pure fantasy and reflect the longings of a lonely child desirous of an all-good and protecting parent. At times the fantasies and mythologies are active reconstructions of the truth the child has known. Death provides an opportunity for recreating the lost parent and the destroyed relationship. The child can now invent a world of his or her choosing.

Sometimes the personal mythologies, developed after the death of a parent, are short-lived. They serve to help a child bridge the time of most intense and acute mourning. Other times the mythologies last a lifetime, forming the core of a worldview that a child carries into adulthood, sometimes as a treasured legacy of the past, sometimes as unwanted baggage.

The Lost Parent

Early death robs a child of real experiences with a mother or a father. When death occurs very early there may only be one or two memories, sometimes no memories at all. Repeatedly, men and women described their lost parents in glowing idealized terms. They were wonderful men and women, generous, funny, sensitive, one of a kind. Virginia Woolf gives a characteristically romantic description of her mother: "She had been happy as few people are happy, for she had passed like a princess in a pageant from her supremely beautiful youth to marriage and motherhood, without awakenment."[4] Woolf's mother is a character from a fairy tale. She is beautiful and young, a fairy princess. She is also happy. Few people remember or care to remember any pain or sadness in the lives of parents who die young. Although she idealized and immortalized her mother, Woolf was very aware that the impact of early death had created an unreal image for her: "Youth and death shed a halo through which it is difficult to see a real face."[5]

Not only do the images of lost parents tend to be idealized, they are also frozen in time. Death robs a child of the chance to see an adult grow and change over time. One way we come to know our parents as "real" people is to begin to see them with weaknesses as well as strengths. This process of humanizing our parents is a gradual one. As we ourselves feel stronger and more capable, we are better able to discard the idealizations of childhood and see our parents as multidimensional men and women. When parents die young, this process of coming to see our parents as real people is aborted. The idealized parent of childhood is frozen in our memory. Many people commented that one of the worst aspects of early death was that it robbed them of a chance to know a changing and more "fully human" parent.

When the parent remains forever young, a child may actually develop a myth of eventual reunion. Author Bruce Duffy, whose mother died when he was eleven, says, "I was nearly thirty-eight, the age my mother was when she died. I guess I had always imagined that at thirty-eight we would converge, my mother and I. Catching her in age after twenty-seven years of pursuit, I thought at last I might better understand her life and what she felt when she left: I awaited that day when we would not just be mother and son but simply Joan and Bruce, as if we'd met at some raucous party of the memory."[6]

Children invent not only a perfect, idealized parent, but also a parent who meets their particular and unique needs, a parent perfectly matched to their own developmental requirements. Troy's mother died when he was an adolescent, a boy beginning to rebel against the traditional values of his conservative southern family. Troy wore his hair long, smoked marijuana, spent hours writing poetry, and became intrigued by his own awakening bisexuality. Throughout his late adolescence and his early twenties, Troy comforted himself with a vision of his mother: "She was a free spirit, a rebellious woman far ahead of her time who would have supported her son and understood his own search for identity." Troy invented a mother whose personality and whose acceptance would allow him to explore his own developing self in a variety of directions.

Almost twenty-five years after her death, when Troy was packing up his father's home, he discovered a box of letters written by his mother. In the letters, his mother talked about her traditional values, her devout Christian faith, and her desire for a stable and conventional home. The woman who emerged from the letters was very different from the lively, free spirit Troy had imagined. As an adult, secure in his own identity, he was able to see his mother as the woman she had been, not the woman he needed her to be while he was growing up.

Because Liz was only four when her mother died, she was left with few memories. Her only images are of the happy, beautiful woman who used to sit and sew fanciful hats decorated with colorful buttons. Liz was named for her mother, and she remembers being called "baby Liz." After her mother's death, Liz spent time as a child imagining that she had been the treasured and loved child of this woman who had died so young.

Liz's father was overwhelmed by his wife's death, and he quickly remarried, this time to a prim and sour woman. Liz desperately needed to hold on to an image of a happy, loving mother, a mother who would have been able to embrace not only her, but life as well. Liz can clearly remember hearing her stepmother's repeated admonition, "Liz, don't ever marry a man with children, it will ruin your marriage." Liz was not very old before she realized that her stepmother saw children in general, and her in particular, as a burden. When she imagined her own mother, Liz envisioned a woman who would not only have loved being a mother but would also have loved her dearly.

It was not until she was herself a woman well into midlife that Liz felt secure enough to begin to dismantle the myth of her happy and perfect mother. Liz went on a quest to discover just who her mother really was. She looked at old pictures and questioned relatives who knew her mother. Liz discovered not the happy mother of her imagination, but rather a woman who was depressed and burdened, one who had never recovered from earlier losses herself.

Prior to marrying Liz's father, Liz's mother had been happily married to another man. She had had three children and her life was the picture of domestic bliss. In her early thirties, tragedy struck twice. Her youngest son was killed in an accident, and six months later her husband died. In the letters and mementoes that Liz uncovered, she came to know her mother's anguish and pain at the loss of both her child and her husband. Barely recovered from her twin losses, Liz's mother met and married Liz's father. Even in their wedding pictures, Liz's mother looks unhappy and heartbroken. Liz says about the face she saw in the pictures, "It was the saddest face I have ever seen." It was not long after her second marriage and Liz's birth that Liz's mother died. In retrospect, she now seems to Liz like a woman who gave up on life, a woman so beaten by her own devastating losses that she had no energy to invest in a new marriage and a new baby.

When Liz finally saw the truth of her mother's life, she wailed in pain. Liz spent months crying, not only for the loss of her mother, but for the loss of her myth, the myth that had sustained her through much of her childhood. When her pain subsided, Liz felt a surprising sense of calm. At last she felt ready to bury her mother because at last she had been able to know her mother.

Both Troy and Liz invented and nurtured images of ideal parents because they needed to in order to survive in a hostile world. For the same reason, some children use the occurrence of premature death to repair the image of a parent they knew to be less than ideal, to create, as one woman said, "a new and better version of my father."

Eleanor Roosevelt lost both of her parents before she was ten years old. Despite a contrary reality, she transformed her father into an ideal parent: "He dominated my life as long as he lived, and was the love of my life for many years after he died. . . . With my father I was perfectly happy. . . . He was the center of my world and all around him loved him."[7] In her idealized reminiscence, Roosevelt chooses to forget that her father was a man with many weaknesses, an alcoholic who was estranged from her family at the time when Eleanor's mother died. He was a man who, despite his promises, continued to disappoint his daughter with his irresponsible behavior. Many promised visits, for example, failed to materialize because of his drunken binges. Death gave Eleanor Roosevelt the opportunity to create the father she wanted.

A poem that Roosevelt carried with her years later, after the discovery of her husband's infidelities, gives a clue to her myth-making capacities.

> The soul that has believed   And is
> deceived
> Thinks nothing for a while,   All thoughts
> are vile.
>
> And then . . .
>
> Finding the pull of breath
> Better than death . . .
> The soul that had believed
> And was deceived
> Ends by believing more
> Than ever before.[8]

Roosevelt clearly applied this same philosophy to her father, a man whom she continued to believe despite his deceit. Rather than being crushed by her father's betrayal and his disappointing behavior, Roosevelt believed even more strongly in the image of a perfect and loving father. Roosevelt's biographer Joseph Lash conjectures that her tendency to "overestimate and misjudge" those she loved continued throughout her life and caused her disappointment.[9]

WANDA'S STORY

Wanda had grown up with the sense that she had two fathers. Some of the time her father was a responsible businessman who provided well for his family, and was fun-loving, generous, and caretaking. Other times he was an alcoholic father whose week-long binges would throw the family into disarray and fear. Wanda was seventeen when her father's death in a boating accident allowed her to bury her alcoholic and irresponsible father, leaving only the memory of the good and loving "Daddy."

When he would drink, Wanda's father lost all control. He failed to come home for weeks at a time. He neglected to pay bills and to take care of his responsibilities. All of the family's money, even the grocery allowance, was used to pay his bar bill. Wanda remembers one occasion when the three children gathered around the dinner table and had to make do with a few stale biscuits. If her father reappeared during a binge, his behavior would be out of control. He would rage around the house, screaming, fighting with her mother, and then falling asleep in the middle of the living room floor. Occasionally he would go out in the neighborhood and stumble into someone's yard, sometimes threatening to bang on the windows and break down the door. Often the police would be called; sometimes neighbors would have to join in restraining him.

As the only daughter in her family, Wanda had a special relationship with her father. She always thought that if she loved him enough and paid enough attention to him, she could somehow fix him—a myth about relationships that regrettably Wanda took into her first unsuccessful marriage. As a child, Wanda was known as "Daddy's little girl," and when her father was feeling good and had sufficient money he would always buy special presents for his beloved daughter. Wanda reciprocated. When her mother would periodically throw him out of the house, it was Wanda's mission to sneak him food and supplies.

As a girl, Wanda had never been able to reconcile these two conflicting images of her father. For her, he was both the out-of-control, abusive alcoholic and also the generous and loving father. When he died, Wanda buried her alcoholic father. In her mind and her imagination, she kept alive the man who had been her support and her patron. Wanda had been unable to "fix" her father while he was alive. Death gave her the opportunity to repair him to her liking. When she tells people about her father, she only remembers the popular, funny, gregarious man who loved to sing in the church choir. Unlike Troy and Liz, who came to realize that the image of the ideal parent was an invention of their own imaginations, Wanda continues, as a woman in her midforties, to believe in her "perfect" father.

And like Eleanor Roosevelt, she too tends to hold idealized and often unrealistic views of all those for whom she cares.

Kitty, whose father died after a long illness and a short but difficult life, had a somewhat easier time "fixing up" her father's image. Ten priests eulogized her father at his funeral as a "salt of the earth," hardworking man. Kitty had much support for starting to see her father as a tragic figure destroyed by a rough life. She says, "Death miraculously cleansed him of any bad qualities." When she thinks of her father now she imagines a man who understands and respects the work she does, who is proud of her and who forgives her for any mistakes she makes because he knows that she tries hard. The father who failed in his many attempts to give up the cigarettes that eventually killed him has disappeared. His small-town prejudices were forgotten along with his many misguided business ventures that nearly bankrupted the family. His passive voice that had failed to ever tell her of his love and concern vanished on the day of his funeral. Kitty's "remembered" father is indeed "a new and better dad."

Myths about the Self

In the same way a child is likely to create a myth about the parent who has died, he or she may create a set of false beliefs about the self. These self fantasies seem to fall into two distinct categories: fantasies about who the child is, usually tied to some notion of bad karma or culpability for the parent's death, and fantasies about who the child might have become if the parent had lived, replete with images of an ideal self who would have been nurtured by the relationship with the now deceased parent.

The mythologies of bad karma and personal responsibility for the parent's death often occur when there is a history of multiple losses and tragedies. Charlotte Brontë lost her mother to an early death. Soon after, her two older sisters were buried in companion graves, and several years later Brontë survived the deaths of her brother and her two younger sisters. Following her later losses Brontë wrote, "I am driven often to wish I could taste one draught of oblivion, and forget much, that while mind remains, I shall never forget."[10] Brontë found little respite in her life from the loss and tragedy that seemed to be constantly at her heels. She believed herself to be doomed to a life of sorrow and loneliness. She could not change her unlucky destiny, merely bear her lot with as much dignity as possible. Shortly before her marriage she wrote, "The evils that now and then wring a groan from my heart, lie in my position, not that I am a single woman and likely to remain a single woman, but because I am a lonely woman and likely to be lonely. But it cannot be helped and therefore imperatively must be borne and borne, with as few words about it as may be."[11] Charlotte Brontë wore the taint of death and loss throughout her life.

JOCELYN'S STORY

Jocelyn has buried so many relatives that Brontë's words might well be her own. Jocelyn was born into a large farming community and grew up with a warm and diverse extended family. As a very young girl, she was the doting companion of her strong and forceful grandfather, who took her with him as he made his daily rounds of the farm. Jocelyn first encountered death when she was only five years old, when her grandfather died. Because he was her grandfather, however, and not her father, his death was mourned but did not send shock waves throughout the family. When only three years later his eldest son, Jocelyn's father, died tragically of a slow illness, the family and Jocelyn were bereft.

Jocelyn remembers being her father's constant companion just as she had once been her grandfather's. She was a tomboy, and she followed her father around "like a little puppy." He would take her swimming, play softball with her, and treat her like his special little girl; Jocelyn's final memories of her father are of a thin man who could barely wave to her from the window of his hospital room.

When she was not quite eight years old, Jocelyn began to believe that "the people I love die on me." At her father's funeral, Jocelyn remembers being comforted by her father's younger brother, a funny, warm man whose skills as an actor allowed him to entertain his nieces and nephews with stories and charming impersonations. Jocelyn's uncle told her not to worry, that she would always have him now that her father was gone, and that he would be there to love her and to take care of her. Jocelyn remembers feeling numb when one month to the day after her father's death, this uncle dropped dead of a sudden heart attack. Jocelyn was now convinced. "There is something about me, perhaps something about the essence I excude, that causes the people I love to die."

Following the death of her grandfather, her father, and her uncle, Jocelyn, her mother, and her siblings moved away from the farm to a nearby town. Although she was an African American girl from the country, Jocelyn formed an intense friendship with a little White boy from the city. Despite their surface differences, Jocelyn and this boy shared something very important: they had both lost their fathers. They became constant companions, and their conversation frequently centered on their fathers and the loss they shared. As the stories of their missing fathers grew, Jocelyn often imagined that she and this little boy had the same father; their stories, their memories, and their fantasies were so similar. Each used to say to the other, "Don't worry, it doesn't matter that we don't have fathers, we have each other."

Children who lose parents are driven in their search for someone who will understand the loss. Adults often do not know the correct words to use when talking to children about their bereavement. Only another child who has suffered a similar loss seems an appropriate kindred spirit.

Three years after she and her friend formed their bond, Jocelyn was left alone once again. Her little friend and his family moved to another town. His mother was remarrying and the family was relocating to be near her new husband's family. Although this time it was not death that took Jocelyn's friend away, she felt abandoned and empty nonetheless. She spent many days walking by her friend's house, hoping that he might still be there, wishing to catch a glimpse of him, imagining that he might return to retrieve some forgotten object.

The search for her lost friend parallels the search many children engage in for the lost parent. In reality the parent is dead, but in fantasy the parent lives on and the child finds him- or herself searching down each new street for a glimpse of the missing mother or father. It is not surprising that by the time she entered adolescence, Jocelyn believed it was dangerous for her to love anyone. Her hypothesis that "the people she loved leave" was a core part of her personal belief system.

Although she is only forty, as an adult Jocelyn has already lived through the deaths of her mother, her sister, her aunt, and her half-brother. Each time Jocelyn, like Charlotte Brontë, felt assaulted by the force of death. She is convinced that it is her fate to be someone who loses those she loves. Jocelyn did not see herself as causing the death of these loved relatives, rather, it seemed to her that death was a part of her life, inextricably tied to who she was, and that it was impossible for her to move through the world without dragging the shadow of death behind her.

Some survivors of early loss harbor more personal and more causal fantasies about responsibility for the death of a loved one. After the death of her mother when she was only five months old and the loss of her father fifteen years later, Tessa was convinced that people left her because she was bad. She reasoned that if she could just be good enough people would not abandon her. She was not quite sure what "good enough" meant, but she developed a series of elaborate rituals and routines, which she needed to follow perfectly, in order to prevent someone else from dying.

When Tessa was only ten, her father had his first stroke. That is when she began to believe that if she could be perfect she could save her father from death. When her father suffered a second stroke four years later, Tessa kept vigil in his hospital room. The nurses reinforced her fantasies by telling her that her father ate and responded only when she was in the room. Occasionally Tessa would be unable to sit by her father's side in the hospital, and she would worry that something awful might happen. On the day her father died, Tessa had been unable to go to the hospital because of after-school activities. Although no one blamed her for her father's death, Tessa blamed herself. Regardless of how well she did during the rest of her early adulthood, Tessa felt like a failure on the inside. The outside person might succeed, win awards, marry, and have a family, but the woman on the inside felt as if she had failed in her most important task: keeping alive those she loved.

In midlife, Tessa received counseling to help overcome her belief that some failure in herself had caused the death of her parents. Although at that time she fully believed that the split inside herself had healed, several years later when her husband had to have surgery, Tessa kept vigil in his hospital room. As she said, "I know I can't cause him to live or die, but I can't take the risk of being left with the guilt if anything bad happens."

More common than myths about personal responsibility or bad karma are the fantasies children evolve about who they might have become if their beloved parent had lived. Like the fictional character Terry Malloy in *On the Waterfront,* many people live with the fantasy, "I could've been a contender." They think, If only my mother or father had survived he or she would have helped me to become my very best self. I would have been someone special, someone accomplished and successful if I had had the support and guidance of my parent.

At times these illusions about the self are pure fantasy, as invented and fabricated as the images of ideal parents. Occasionally they are based on some real information about the parent who died, an apocryphal story that leads the child to believe a parent would have performed in a particular way. Perhaps more than anything, these fantasies reflect a child's sense that something good died when the parent was taken away, that some spark inside the self that needed parental guidance and nurturing went out with the parent's death.

REGGIE'S STORY

Reggie was only three years old when his father was killed in a violent car accident. He has been told by relatives that when tragedy struck, his family was poised for success. Reggie's mother and father had just bought a home in a beautiful suburban community. He and his sister were healthy, thriving children, and his father had just been featured in a local news story on African American executives on the rise. It was easy for Reggie to mythologize his family story and to create for himself the image of a perfect father who would have provided guidance and mentoring to his young son.

Throughout his childhood, adolescence, and early adulthood, Reggie frequently thought to himself, If only my father had lived, I'd be somebody special. He imagined that his parents would have belonged to the local country club and that he would have been part of a select and "cool" group of people. Instead, Reggie always felt somewhat like an outsider, desperate for the approval of the popular clique. Reggie imagined that he would have shared in his father's elevated status and that that status would have given him a special role with his peers. As Reggie floundered throughout high school, he fantasized that if his father were alive, his father would not only have given him advice, but would have provided the necessary structure and guidance to keep Reggie on track. Repeatedly, conversations that began, "Son, when I was your age," would filter through Reggie's mind. His father would share stories of his own boyhood, and those stories could be used by Reggie as guides in making decisions and planning for his own future. When he found himself more interested in the social side of school than in the academic, Reggie imagined another conversation in which his father said to him, "Son, school isn't supposed to be fun. It's hard work and you've got to knuckle down." Reggie would look admiringly at his father, nod his head, and say, "Okay, Dad, I've got it."

In reality these conversations might never have occurred. The young son would probably have been more rebellious and less easily led by his father's words of wisdom. Yet, in his fantasy life, Reggie imagined his father's guidance bringing out his own best talents.

Reggie also believed that his father would have wanted to create a son of whom he could be proud. Reggie could just picture his father standing around the corporate board room, wanting to brag about his son's latest athletic or academic accomplishment. Needing a successful son, Reggie's father would have "cracked the whip." He would have made sure that Reggie studied and did his very best. Although in midlife Reggie is now a successful businessman, he believes that he would have become somebody "truly special" and that he missed his opportunity to "be a contender" when his father died.

For Vincent, fantasies about the "person he might have been" focused on who he would *not* have become if his mother had lived to provide guidance and to keep him on the right track. Although Vincent's father was a hardworking man, he spent little time with his young son after his wife suddenly died. Vincent's father had lost his own mother when he was a boy, and consequently he had no firsthand knowledge of what a boy might need from a mother. He reasoned that as long as he kept a roof over Vincent's head and food on the table, he was providing his son with a good life.

Unfortunately, Vincent needed more guidance and involvement to stay free of the rough and destructive elements in his neighborhood. Searching for companionship and acceptance, Vincent quickly fell in with a drug-using crowd. Recreational drug use led rapidly to an addiction, which haunted Vincent for much of his adult life. Vincent does not know whom he would have become if his mother had lived, but he is convinced that he would not have become drug addicted and destitute. His mother's guidance, Vincent reasoned, would have kept him safe from the temptations of the street.

Although no one else I interviewed suffered as many personal setbacks as Vincent, many people felt that they had been unable to parent themselves as well as they imagined they would have been parented by the one who died. Repeatedly, interviewees said, "I just know she or he would have done a better job in raising me than I was able to do for myself."

Fantasies about the Relationship That Might Have Been

Because the early death of a parent is about absence and loss, it is not surprising that children develop myths about the relationship that might have been. Not only the parent and the self are idealized, but the connection between the two also becomes part of the fantasy. Especially for children who hardly knew their parents, it is of foremost importance to believe that an actual connection between the child and parent existed. Children will often search for pictures, pictures that depict the parent holding an infant son or daughter, some visible sign that the two were in fact linked.

Heiress Gloria Vanderbilt, whose father died when she was an infant, used to play a game in which she imagined that her father had left behind an important letter just for her: "My favorite [game] was that he had written me a letter, a really long one, and hidden it in some secret place for me to find. Maybe, even, there would be a knock on the door and, standing outside, there would be the postman with a letter, special delivery, addressed to me, from Guess Who."[12] Vanderbilt's fantasy is a poignant example of a child's need to invent a connection with a parent she never knew. Because the fantasies of the connection to the lost parent grow in a field marked by absence, they often reveal what was missing in the child's life. These are fantasies of a longed-for but never known connection.

Tracy, who was left to raise herself with only a neglectful father for a parent, imagined a mother who would have mentored her into womanhood. Her mother would have taught her, she imagines, the things she needed to know in order to become a woman. Mostly Tracy has a vague sense that she is missing some important information necessary for her own adult development, some information that other women have and that can only be imparted by a mother. Occasionally, some specific behavior will remind her of what she does not know. Tracy can recall visiting a friend one day and having coffee while the other woman folded her laundry. Tracy remembers watching this very simple behavior and thinking to herself, No one ever taught me how to fold laundry. I didn't even know you were supposed to do that. She remembers being flooded with a sense of emptiness and then crying as she and her friend continued their conversation. Tracy was crying for all she had missed in being a motherless girl—the guidance and mentoring of an adult woman who would have shown her the way to grow into adulthood herself.

Tracy has two sets of wedding pictures that symbolize for

her what she lost when her mother died. One set is of her mother and father, and the pictures show a lovely bride in a traditional long white gown with flowers in her hair. The other set is of Tracy and her husband. The photos, in Tracy's words, depict a "typical hippie wedding." Tracy is standing on a hillside in a long, flowered skirt. While many couples married in the late sixties had similar ceremonies, Tracy is convinced that her unconventional wedding reflected the lack of a mother's guidance as much as it did the spirit of the times.

While Tracy imagined a lost relationship that would have been filled with womanly lore, Ted only envisioned a father who would have supported him in becoming himself. After her husband died, Ted's mother became terrified of sustaining another loss. She lived a conservative and modest life, and Ted remembers that she was unwilling or unable to support anything even remotely risky. As long as Ted chose the safe option, his mother was able to offer support and encouragement. Whenever he ventured, even slightly, from a safe path, Ted's mother became frightened and critical of his choices.

Although Ted was bright and did well in traditional academic subjects, he loved playing music and wanted to pursue a career as a musician. Nothing seemed riskier or less safe to Ted's mother than a career in the arts. She withdrew her support from Ted, and became openly hostile to his plans. Throughout his struggle with his mother, Ted would often think to himself, If my father were alive, he would have allowed me to do what I wanted. He would have supported me in following my dream.

Ted's fantasies about his father grew in part out of his desperate need to believe that there was someone who would have supported him and nurtured him. They also, however, grew out of a rather routine story that had achieved legendary status within the family. Early in their marriage, Ted's mother had very much wanted to go to graduate school. She could not, however, imagine how she might raise her children and attend school at the same time. Her husband told her not to worry about her responsibilities at home; he would take care of things. He would let her do what she felt she needed and wanted to do for her own career. This story enshrined Ted's father for all time in the pantheon of supportive parents. Certainly a man who was willing to support his wife would have done no less for his son. Ted's father had also been known as a warm, outgoing, and spontaneous man who loved to sing and joke, and Ted could not imagine that his father would disapprove of a career in music.

Without a supportive parent to combat his mother's fears, Ted did not feel strong enough to pursue his own interests and desires. Instead, he opted for a safe career as a civil servant, one of which his mother could approve. For many years Ted was haunted by the feeling that he had betrayed himself, lacking the courage to pursue what was right for him.

In his midthirties, Ted's fantasy of the supportive father materialized in one of his dreams. The dream was set in some unknown city on a foggy and mysterious morning. Ted was sitting in the lobby of a large apartment building. As he looked out the window, a long limousine pulled up. The door opened and Ted's father stepped out. He walked up to his son, a son he had never known, and shook Ted's hand, saying, "I just wanted to say hello and see how you were doing." He looked at Ted, nodded, and said, "You seem to be doing just fine, son. I'm sorry. I can't stay long." With that parting, Ted's father returned to the limousine and drove away. When he awoke, Ted felt a sense of calm, as if he had finally received the unconditional support for which he had longed most of his life. The dream felt soft, beautiful, and sad.

For Victor, the lost relationship he imagined having with his mother was not supportive but energizing. Victor's mother, who died when he was ten, had been an active, dynamic woman. She was, he said, "The fuel that drove the engine." When his mother was alive, Victor was an active little boy. He took piano lessons, played sports, and did well in school. In part, his accomplishments were driven by his mother's enthusiasm and her interest in the welfare of her only child. She helped Victor with his homework, made sure he practiced piano, and drove him to his baseball games. "I progressed," says Victor, "in part through her interest in me and because of her overwhelming joy in my success."

Victor tried to motivate himself after his mother died, but with no success. "It seems," he said, "that I have never really been able to focus since she died. My own energy has never been enough." It may well have been that if Victor's mother had lived longer he would have internalized some of her enthusiasm and her energy. As it was, her early death left him feeling that he was incapable of forward movement without a strong and powerful motivator to push him along.

Throughout his life, Victor has both sought and feared relationships that are similar to the one he had with his mother. He longs for another partner who will guide, direct, and energize him the way his mother did. Yet he fears ever again becoming so dependent on an external source of power and energy, for he knows too well how deadening it feels if that source is withdrawn.

While for most children, the imagined relationship with the lost parent grows out of their own sense of absence and longing for what might have been, at times the myth is fueled by family members. Relatives encourage the child to believe that a certain special relationship existed between him or her and the lost parent, believing that such a myth will ease the child's sense of loss or possibly serve to guide future development.

NOAH'S STORY

Noah was only six months old when his father died, but as soon as he could understand, he was told the story about the special relationship that existed between him and his father. Early in his mother's pregnancy, Noah's father was diagnosed with a serious illness. The doctors urged him to undergo surgery that might save his life. Noah's father refused. He insisted that he would not receive treatment until after his child was born. The surgery was risky and could itself be life-threatening. Noah's father wanted to make sure that he survived to see the birth of his child. When Noah's mother told him this story, she used it as an example of how much his father had cared for him.

Noah was raised in a very religious Christian family, and it did not take much for him to see his father as the martyred Christ, the man who gave his life so that his son might live. If his father had literally died out of caring for him, then, Noah reasoned, he would have to live an exceptional life. He kept thinking when he was a young boy, I need to be something special. I have to perform. I should be an athlete, an intellectual, a man of God. My life has to count.

In high school, Noah was not only an outstanding student academically, but he was known as "Mr. Extracurricular." He was an athlete, a musician, and a class leader. At Christmastime, he would send a list of his accomplishments to his friends. He did this in a humorous format designed as an imaginary "to do" list in which he would list the things that he had set out to accomplish, giving himself check marks where he had succeeded. While he did this with only mock seriousness and his friends often found it entertaining, Noah was driven by his own inner sense that he needed to achieve in order to justify what he believed to be his father's ultimate sacrifice.

Following his graduation from a prestigious college, Noah entered an aggressive and growing young business. By working sixty to seventy hours a week, he quickly rose within the firm, and by the time he was thirty, Noah was making a large salary and had the promise of becoming a manager within his company. And then abruptly, his successful world fell apart. Noah was assigned to a new supervisor who found his driven and sometimes arrogant manner to be offensive. She told him that although his job performance was outstanding, she did not like his attitude and as a result she was going to let him go. Noah remembers feeling devastated; for one of the only times in his life he broke down and cried. Noah had dedicated himself to being perfect, to succeeding beyond anyone's expectations. Only that level of accomplishment would justify his father's death. When he was fired, albeit somewhat capriciously, Noah felt as if he had failed. He spent the next year of his life reassessing how he was living. Noah realized that he had been driven by his own personal "mission impossible." He set off on a journey to try to find out who his father really was. He only knew his father through this myth of sacrifice. Noah drove around the country talking to surviving relatives and people who had been friends of his father's, trying to understand who this man was and what had caused him to make the choices he had. Noah's journey ended with his finally being able to separate his father's life and death from his own life. At the end of the year, Noah felt that he had reclaimed his own right to live. He no longer needed to be a superstar in order to vindicate his father's early death.

When he went back to work, Noah made some dramatic changes in the way he lived his life. He accepted a job that did not demand a seventy-hour workweek. He now balances his life among work, friends, and entertainment. Noah also contacted some business associates toward whom he felt he had behaved badly. Although these colleagues were somewhat baffled by Noah's overture, he took each out to lunch separately and apologized for past misdeeds. Achievement and accomplishment were no longer at the top of Noah's list. Rather than feeling that his father's life had left him with the demand to be the very best, he now reasoned that there was only one lesson to be learned from his father's untimely death: Life is short; one must be true to one's self.

In most cases, the fantasized relationship between children and deceased parents is idealized and positive. However, some children imagine a less than ideal relationship or even no relationship at all. They simply construct a scenario that allows them to avoid the pain of mourning.

When Allison's father died following a sudden stroke, she felt that she had no reason to feel bad because she and her father had no relationship. "The myth I created for myself said, 'I never really cared about him. He never really cared about me so it's no great loss.' " She did not cry at her father's funeral, and she remembers joking in a cavalier and hard way about his death. When anyone would ask her about her father she would respond, "Yeah, the old man croaked." Her brash response may have surprised some of her friends and relatives, but it was her way of saying to the world, "This doesn't bother me at all."

Although her fantasy that she and her father shared no relationship and that his death left her untouched may have helped Allison through the first months and even years of her mourning, it has not served her well into adulthood. It has caused her to feel separate and different within her family. Allison's mother and siblings mourned openly after her father died. Her bravado and denial, which clearly were her own way of dealing with her loss, were seen as a sign of callousness and indifference.

Writer Bruce Duffy, who adopted a similar persona after the death of his mother, says that his cavalier attitude put a wedge between him and his father that the two never overcame: "What irked him (my father) then was my 'unfeelingness' as he put it. He hated the fact that her death seemed to pass clean through me, leaving precious little grief that he could see and only my wild, obnoxious propensity to laugh at inappropriate times."[13]

Allison's bravado served as well to make her an outcast within her own family. Her "tough guy" persona, which masked her inner vulnerability, has made it hard for Allison to establish close relationships. Despite the pain she carries inside of her, she seems to casual observers to be an unfeeling and hard woman. Allison has also suffered as an adult because her myth has grown too powerful. She freed herself from having to mourn for her father because she reasoned "he had never loved me anyway." As that myth seeped into her core she felt increasingly like an unlovable woman. Allison's father died so long ago that it is no longer possible to uncover evidence of love between father and daughter. Allison is left only with her created mythology, a mythology that tells her she was unlovable as a girl and is unlovable still.

The personal myths that children create out of the ashes of their despair serve to organize the world for them. These myths are difficult to discard as one enters adulthood. Frequently these personal mythologies form the core around which one establishes a sense of self and a sense of relatedness to others.

Idiosyncratic Myths

When a child constructs a personal mythology he or she does so with immature cognitive abilities. A child cannot help but reason as a child—sometimes attributing causality where none exists and frequently asking "why" when no answer exists. Consequently, new worldviews are often constructed on a faulty foundation. In an attempt to make sense of the loss, some children will fashion an idiosyncratic view of the universe that is held to tenaciously despite subsequent contradictory experiences. While it may not be surprising to learn that children construct sometimes illogical explanatory systems, it is remarkable that many survivors of early loss continue to hold these beliefs into adulthood.

Don't Be Prepared

Jenny was only eight when her father died, but she remembers clearly hearing her mother tell her that one must always be prepared for the worst. Jenny was the only child of her very successful and glamorous parents. Although she had been trained as a teacher, Jenny's mother lived the life of a socialite while her husband was alive. When Jenny's father died, the family's fortune and lifestyle changed dramatically, but Jenny's mother felt comforted by the fact that she could return to her career as a teacher. "See," she told her young daughter, "you must always have something you can fall back on." This lesson was designed to motivate Jenny and to inspire her to live her life prepared for the worst. Jenny, however, took her mother's lesson and applied the reasoning of a little girl. Perhaps, she thought, the reason my mother was cursed with adversity is because she was prepared to handle it. Maybe if I am not prepared nothing bad will happen to me.

Jenny has lived much of her adult life trying hard not to be prepared. She is the mother of four children and is a very bright and lively woman. Yet she has never pursued any interests for longer than one or two years. Jenny wants to make sure that her interests remain hobbies and never blossom into a career. She attributes her propensity for switching her attention to the fact that she has multiple interests and talents. While her explanation may certainly be part of the reason, the other reason she switches her focus so frequently is that Jenny does not want to be prepared for widowhood.

In her role as homemaker as well, Jenny insures that she never plans too far ahead. She has raised four children into adulthood, yet she has managed to avoid any long-range planning or any careful preparations for the future. While her adult self knows that her motto, Don't be prepared, is an immature and childish one, Jenny cannot abandon her view of the world, consolidated in childhood, that tragedy happens only to those who are ready to handle it.

Don't Let Yourself Be Too Happy

The lesson that Paula learned at age sixteen from her mother's early death was that one should never be too happy.

Following a bitter divorce, Paula's mother worked for many years in order to establish her own independent identity, struggling to free herself from the influence of her controlling and critical older brothers. She established a business of her own without the support of her alcoholic ex-husband. Shortly after her fortieth birthday, things seemed to be coming together for Paula's mother. She was financially successful, running her own business, and enjoying a sense of accomplishment and independence. After many years of living alone, she had finally met a man whom she loved and with whom she felt she could share the rest of her life.

Although her mother never voiced these sentiments, Paula could not help but feel that life had played a dirty trick on her mother. Her mother had worked for years to build a happy and independent life, and just when she was on the verge of being truly happy, cancer came and took her life away. Paula took her mother's experience and reasoned that it was unsafe ever to be too happy. One could have a successful career or perhaps one could have a fulfilling love life, but one dared not have both. Too much happiness would tempt the fates and subject Paula to the same early death that had taken her mother away.

Lightning Won't Strike Twice in the Same Place

Although Felicia was shocked by her mother's sudden death, she comforted herself with the belief that if God had taken her mother early, he could not possibly take her father as well. Felicia consoled herself with the thought that she now had a deal with God. Her mother was gone but she would have her father forever. Imagining life to be some giant balance sheet in the sky, Felicia assumed that her debit column was already full. Rationally she could articulate that her beliefs were silly. Of course no one could live forever, and someday her father too would die. Yet emotionally Felicia was absolutely convinced that lightning would not strike twice in the same house.

Felicia's father lived and thrived for almost twenty-five years after her mother died. Yet when the surgeons came to tell her and her brothers that her father's condition was serious and the prognosis was poor, Felicia flew into a rage. She heard herself saying out loud words that seemed absurd coming from the mouth of a grown woman: "I paid my dues. My father is not supposed to die." It took Felicia many months and much support from friends and relatives to begin to accept her father's death and to put to rest her personal myth of a universal balance sheet.

Following the devastation in Nazi Germany, what plagued many survivors was their inability to create a myth powerful enough to explain the devastation they had witnessed. In order to survive catastrophe, individuals must construct theories to explain the world. At times, these explanations remain viable for only a short time. They serve as "positive illusions," designed to carry children through the worst phase of their grieving.[14] In some cases, they become consolidated into myths that last a lifetime. Often these myths merely hover in the background of one's consciousness and only surface when particular circumstances bring them to the foreground. In other cases, the myth is so pervasive that it is always present, and it exerts a powerful influence on all aspects of adult life. Regardless of their impact, however, children may have no choice but to make myths. The alternative to bringing some order to the chaos of early loss is to live in a state of constant despair.

PART II

Adult Milestones

CHAPTER 5

~

Creating the Self

THE FUNDAMENTAL TASK OF EVERY man and woman is to create the self. How do we take the raw material of childhood and turn it into a cohesive adult self? More than in probably any other task, a child feels the loss of a parent in this daunting assignment. A parent, especially the same-sexed parent—a father for a boy and a mother for a girl—serves as a living example of how to be a person. The loss of that parent leaves the child frighteningly alone.

We learn how to be people by following the examples set forth by our parents. We learn by taking that example, trying it on for a time, discarding the elements that do not fit, perhaps even tearing it to shreds before we can arrive at a sense of self that feels personally meaningful and authentic. As one man, orphaned in infancy, said, "My father would have been a model, a guide. At the very least, someone I could rebel against." In the absence of a parental model, a child creates the self in a vacuum. There are few guidelines, and equally important, there is no wall, no outer limit that says to the child, "You can go this far and no farther."

Without a parent to guide the way, some individuals turn to their own imagination in the task of creating the self. Author Charlotte Brontë invented a whole world, an imaginary town in which relationships and dramas were enacted. Later in her life, Brontë commented that her lifelong fascination with the complexities of human character began when she was only five years old, not coincidentally, her age at the time of her mother's death.[1] As an adult, Brontë wrote about the imaginary world she had created in childhood: "It is very edifying and profitable to create a world out of one's own brain and people it with inhabitants who are like so many Melchisidecs—'Without father, without mother, without descent, having neither beginning of days, nor end of life.' By conversing daily with such beings and accustoming your eye to their glaring attire and fantastic features—you acquire a tone of mind admirably calculated to enable you to cut a respectable figure in practical life."[2] Brontë invented a world out of her imagination and then she used her invented characters as models and guides to create her adult self. Not surprisingly, Brontë's imaginary characters were orphans. They too had no models or guides for how to be become adults. With the skill of a great writer, Brontë was able to manufacture characters from her imagination and then take those same characters back into herself as models for how to become a woman.

Several people I interviewed used similar imaginary techniques in order to create themselves. One man read all the adventure stories he could find, not merely relishing the excitement of the plot, but also learning how to become a man from the exploits of the characters. Another man spent hours watching television, in part, he says, to numb himself from the pain he felt, but also in part to collect an inventory of characters that he might use in the creation of himself. It was as if he had an imaginary file of index cards, each one listing and describing a particular personality, and throughout his life, he would draw on this file of characters in order to fashion his own unique self. The creation of the self out of one's imagination was likened by a friend of Charlotte Brontë's to growing potatoes in a cellar.[3] One must bring forth the self out of darkness with little nurturance or assistance from the outside world.

Some survivors of early loss were able to continue to use the parent as a model long after he or she had died. In these cases, the child remembered some special message delivered by a

mother or father, a message that then served as a guide for how
to live life. Arthur Ashe, whose mother died when he was a
boy, recalled telling a group of young people "about the morality of the decisions they might make in life. I usually tell them,
'Don't do anything you couldn't tell your mother about.' "⁴
Although she died when Ashe was only seven, Ashe's mother
continued to be a guiding image for him throughout his life,
and he tried actively to live a life that would please the mother
he kept inside his own imagination.

After her mother died, Eleanor Roosevelt's father described
for her what their blissful life together might be like once she
acquired certain attributes and qualities that would transform
her into the woman with whom her father could share his life.⁵
Roosevelt remembered her father's prescription, and throughout her life, she tried to be the woman he wanted her to be.
This internalized model of womanhood became the guide that
Eleanor Roosevelt used in creating herself.

When Eleanor was only eight, her mother died, and her father died two years later. Long after her parents were dead,
Eleanor Roosevelt wrote: "I knew a child once who adored her
father. She was an ugly little thing, keenly conscious of her deficiencies, and her father, the only person who really cared for
her, was away much of the time, but he never criticized her or
blamed her; instead he wrote her letters and stories, telling her
how he dreamed of her growing up and what they would do
together in the future, but she must be truthful, loyal, brave,
well-educated, or the woman he dreamed of would not be
there when the wonderful day came for them to fare forth together. The child was full of fears and because of them lying
was easy; she had no intellectual stimulus at that time and yet
she made herself as the years went on into a fairly good copy
of the picture he had painted."⁶ Without either a mother or father to guide her, Eleanor Roosevelt used her memory of her
father's image of what he wanted her to become in order to
create herself into womanhood.

One man recalls being haunted for years by what were re-
puted to be the dying words of his father: "Tell Brian to take
care of his little brother." Brian was only three years old when
his father died. Yet these words, the only real advice he was

ever given by a father he never knew, became important for Brian as he began to figure out how to become a man. He took these parting words to mean that he must be both successful and responsible. And in fact, achievement and responsibility became the building blocks of Brian's adult self.

In the absence of any real memories of a lost parent, many individuals undertake a quest for their historical roots. Several men and women described searching through family record books, personal diaries, and old letters in an attempt to gain a sense of who the lost parent really was. Some individuals sought out relatives and interviewed them, attempting to gather data about their dead mother or father. This quest was often driven by an ambiguously defined desire to "know my parent." Survivors of early parental loss often held the belief that some missing piece of information about the dead parent might hold the key to their own development. "Knowing" the lost parent meant that they might be able to know themselves.

Philosopher Friedrich Nietzsche, whose father died when he was not quite five years old, undertook the writing of his autobiography when he was only a boy of fourteen. In order to write what was to be *his* autobiography, Nietzsche solicited anecdotes from many of his relatives about his own father. The book, rather than being the story of the young Nietzsche, became a collection of stories about Nietzsche's father. The philosopher later said that his desire was "to write a little book and then to read it myself."[7]

For a boy of fourteen, it is not surprising that his own life's story is entwined with the life story of his father. The boy has not yet started to break away and to become an individual different from his own father. Although Nietzsche wrote a public document, he was driven by his desire to read it himself. He was collecting information that he might use to understand who his father was, and to see who he himself might become.

When a parental role model is nonexistent or so vague as to be of little use, many individuals turn to substitutes—mentors, or surrogates—who serve the same role a parent might. Throughout his life, Nietzsche searched for symbolic fathers, men of genius and stature who might guide him in the task of becoming himself: "I always believed that at some time fate would take from me the terrible effort and duty of educating myself: I believed that, when the time came, I would discover a philosopher to educate me, a true philosopher whom one could follow without any misgiving because one would have more faith in him than one had in oneself."[8]

Certainly the young child, and even the early adolescent, believes in parental power, especially as it relates to the life of the child. This faith in the invincibility of the parent gives way to the rebellious questioning of adolescence. Nietzsche's relationship to his mentors, the philosopher Schopenhauer and the composer Richard Wagner, illustrates the child's ultimate struggle against an idealized and loved parent. At first the parent seems perfect, unable to do any wrong, a perfect model of how to be a person. Then the idealization crumbles and the child rejects the parent's model; the child must find his or her own way to live a life that is personal and authentic. Eventually the child is able to return to the parent, not as an ideal, but as an example, one example among many of how to become a man or a woman. One man talked about finding older men, usually ten or fifteen years older than he, and watching them, not because he wanted to become them, but because he wanted some glimpse into the future, some sense of what might lie ahead given that he had been robbed of the example of his father when he was a young boy. He did not view these older men as ideals he himself needed to emulate; rather, they were living examples of how a man might live his life.

When he was a philosophy student, Nietzsche would spend hours during lectures watching the way his professors taught. He was as interested in "how they did it" as he was in what they had to say.[9] A child certainly needs practical and concrete information from a parent, but perhaps more important than knowing how to change a tire or how to bake bread, a child needs to know how to be a person in the world, and it is this process of becoming more fully human that Nietzsche sought in the examples of his professors.

Nietzsche suggests the complicated symbiotic relationship between a parent and a child in his birthday tribute to Wagner. "It is an incomparable good fortune for one who has been feeling and stumbling along on dark and foreign paths to be led gradually into the light, as you have done with me. I cannot therefore honor you in any other way than as a father. So I celebrate your birthday also as a celebration of my own birth."[10] Nietzsche was well aware of the intimate and essential relationship between a father and son, a relationship of which he was deprived and which he sought throughout his life in substitute relationships with mentors and teachers.

The task of creating the self is a daunting one. Adolescence and early adulthood are characterized by crises of identity, struggles in which young men and women try to find a balance between incorporating parental goals and values and creating a self that is uniquely their own. When there is a living parent, a child must balance the desire to please the parent with the need to be his- or herself. "Pleasing" a parent too much can mean becoming a carbon copy of the parent's image of who the child should be. To displease a parent too much, on the other hand, might risk the affection and approval that even a grown child still seeks. The desire to maintain a relationship with the parent serves as a counterbalance to the need to break free of existing guidelines and demands. Children with living parents may sometimes feel limited in just how far they can stray from the path marked out by a mother or father.

Biographers have suggested that Charlotte Brontë was free to create the rebellious and free-spirited character of Jane Eyre in part because both Jane Eyre and Charlotte Brontë were motherless women.[11] Only a woman who did not have to worry about displeasing her mother could create an image so individual and so outside of traditional bounds, a character that some reviewers chose to label as "dangerous."

If most of us rely on parental models to create the self, then what is the experience like for a motherless or fatherless child who must embark on the journey of becoming a person without a guide to lead the way? Survivors of early loss describe their feelings about being so emotionally on their own as ranging from *exhilaration* and *determination* to *resignation, a sense of being overwhelmed,* and *a feeling of being out of control.*

For some, the freedom of creating the self with no or few constraints is exhilarating. The task of choosing among all possible options is heady and exciting. For others, determination is mixed with a defiant and angry "I'll show you" to a world that left them bereft. Still others are quietly resigned, prepared to take on a task they assume more out of necessity than enthusiasm. For some individuals, the task of creating the self without clear guidelines and models is overwhelming. They approach adulthood with a feeling of fear and trepidation. Still others feel dangerously out of control at the prospect of having to create the self with no boundaries or outer limits. However daunting the task, orphaned children have no choice but to "grow potatoes in the cellar."

Exhilarated

Philosopher Jean-Paul Sartre described the early death of his father as his greatest piece of good fortune. "The death of Jean Baptiste was the big event of my life. It sent my mother back to her chains and gave me my freedom. There is no good father, that's the rule. Don't lay the blame on men but on the bond of paternity, which is rotten. . . . Had my father lived, he would have lain on me at full length and would have crushed me. As luck had it, he died young."[12]

Sartre believed that he would have been both doomed and limited by his father's expectations, desires, fears, and insecurities. His father would have forced him to become a duplicate image of his own life, teaching him to respect traditions and to "know [his] rights and [his] duties."[13] These obligations to the past would have guided Sartre's creation of himself, serving as powerful limits on his own possibilities. Sartre declared, "My luck was to belong to a dead man."[14]

In his philosophy and in his life, Jean-Paul Sartre was passionate about creating the self. Sartre believed that we are what we make of ourselves, and in the absence of a controlling father, we can become whatever we choose. Sartre's insistence that the past had no influence on his own life extended to his own immediate past and to his own work as well as to the distant past and the life of his father. Once a work was completed, Sartre refused to acknowledge its importance and its impact. Once the past was gone it was finished. All that mat-

tered was the future, and Sartre was continually pushing himself into the future, intent on constantly creating and re-creating himself. "I never stop creating myself. I am the giver and
the gift."[15]

As a young boy, Sartre aspired to be the person who "knew
the most things,"[16] a goal that seemed reachable to a boy who
had no father. There was no authority. No dragons to slay; no
kings to honor.[17] In a world without the demands of authority,
Sartre could indeed become the person who knew the most
things and who created his own reality.

Rather than being overwhelmed by his freedom, Sartre was
exhilarated by it, excited by the prospect of becoming a person
who had no ties to anyone except himself. Once after visiting
the philosopher Martin Heidegger, Sartre defiantly refused to
acknowledge any debt to a man who many believed was his intellectual mentor. When he arrived at the train station after his
visit, Sartre was greeted with a bouquet of roses, a gift from
Heidegger and a token of the philosopher's appreciation for
Sartre's visit. Sartre took the roses and threw them out the
window of his train compartment, unwilling and unable to acknowledge any debt or connection to another thinker or philosopher.[18] Though Sartre had pupils and disciples, his world
had no place for fathers.

Sartre's autobiography, which was eventually entitled *The
Words,* was originally entitled *Jean-Sans-Terre,* which means
"Jean without possessions or without inheritance."[19] Sartre
liked to think of himself as the man who had come from nothing, one who was totally self-made and self-created. Throughout his life, Sartre was preoccupied not only with creating his
own story and his own identity, but also with creating his own
obituary. He wanted to control not only the way he lived his
life, but also the way in which he would be remembered after
his death.[20]

Jean-Paul Sartre was a creative genius, a provocative and
original thinker. He seemed to delight in defiantly denying that
his past or his history had any impact on his self. He could say
out loud what for most is unthinkable, that the death of a parent was a wonderful piece of good fortune. Even if a child feels
excited to be free of parental limits, he or she may be uncom-

fortable about saying so. Exhilaration is not a usual, much less an acceptable, response to the death of a parent.

For Charles, who was fifteen when his mother died, his sense of excitement on the day of his mother's funeral made him uneasy. He felt guilty to be feeling almost euphoric as his mother's casket was being lowered into the ground. He remembers leaving the funeral party at the cemetery and wandering off for a long walk. "I was upset but I was so excited. I saw it as an adventure. I said to myself, 'You'll be on your own. Wonderful things are going to happen.' Suddenly I was a man. There was nobody telling me yes or no or maybe or anything else. I thought, This is you now. It's your life. And I felt exhilarated." As he told me of his response to his mother's death, Charles could not help adding that he felt guilty saying those words out loud. A son is not supposed to feel freed and excited when his mother dies.

As a man of thirty-five, twenty years after his mother's death, Charles has maintained his sense of excitement and ownership about his own life. He believes that he can do anything he wants and be anything he desires. This is his life and he embraces it fully. As an adult, when he has been faced with adversity Charles has always thought to himself, I can handle anything. He was quick to point out that he does not believe that he can "fix anything," that is, change it so that it will be more to his liking, only that he can survive whatever trials life puts in his way.

Although Jonah's first thoughts following the death of his mother were trepidation at being left alone with his abusive father, he quickly took charge of his own life and began to feel excited at the prospect of "creating myself": "After my mother's death, I discovered that my father wasn't God and that I could be different from him." For years Jonah's mother had interceded with his abusive father. While she served to protect Jonah, she also left him with the belief that his father was powerful and untamable. Once his mother was gone, Jonah learned that he could cope with his abusive father, and that discovery freed him to begin the process of creating himself. Jonah says, "I am the product of my own imagination. I created a vision of what a man does in life and then I tried to do it. I dreamed myself into the future as a teacher, a lawyer, a husband, and a father. I have always set my own standards and tried to meet them." After Jonah decided that he could not tame or please his father, he decided that his father's standards, guidelines, and expectations were irrelevant to his own development. "I began to set the standards myself."

In talking about his life, Jonah says, "You create an image and you live up to it and then you do it again. It enables you to do things you wouldn't otherwise be able to accomplish." Jonah creates an image from his own imagination, from his experience with other men, and from his vast knowledge of literature and fiction. That image serves as his own ideal, selected by him and not imposed by anyone else. It is that image that Jonah tries to approximate. For Jonah, the process of creating the self does not stop with a single image, however. As soon as he feels he has successfully approximated one ideal, he creates a new image, which then serves as his next milestone in the journey of creating himself. Each time the creative process that drives Jonah into the future is of his own making: "I plan my own life. I will invent my retirement just as I invented my adulthood. This is my life, I made it and I am excited about it."

Self-doubt seems almost absent from these stories of individuals who were excited by the prospect of creating the self. These individuals feel that they have no one to answer to other than themselves. They experience a sense of pride mixed with bravado as they talk about the pleasure they have taken in creating their own identities. As Sartre said about himself, "I faced my Destiny and recognized it: it was my only freedom. . . . In short, I did not quite manage to pigeonhole myself."[21] For the man or woman who feels excited at the prospect of creating the self, there are no limits. All things seem possible.

Determined

In some individuals, two separate responses to early loss combined to create a feeling of fierce determination to the task of creating the self. The first was anger. These individuals felt furious either with the dead parent who had abandoned them or with the surviving caretakers, who were seen as uncaring, incompetent, or neglectful. This anger was then mixed with resolve, resolve to "show" an unfeeling and unloving world that one was indeed worthy and lovable or resolve to use their own lives as a vindication of the parent who had "abandoned" his or her responsibilities by dying young.

When actor James Dean's mother died, she left a nine-year-old boy with a father who felt overwhelmed at the prospect of raising a son. Dean's father put his wife's casket and his young son on the same train, sending them both back to their hometown, where he hoped his son would be raised by members of the extended family. Although Dean seems to have been well cared for by his aunt and uncle, he became determined to succeed in defiance of the mother who had died and the father who had abandoned him.

When he was asked why he became an actor, Dean replied, "Because I hate my mother and father. I wanted to get up on stage . . . and I wanted to show them. I'll tell you what made me want to become an actor, what gave me that drive to want to be the best. My mother died when I was almost nine. I used to sneak out of my uncle's house at night and go to her grave, and I used to cry and cry on her grave—'Mother, why did you leave me? Why did you leave me? I need you . . . I want you.' "22 Eventually Dean's cry turned into a defiant promise to himself: "I'll show you for leaving me . . . fuck you, I'm going to be so fuckin' great without you!"23

Dean's anger at the mother who had died and the father who had abandoned him inspired him to create a self that would be recognized and admired everywhere. Throughout his short life, James Dean was obsessed with the process of creating and inventing himself. As he traveled around the country, he would pick up pieces of personality, stylized affectations that he would make his own, carefully constructing and creating his own persona, his own self. A friend of Dean's said that he seemed to be always writing his own biography, actively attempting to complete the job of creating himself.24 Dean repeatedly had himself photographed, then he would spend time studying the photographs as if he were studying the image of the man he wanted to become.

Eleanor Roosevelt was similarly determined to create herself. Left orphaned by the early deaths of both her mother and father, Roosevelt was determined to make something of herself, not only for herself, but also to vindicate her father, who died an irresponsible and dissipated alcoholic. Roosevelt's biographer Joseph Lash writes, "Because of her overwhelming attachment to him, she would strive to be the noble, studious, brave, loyal girl he had wanted her to be. He had chosen her in a secret compact, and this sense of being chosen never left her. When he died she took upon herself the burden of his vindication. By her life she would justify her father's faith in her, and by demonstrating strength of will and steadiness of purpose confute her mother's charges of unworthiness against both of them."[25]

For years after Armand's mother, his only parent, died, he heard relatives malign his mother as a careless woman who had not taken care of her own health. He also listened to these same relatives as they repeatedly told him, "You will make nothing of yourself. You're no good, just like your mother." Although he was only a small boy, Armand would huddle with his younger sister and they would talk of how they would succeed in the world just because everyone was expecting them to fail. The two orphans made a pact with one another: "If I am successful, I will take you along and you'll do the same for me." After their mother's death, Armand and his younger sister were sent to live with a great-aunt who seemed to take pleasure in reminding them that they were only with her because no one else wanted them. Despite years of physical and psychological abuse, Armand held to his pledge to make something of himself, not only for himself, but also in memory of his mother who had died so young.

When he was only fourteen years old, Armand decided that he could no longer endure the abuse in his great-aunt's home. He packed his bag and ran to his older brother, who lived in a rough and dangerous neighborhood. After only a few months, Armand decided that growing up in such an environment offered him little chance for the success of which he dreamed. Although he was only fourteen, Armand did a careful survey of the high schools in his neighborhood. He decided which would be best for him to attend. Then he found a distant cousin who lived in that neighborhood, went to her, and proposed that she allow him to live in her house in exchange for his paying room and board. "After that," says Armand, "I was never a child again. Never."

The same strength and determination that allowed Armand to leave an abusive situation and to take charge of his own life led him eventually into military service, where he would receive training and financial support, and finally to a community far from the one in which he had grown up. After his discharge from the army, Armand moved to a new city. There, as part of the process of creating himself, he consciously decided to change his name. He no longer wanted to be associated with the poor boy who had grown up without the love of a mother or father. As a man and as a member of the gay community, Armand would now create a family and a world that could be uniquely his own. "Because of the gay community, I now realize that family does not have to be the people who have the same blood as you. They can be other people; people who are your friends, these people become your family. The people you see every day. The people who are in your life and you are in their lives. I can now make the family that I want to have."

Since being orphaned at the age of four, Armand has been determined to create himself and to prove to his abusive and negligent relatives that he has become someone worth loving despite their treatment of him. He has provided for himself the things he needs in order to survive. As a young boy he would often say to his sister, "You tell me that you love me and I'll tell you that I love you. Children need to hear that they are loved." Without anyone guiding him or telling him what he needed in order to become an adult, Armand knew intuitively what was necessary for his own survival and he has been determined to create a loving world for himself.

COKIE'S STORY

Cokie first began taking care of herself and her mother when her mother was first diagnosed with cancer. Even at the young age of nine, it was obvious to Cokie that her alcoholic father would be unable to provide her mother with the care she needed. For six years Cokie was her mother's nurse and constant companion. She helped with the cooking, took care of her younger sister, and stayed up late with her mother watching movies and talking. When her mother's pain became so intense that she needed an injection of morphine, one of the few things Cokie could not do, she would page her father. He would come home, administer the shot, and return to the bar with his friends.

Cokie was determined to raise herself and to care for her family in the best way she knew how. "I absolutely felt that I was capable and I did not need any help at all. This is what I must do. Others have done it before. I could do it now." In her fierce determination to create herself, Cokie became a little adult. She was barely an adolescent, yet she had already assumed the responsibilities and commitments of an adult woman.

Some authors have speculated that what gets called a "pseudoadult personality" is born out of a desire to identify with the lost or dying parent.[26] Cokie's prematurely adult self was born more of a desire to survive in a world that might easily have defeated her. After Cokie's mother died, her father left her and her sister alone for a week while he went off on a vacation. Cokie was not especially surprised since her father had been only minimally involved with them in the final months of her mother's life. Although she was only fifteen, Cokie went about the business of negotiating with various relatives, discussing the possible child-care arrangements for her and her younger sister. When her father returned home from his trip, he begged Cokie to stay with him, promising to make a better life for her and her sister and telling her how much he needed them in his life. Cokie acquiesced to her father's request, but told herself that her primary goal was to survive and to take her young sister with her.

Although she continued to go to school, Cokie's life resem-

bled that of a working mother. She would go to school during
the day but quickly come home in order to be there when her
younger sister arrived home from grade school. Cokie felt unable to participate in any after-school or extracurricular activities. She had extra activities of her own: the care of a home
and the raising of her young sister.

When Cokie was eighteen, her father had a serious car accident. For six months she was the sole caretaker of her younger
sister. Cokie used this opportunity to move away from her father's home. As a high school graduate, she was able to get a
job and to rent an apartment of her own. Cokie took her sister
with her and they set up home in a small one-bedroom apartment. Cokie worked during the day and took care of her sister
in the evenings. She felt no resentment for this arrangement.
She had grown accustomed to her role as older sister and caretaker and felt committed to doing a good job. Cokie lived the
life of a busy single mother: working during the day, preparing
meals in the evening, making sure that the home was a comfortable and nice place for her young charge.

In the summer, Cokie, like other mothers, began to prepare
for her sister's summer vacation, interviewing various day
camps and selecting the one that seemed best suited to her sister. When she herself began to date, Cokie had to explain that
she came as a "package" deal. Anyone who wanted to go out
with Cokie would have to get to know and eventually love her
little sister. Many young men were deterred by this arrangement, but Cokie insisted that she would not leave her sister behind. When Cokie was nineteen she met a man who felt willing
to date her on her terms. On their very first date Cokie, this
young man, and her eleven-year-old sister went out for ice
cream. Cokie was pleased that the man seemed able to accept
her young sister as part of the deal.

When six months later this man asked her to marry, Cokie
decided that this might at last be a chance for a life of her own.
She packed up all of her belongings, including her younger sister, and she and her boyfriend drove to a town in a southern
state where he had relatives. They rented an apartment, obtained a marriage license, and only then did they phone Cokie's
father. Initially he pleaded with Cokie to return, saying once

again that his children were important to him. This time, however, Cokie ignored his empty pleas. Cokie was determined to have her own life, free of the neglectful father who had abandoned her and her sister when her mother died.

After Cokie and her husband married, she became the legal guardian of her sister. Cokie not only successfully raised herself, creating the adult woman she eventually became, but also raised her younger sister, who now looks to Cokie almost as if she were a mother. In her early thirties, Cokie severed all ties with her father. Her anger at him for failing to help raise her and her sister made it impossible for her to continue any contact. She no longer wanted or needed anything from him and she had proven that she could survive without him. Although she is now only in her midforties, Cokie and her husband are planning for an early retirement. When one considers that Cokie began being an adult woman when she was only nine years old, retirement at age forty-five begins to make sense.

One senses, however, that Cokie's determined struggle to create herself despite her father's selfish neglect has not been without its costs. She did manage to raise her sister and build a life for herself, but she missed much of her own adolescence and early adulthood. Her efforts have left her exhausted, and rather than anticipating a creative midlife, she longs for a time when life will be less of a struggle.

Resigned

For some, the task of creating the self is taken on with a sigh of resignation. These survivors of early loss feel neither excitement nor defiance. Instead, like good soldiers who must do a job that no one else much relishes, they act out of necessity. The child is presented with a situation that calls for action; there is no choice. One either creates the self or lives in a world of chaos.

Rock star Madonna, the quintessential image maker of the 1980s, felt just such resignation on the death of her mother. When asked to describe the impetus for her competitiveness, Madonna attributed some of it to the death of her mother when she was only six: "After I got over my heartache I said, 'I am going to be really strong and if I can't have a mother to take care of me, then I'm going to take care of myself.' "[27] Her mother's early death also taught her that life was short and that one could not and should not wait for the things that one really wants. Necessity caused Madonna to have to create herself. There was no mother to guide her and to nurture her choices. She alone was left with the responsibility of inventing and reinventing the woman she would become. While necessity began the process, Madonna's own pleasure at creating her public image clearly continued to drive the process of creating the self.

Another survivor, Jake, with less flair for the dramatic, talked about having a similar sense that he had no choice but to become his own person. "When I was growing up I could do a lot of things by myself perfectly well. I would often go out and play basketball, bounce and shoot for an hour by myself, or go out on the golf course by myself. I could probably spend more time by myself and do things on my own more than most people my age could, and I enjoyed it. I still enjoy it. It may be that I developed this sense of myself because of necessity." In the absence of a father to mentor and guide him, this man learned how to take care of and nurture himself.

Clare recalls feeling quite unprotected in the world when her father died. Her mother was a self-absorbed woman, concerned with what members of the community thought of her and her family. As a result, Clare recalls not receiving much attention from her mother once her father died. The experience of being on her own and being left to her own devices convinced Clare that she could endure a lot. She knew suffering, discomfort, and inconvenience firsthand, and she learned that she could cope with these by "just putting my head down and forging ahead." Because she received little attention from her mother and was often left to fend for herself, Clare invented an interior world that became "quite portable," a world in which she could invent herself and imagine possibilities for her own life.

Desiring to gain attention from her friends and classmates, Clare invented an imaginary boyfriend, complete with a fatal illness. She told her friends about her doomed lover and remembers being not only pleased with the attention she received, but also intrigued that she could invent a world and then use that world to get what she needed from other people.

After her father's death, Clare felt alone and frightened much of the time, yet she was resigned out of necessity to forge ahead. "I do what I have to do. I summon all my courage and I attend to the tasks that I have to attend to but with enormous energy expended. Sometimes I slink back until I build up my required head of steam and then I can go at it again. But I don't go out thinking, I can do it all. Part of me thinks I can do it, but part of me thinks I can't. Another part of me thinks I'll be laughed at, I'll be rejected. I know that I'm highly skilled in my profession, yet I keep thinking that I'm going to be found out. That's how it plays itself out. I do what I have to do. I earn a good living. I'm inventive. I basically take care of myself." Clare, like many of those who create the self out of necessity, feels burdened by the task of having to be her own inventor. By all standards, she has succeeded quite well, but sometimes she wishes that the burden could be shared by another, a strong and available parent who might have been there to guide her on her way.

DON'S STORY

When his father abandoned the family, Don became the man of the house out of necessity. His older brother was already an out-of-control teenager, and Don's mother felt overwhelmed by the prospect of raising her three sons. She turned to Don, the son most like her, as the logical choice to replace his father. Don says, "Virtually all of my father's responsibilities fell to me. I was paying the bills, orchestrating the shopping, trying to control my brother's acting out. When my brother would leave the house, my mother would send me to watch him, making sure that he did not get into any trouble." As a boy of eleven, Don resolved to be a responsible man, a man of whom his mother could be proud. "I did what my mother asked because there was no one else." If Don's father had not died when Don was only sixteen, five years after he had already abandoned the family, Don's story would be about the trauma of abandonment, not about early death. But for Don, abandonment and death became permanently entwined and came to mean loss without the chance of reunion.

Throughout his life, Don's motto has been: A man takes care of himself. This is in part what he learned from his father's failed example. Don's father had been unable to take care of his family when he lived with them, when he abandoned them, and ultimately when he died. Don saw how important it was, not only to his mother, but to the family's very survival, to have a responsible man at the helm. In the wake of his father's abandonment, a man was born. Don says that the boy he was at the time went underground. As an adult, however, his close friends fondly refer to him as "the boy," aware that he harbors a childish inner self kept very separate from the adult person necessity forced him to become as a young child.

Don's father's example serves as a reminder of how a man should not behave, and whenever Don feels himself slipping into being irresponsible, lazy, or doing less than he might be able to do on the job, he gives himself a pep talk, boosts himself up, and pushes himself back into the world. Don is his own cheerleader, his own mentor, and his own guide.

When he was in high school, Don was eligible for the free lunch program because his family was on Welfare. He chose, however, not to take charity from the school. Instead, he devised a small business, buying bubble gum at discount and selling it to his friends at full price. His little business, which became the first of many entrepreneurial ventures, allowed Don to pay for his own lunch and to nurture his sense of being a responsible, self-supporting man.

In his career, Don is very successful. He manages a large corporate division and supervises hundreds of employees. Whenever he is presented with a task by his superiors, his immediate response is, "Just tell me what I have to do and I'll do it." When he hears colleagues complain about having to make cuts in their operating budget, Don is always surprised. He does not understand why other people cannot just buckle down and do what needs to be done. Don's experience growing up has convinced him that he has the inner resources to make bricks without straw. He is able to do what needs to be done even without the resources. As a young boy, he did not have the knowledge or the skills to be the man of the house. Yet necessity forced him to do the best he could.

Like many who feel resigned to be their own mentors and creators, Don has often felt burdened and drained by the experience of having to raise himself. Despite his many successes, Don knows that it takes all the energy he has to be so responsible for his own life. At times, he fantasizes about staying home and letting his wife support him, but he is too accustomed to relying on himself and too afraid of feeling dependent and vulnerable to indulge that fantasy for very long.

Overwhelmed and Panicked

For some individuals, especially those who are orphaned very young, the task of creating the self seems overwhelming. Not only are there no models and no guides, but the young child feels bereft of the inner resources to take on the task of becoming a person. Many of those who felt overwhelmed by the task of creating the self saw themselves as being underachievers. They assumed that they had been held back in their own development by the lack of a parental model and guide. Often they felt behind their peers, as if things came late to them and the task of having to learn things on their own was so overwhelming that it cost them dearly in time and energy.

Author Richard Rhodes remembers being overwhelmed at the task of creating himself when he was left alone with a neglectful father and an abusive stepmother following his mother's suicide. Rhodes searched desperately for the rules that would make a secure and safe middle-class life. He remembers reading Emily Post's book of etiquette, trying to find a prescription for how to live a life and become a person.[28]

Many people who are overwhelmed at the task of creating themselves feel scared and frightened. For one man, Jerome, the feeling of being scared was crystallized in the image of him having to run home every day across a barren field in order to get to his grandmother's house. Jerome's father died when he was an infant, and his mother left him in the care of relatives until he was six. Although he was surrounded by aunts, uncles, and cousins, Jerome remembers thinking, I'm the only one here with my last name. There are no others like me. Knowing that he was vulnerable, his cousins would make a game of teasing Jerome as he ran from the ball field to his grandmother's. They would tell him that ghosts and goblins waited in the field for him on his way home. Jerome remembers being terrified, a terror that was part of his childhood. Yet he also remembers feeling that he had no choice but to run across the field. Although his memory pertains specifically to his after-school activities, it also serves as a metaphor for Jerome's feelings about having to become a man on his own. He felt scared, overwhelmed, yet as if he had no other option but to run across that field. There was no other way to get where he had to go.

Being scared followed Jerome into adolescence. This time, it was not the ghosts in the field, but rather his own inability to accomplish the tasks that lay before him. Jerome was a smart boy, and he did well in school. Yet he felt frightened of trying anything above and beyond his regular curriculum. Once he remembers watching the other boys practice for a track meet. When Jerome thought no one was looking, he tried the high jump and, to his surprise, did quite well. One of the coaches came over to him and said, "Son, that was a good job. Why don't you try out for the team?" Jerome, rather than feeling pleased at the coach's encouragement, felt frightened. How could he possibly do something like that? He remembers thinking that if he had a father he would have someone to reflect back his own strengths and weaknesses, someone who could serve almost as a barometer, telling him at what he was good and at what he was not. In the absence of external validation from someone who loved him and someone he trusted, Jerome felt frightened to reach beyond safe boundaries.

Once when an uncle gave him some advice on how to shoot baskets, Jerome remembers, "I latched on to it like it was gold. I was so hungry for someone to tell me how to behave." When he graduated from college, Jerome did not know how to avail himself of the career counseling provided by his university. He felt so unsure of himself that he did not know where to look for the guidance he so desperately sought. In retrospect, he now feels he made the wrong choice and spent almost ten years in a career for which he was not well suited. When he eventually changed to a career in public service, one that felt more comfortable and more authentic for him, Jerome remembers thinking, I'm behind schedule.

This sense of not doing things on time has pervaded Jerome's adult development. He always feels that somehow he cannot do things as fast as other people or with as much confidence as others. Despite many successes in the world, Jerome has still failed to develop an internal sense of himself that is secure enough to give him the confidence to take risks and to move forward in his own life.

For other individuals, the sense of being overwhelmed by the task of creating the self focuses specifically on how to become a man or how to become a woman. These individuals feel that only their same-sexed parent could initiate them into the world of adulthood, and when this parent dies young they feel deprived of the only viable guide they had for their journey into manhood or womanhood.

BRIAN'S STORY

When Brian passed his forty-first birthday, he became a man who had lived longer than his own father. He was awed by his own chronological age, unable to comprehend how he could possibly be "older" than his own father, since, at least in part, his image of himself was forever frozen as the young three-year-old boy who had been devastated by the sudden death of his father.

Regardless of whether he is working, relating to his wife and family, or pursuing one of his many interests, the question, What does it mean to be a man? forms the subtext of Brian's story. While he has an uneasy sense that he does not have the answer to this all-important question, Brian, like the knights who went off to search for the Holy Grail, is convinced that the image exists. Somewhere there is a template for how to be a man.

As he talked about his life, I was reminded of the fairy tales of young boys who go off to seek their fortunes. The story invariably begins with the death of the boy's father, an event that both frees him and impels him on his quest to search for his own identity and to seek his fortune. Should the young boy ask for a clue about the object of his search, he is told, usually by an older man or a wizened woman, "You will know it when you see it." Brian's quest has been marked by the same self-given advice and belief. Although he cannot describe the image of manliness he seeks, Brian is convinced "he will know it when he sees it."

When talking about himself, Brian says, "I don't often think of myself as an adult male. It's not that I'm a little kid, it's just that I'm outside of the normal stream of adult male development." Brian refers to himself as his own creation, a thing unto itself, and he is aware that in the absence of a parental model, he must forge his own path.

For many years, Brian has sought to discover the signposts of adult male development. He reads books, talks to other men, and seeks out mentors, always looking for someone who might teach him what it means to be a man; he wants someone to guide him on his quest, to make his journey easier. Brian is a lover of maps and has a collection of maps from far-off places. The maps interest Brian not only because of their practical utility, but also because of their clarity and power. The maps hold the key of how to get from here to there. And this is exactly the nature of Brian's journey; he longs to get from the "here" of insecure boyhood to the "there" of confident manliness. If Brian can just find the right map, if he can just study the course carefully enough, the road would be laid out for him and he could proceed on his way.

Because his image of manliness is vague and insubstantial, Brian often looks to other people to confirm that he is on the right track. Some of Brian's professional competitiveness derives from just this need to measure himself against other people. One way that he judges his own adult accomplishment is to look at other men his age and see how he compares. This need for external affirmation persists despite Brian's suspicions that only boys, not men, need external approval and confirmation of their worth and his equally strong belief that first and foremost, men are true to themselves and that satisfaction for them comes from within. His hero is a mythic figure whose self-containment, maturity, and self-confidence may be unattainable for a flesh-and-blood man.

Some of Brian's sense of what it means to be a man comes from his few remaining memories of his father, memories which themselves have taken on mythic proportions. In one fragment, almost like a dream, Brian remembers his father taking him to an amusement park where a man wrestled an alligator, eventually taming the creature by putting a stick in its mouth and thus rendering it powerless. The image of a powerful man, capable of taming out-of-control forces, has been central to Brian's understanding of what it means to be a man, and it has been instrumental in his choice of a rather unusual career. Brian is an international expert and consultant on the management of disasters. His firm is enlisted to manage natural and social disasters caused by earthquakes, fires, and social upheaval. Like his hero Teddy Roosevelt, Brian charges in with a team of skilled professionals, social planners, doctors, nurses, and engineers and sets up a system to manage the catastrophe. His career is not only unique and highly creative, but in his work, Brian took one of his only memories of manliness and turned it into a life's passion.

When he was a small boy, Brian engaged in a series of compulsive rituals. Each night he would check the house thoroughly, making sure that it was safe from robbers, burglars, and kidnappers, and he would say a special prayer, listing all of the people in his life who were important to him and asking God to keep those loved ones safe from evil doers. Only when he had said the prayer in the right order, after having checked all of the available hiding places in the house, would Brian feel safe to go to sleep.

Brian's second memory of his father is of his father lifting him high into the air so that he, Brian, could touch the ceiling. His father was a big man, and Brian's memory captures the feeling of a little boy being bolstered and supported by someone who must have seemed both powerful and secure. In describing the perfect mentor, Brian seeks someone "who will be vested in his growth, development, and success forever," someone who will always support him, just as his father quite literally held him up and let him reach for the sky when he was a little boy.

While growing up, Brian always had the sense that he had something "big" to do and was always pleased and a little surprised when he seemed to succeed. In his career Brian has repeatedly had a similar experience. He takes on a new challenge, not sure that he has the skills or the competence to accomplish the task successfully, and then is pleasantly surprised when he rises to the occasion and does what needs to be done. As a young boy, Brian rose to the occasion and performed like a little man. He quickly learned to play by himself while his mother was at work, he never cried or whined, and he entertained his mother by reciting all the things he had learned in school. He was praised and rewarded, yet he was never quite sure what he had done or how he had done it. Consequently, he never attained a clear sense of how one succeeds in the world. He only knows that if he works hard enough and tries hard enough he will somehow stumble on the successful course of action. While he has done this repeatedly throughout his life, Brian does not have an enduring sense of himself as a man who is competent and able to solve problems. He continues to feel that he is the little boy assigned a task that is too big for him, who, through perseverance and good luck, manages to triumph.

Throughout his life Brian has searched for mentors, men to whom he could turn, men who could teach him how to be a man. He says, "I always looked for experts and then associated myself with them." It seemed that the world was divided "into people I could learn from and people that I couldn't." While ostensibly Brian was looking for particular content knowledge, he was also looking for men who could answer for him his primary question: What does it mean to be a man?

Some of the men he chose to learn from were engaged in physical, stereotypically male behaviors—men who worked construction, drove trucks, sailed the seas. Brian was fascinated by men who used their physical strength to make their way in the world. When I asked Brian if he thought that he sought out these men because they were stereotypical men, he said no; instead these men represented alive, vital energy to

Brian. The more he and I talked, the clearer it became that what was so attractive about these men was that Brian knew they were alive. Brian grew up with the image of a dead man for a father. He now wanted living, sweating, lusty men for models.

When Brian was ten years old, his mother remarried, and Brian remembers feeling excited and hopeful that his new stepfather would fill the role of father for him. Regrettably, Brian's mother was not interested in her new husband's taking on the role of father with her sons, and she interposed distance between her husband and her sons. Brian's stepfather was also not a nurturing or emotionally available man, so he willingly ceded to his wife's wishes and did not invest much energy and time in his two new stepsons. Brian remembers feeling terribly disappointed when he realized that his stepfather would not unlock the door to maleness for him. He had been hungry for someone to fill the role of father, and his stepfather would not be the person to do that. Brian remembers being twelve years old and sitting alone in his bedroom, overcome by grief, sobbing and crying, realizing that his own father was gone forever and that he would never have someone to fill the role of father for him; forever would he be a fatherless child.

As he has moved into midlife, Brian has spent a great deal of time thinking about what it means to grow older as a man. He has no sense of how a man ages, how a man becomes comfortable at different stages of life. He had no experience of seeing his own father age and feels "as if he is going through uncharted territory." Brian is very aware that his uncertainty about the future puts him at risk for clinging to strategies that were successful in the past. As he says, "I know very well how to be a fifteen-year-old, how to be a thirty-year-old. I'm always in danger of going back to those old ways and trying to repeat my past successes."

In recent years, Brian has come to feel that his life is finally his own responsibility. He is aware that his feelings of greater freedom and personal responsibility have come since he passed the age at which his father died. While this juxtaposition of ages sometimes feels like too simple an explanation to Brian, he does feel freed by passing this chronological milestone. He says, "I have a much greater sense that I'm on the bridge steering my own life. I am where I should be. I should be the captain. I don't need anybody else to help me right now." As Brian says this I am once again reminded of the fairy-tale quest of the young man who, after searching for some ideal image, for some truth outside of himself, finally comes to realize that what he has been searching for is in fact inside of himself. Brian, who for so long has looked for what it means to be a man, is coming to realize that the reflection in the mirror is as good an image of manliness as he will ever find.

Even when they have managed to accomplish the task of adult development—establishing a relationship, parenting a child, and maintaining a career and a profession—some individuals continue to feel lost without a solid anchor and a strong sense of themselves as adults.

Rather than feeling more at ease with the loss of his father as he gets older, Ted actually feels more despairing with each passing year. "The older I get, the more powerful the loss is. It's as if I go deeper, like an archaeological dig, down to another layer, another lost city." Ted has managed to maintain a successful job for many years, yet he works with no passion, feeling that he never had the confidence to "run with his strengths" and convinced that he chose the path he did out of fear rather than out of desire. Ted has become a conventional man. He works nine to five. He has a wife and a child. But he lives within a world that is secured by fragile boundaries, a world that seems as if it could crumble at any moment: "I felt like I had to learn everything myself. I always feel like I am searching and looking. I had no guide, nothing to measure myself against. I hate to sound this way but I feel lost."

Ted continues to believe that there is some answer to the question of how to be a man, an answer that was lost to him when his father died so long ago. Ted regrets that it has taken him so long to find the answers to even simple questions. He is sure that men who grew up with fathers knew the answers to some of these problems long ago and did not have to struggle as hard as he did. At times Ted comforts himself with the knowledge that things do come late for him. He was almost forty when he married, almost forty-five when he had his first child. Both marriage and fatherhood have been a great joy for Ted, and he believes that if he just keeps struggling he will answer finally the question he needs to answer and then have a strong sense of his own manhood. What worries Ted is that he might be a very old man when he figures out how to live his life, and then, like his father, he will not have very much time.

Out of Control

Parents not only serve as guides, mentors, and examples for their growing children, they also serve as protective boundaries, safety nets that insure that when a child experiments he or she will not fall too hard or reach too far. In the absence of a parental guide, some children find themselves running wild. They do not know how to control their own impulses or how to moderate their behavior. At first, the lack of a parental boundary feels like exhilarating freedom. For most, however, it quickly becomes overwhelming, and the child feels as if there is no wall to contain his or her self.

Keith was twelve when his father died, and he remembers getting little if any advice from his father during the few years they spent together.

Keith's mother and father were well into their forties when they adopted him, their only child. He recalls them as being conscientious absentee landlords, there to make sure he was clothed and fed, but not there for much else. Keith believes that when his father died, his mother went to work and he went wild. When Keith was fifteen, he ran away from home. He remembers standing at the side of the road for most of the night trying to hitchhike a ride. After several hours and no ride, he returned home, physically exhausted but undaunted. His hardworking mother never knew that he had crawled out the bedroom window and had been on his way to the big city.

As an adolescent, Keith drank, stole cars, was truant from school, and eventually was expelled from high school. All he wanted was adventure, and there was no one to stop him from experimenting with everything. Just before his sixteenth birthday, he was arrested for driving with a false driver's license and also charged with driving while intoxicated. Keith realized that his own impulses were out of control, and he was wise enough to know that if he did not find some way to contain himself he would quickly land in reform school. The austere reform school that sat on the hill at the end of his town served as a reminder for Keith of what happened to boys who could not control themselves. To his credit, Keith decided to join the army. From the posters he saw in the town hall, Keith knew that the army turned boys into men, and he was quite sure that he needed some assistance in the task of becoming a man. Once in the service, Keith realized that discipline in the army was different from discipline in the "real world." There were consequences for bad behavior, and one could find one's freedom taken away for a long time if one did not obey the rules. Keith became a good soldier and also completed his high school education while in the service. He managed to get into an occasional fight but never to do anything else that pushed the boundaries of acceptable behavior. The military served as a viable container for Keith, a container that was absent when his father died.

Once out of the military, Keith found his impulses out of control again. This time his wild behavior was not antisocial and violent; it was sexual. Every young woman was a potential conquest, and Keith found himself having many concurrent sexual relationships. One morning he woke up to find a young woman in his bed, a woman he did not know and did not recognize. When they both roused themselves, she explained that they had met at a bar the night before and both gotten so drunk that they could barely walk and that she had come home with him and they had had intercourse. This encounter seemed not only ridiculous to Keith but also somewhat embarrassing. He knew once again that he could not control his impulses on his own and sought an external boundary in order to contain himself. This time he decided to get married. He had been dating a young woman who was interested in marrying him, and shortly after his anonymous escapade, he proposed, and the two went to a justice of the peace and were married. Just as the army contained his adolescent acting out, marriage served the same purpose in young adulthood. Keith became a responsible husband and remained faithful to his wife. The social conventions of marriage were sufficient to control Keith's behavior. In the absence of a parent to provide social restraint and containment, Keith sought containment via external social institutions—the military and matrimony—and in each case he managed to control himself successfully.

College, the usual training ground for young adults, often seems too unstructured for young men and women who feel out of control when faced with the task of creating the self. College encourages intellectual, social, and personal experimentation. While a young man or woman may initially relish that experimentation, the freedom that accompanies it quickly feels overwhelming to some. Young women in particular, who felt that their college-aged sexual acting out might well result in an unwanted pregnancy, felt much safer when they left college for the structure of a job. Several women I interviewed felt that they were able to settle down in the nine-to-five routine of employment in a way that they had been unable to manage in the freer environment of a university.

One woman who had followed the social rules and been a very "good girl" after her mother's death remembers "going berserk" in college. "I didn't know what to do with the freedom. After three semesters, I figured I better leave or it was going to be the end of me." Another woman sought containment in a relationship with a very stoical and emotionless man. Her boyfriend seemed so calm and undaunted by her ups and downs that she felt safe with him. In many ways he performed the functions of a stable parent. Parents try to remain undaunted by their children's adolescent adventures. A good parent knows when to say no but a good parent also knows not to overreact to what is normal testing and experimentation. This woman found a boyfriend who served as a safe buffer for her own out-of-control behavior. His ability not to panic when she felt as if she was losing herself allowed her to feel more contained and eventually more able to control herself.

Certainly, there are a number of people who never manage to contain their own impulses and to find a way to gain the containment that they need in order to grow beyond adolescent acting out. These individuals, none of whom were interviewed for this book, find their way into jails, into homeless shelters, and at times, to an early death on the streets. Despite some severe and often dangerous acting out, each of the individuals with whom I spoke was able eventually to find containment and control in societal institutions such as work, marriage, and the military, institutions designed not only to accomplish a task, but also to insure social order.

The task of creating the self is never an easy one. Children who grow into adulthood with two stable and secure parents still struggle with the questions and pressures of how to become a person. When some of the support and guidance that might be provided by a parent is removed, the task of creating the self becomes more complicated and more difficult. Most of the people with whom I spoke felt that they would not have chosen to go it alone. If they had been given a choice, they would have selected to grow up with the support and encouragement of two loving parents. Yet many likened their experience to the child who is taught to swim by being thrown into the lake. One has no choice. If you want to survive, you learn to swim.

CHAPTER 6

∽

Building Relationships:
The Dance of Love and Loss

WHEN A PARENT DIES YOUNG, the pleasure of loving is tied permanently to the pain of loss. Love and loss are no longer separate and distinct. Like the branches of a vine, they have grown so intertwined that it is impossible to see one without also seeing the other. The young child learns that to love is to lose, or at the very least, to risk losing the beloved. As one woman whose father died when she was three confided, "Deep down I believe all men will leave me eventually."

As each of us grows older, we begin to learn one of life's most important lessons: There is no beginning without an ending; there is no love without the loss of that love. Nothing lasts forever and the things we hold dear eventually leave us. However, for most of us, those lessons are learned when we are old enough to put them in the perspective of a full and complete life. When a child learns such a lesson young, that lesson colors forever the way relationships are experienced.

Imagine for a moment that you are a young child being asked to watch a pair of dancers perform an intricate dance routine. The partners in this metaphorical dance are named Love and Loss. You are an unsophisticated audience, this being the only performance you have ever watched. As Love and Loss glide across the dance floor, their movements are so perfectly synchronized that they hardly seem like two separate dancers. You cannot imagine that these two are ever apart, much less that they might choose to dance with other partners. All you know of the world of dance pairs Love and Loss as permanent companions.

When a child loses a loved parent, the child learns that love and the pain of abandonment are inseparable. As that child grows into adulthood, he or she must figure out how to build intimate relationships with this early reality as a backdrop. As the childish pledge "I'll never love anyone again" begins to wane—as it does in most but not all cases—the adult survivor of early loss must develop a strategy for how to love in a world where loss and abandonment are ever-present dangers.

Troy is convinced that his bisexuality was in part his personal response to the dilemma of how to love in a world where loss is ever present. Troy, who was sixteen when his mother died, was an active and well-known member of his high school community. He was an athlete and a leader in student government. When his mother died, he was surprised by the warm outpouring of support and sympathy, not only from his immediate friends, but from a much wider circle of acquaintances. Thirty years after his mother's death, Troy still has all of the notes written to him by classmates trying to offer their sympathy. Troy remembers thinking at the time of his loss, If I can lose my mother, I can lose anybody. I better not say no to any love that is offered to me. Troy remembers feeling that rather than closing down following his mother's death, he opened himself up to multiple possibilities. Meaningful relationships need not be limited by traditional categories of age, race, gender, and class. Troy believes that his bisexual lifestyle was informed by his early experience of loss. He felt that one could feel love equally in the arms of a man or a woman and one who had lost the love of a mother could not afford to say no to any potential lover.

Most adults who lost parents in childhood do find some way to have relationships despite the connection between love and potential loss. They weigh the risks of losing against the joys of loving, and they devise some compromise that allows them to move forward. Many of the people whom I interviewed commented that it seemed to take them longer than their peers to feel able to enter a long-term relationship. They also reported being less resilient in the face of rejection. One man recalled years of being dejected and unfocused following a rejection by his girlfriend. Interestingly, her rejection of him came because he was unable to make a commitment to her. He was only able to put the loss behind him when a therapist assured him, "Get over it. It's not the worst thing in the world."

Some other survivors of early loss seemed unable to acknowledge the ongoing tension between love and loss. They only felt comfortable seeing one half of the duality. Some saw only love; others focused only on loss. To see both partners in the dance caused them too much anxiety and confusion. Those who focused on love were absolutely determined to love again. They held a belief like the refrain of the once-popular song: "Only love can break a heart, only love can mend it again." It is as if these individuals were defeated on the playing field of love once a long time ago and they are insistent on their right for a rematch. Loss has not jaded them to the possibility of love and human connection. Rather, it has made them determined to find for themselves the comfort and support they once knew.

Those who saw only loss, in contrast, needed to find some way to distance themselves from human connections and intimate relationships. They could not risk being seduced by the joys of love because the pain of another loss was just too great. C. S. Lewis, who for many years turned away from loving relationships after the death of his mother, speaks for many of these individuals when he says, "I had been far more anxious to avoid suffering than to achieve delight. I had always aimed at limited liabilities."[1]

Survivors of early loss must all find some way to solve the problem of intimacy. Most attempt to have relationships despite their belief that love and loss are inevitably intertwined. Others believe that they must selectively see only one side of the duality, focusing only on love or only on loss. For them, to see both is too dangerous and too confusing.

Living with the Tension Between Love and Loss

Those who live with an ongoing awareness that love and loss are connected have a range of responses to the question, How can I have an intimate relationship? At one end of the continuum are those who remain fearful and anxious. They have intimate relationships, but those relationships are haunted by fears of loss and abandonment. Often, despite a lack of confirming evidence, these individuals worry that a friend or lover will leave them suddenly and unexpectedly. At times, even minor separations feel traumatic. One woman commented quite candidly, "I know it sounds silly, but I hate saying good-bye to anyone." My own mother, whose father died when she was seven, always feels just a little bit sad when any of her family or close friends goes away even for a short trip.

At the other end of the continuum are those who accept that love and loss are connected, but who do not let that awareness affect their loving relationships. Just as the committed gardener keeps growing roses even though the flowers are short-lived, these survivors of early loss continue to be open to the possibilities of relationship even though they believe that love and human connection are fleeting. Two men, each of whom had lost a parent in adolescence, were both currently married to women who had serious illnesses. Neither had seen his future spouse's precarious medical condition as a reason to reject the relationship. In both cases, friends and relatives had attempted to counsel against the marriage, suggesting that it was foolish to love someone who might die young. Each responded to these would-be counselors in the same way. Loving a parent who had died young had taught them that one can treasure a relationship that does not last forever. Being sick does not mean that you are unworthy of love or unable to return the love and concern of others. Both of these men were also quite convinced that life came with no guarantees. A wife with a serious medical condition might certainly die early, but a wife who was healthy and robust might just as easily be snatched away by an unexpected event. Both men were also fully convinced that if loss occurred, they would be able to handle it. Having handled the loss of a loved parent when they were still children convinced both of them that they had the inner reserves and strength to deal with death and loss should it strike someone close to them again.

Some psychologists might speculate that in choosing wives who suffered from serious illness these men were merely repeating the trauma of childhood. After talking with both of them for hours, I was convinced that this was not the case. Each treasured the love that he shared with his wife and fully believed that he was richer to have loved this particular woman even if it might mean an eventual loss than to have not loved her at all. For both of them, "love does not need to be forever," it only needs to be as good as it can be while it lasts.

Most survivors of early loss fall somewhere on the continuum between anxiety and acceptance. Despite their fear of losing a loved one, they accept the risks of being in an intimate relationship. Perhaps they worry about abandonment more than they would like, but they do not let those worries prevent them from having relationships. Occasionally, some individuals would construct their relationships in such a way as to minimize their own fear and anxiety. Two common strategies were keeping relationships brief but intense and being the one to leave a relationship first. Both of these strategies were ways individuals managed their anxiety in intimate relationships.

Brief Encounters

Given that death and loss take love away, some survivors of early loss come to believe that all love is fleeting. Since permanence does not exist, the best one can hope for is a series of brief, but intense, encounters. Believing this, these individuals adjust their love lives accordingly. They often have many short affairs, telling themselves that that is all that is possible and also secretly believing that they will limit the pain of an eventual loss by keeping their loves brief.

Harry has been married two times and has had a series of affairs. He reminisces about his past, saying, "I have had zillions of relationships. I get as much as I can very quickly and then

I back off." While he has friendships that go back many years, Harry believes that love is necessarily brief. One has little encounters here and there but then one moves on. Harry is convinced that while love is wonderful, it just does not last very long.

Harry does, however, treasure the memories of the many loving relationships he has had over the years. After almost forty years, for example, he can still remember the few places where he was able to feel loved and cared for after his mother's suicide. An older girl in the neighborhood used to take him for walks, and when he feels melancholy, Harry can still be comforted by humming the song "Sweet Sue," which contains her name. Harry still maintains contact with another family from his old neighborhood who used to let him escape from his abusive stepmother by letting him come into their house and watch television. These relationships may have seemed fleeting, but they were important and loving connections nonetheless.

FELICIA'S STORY

After the car accident that took her mother's life, thirteen-year-old Felicia became her father's constant companion and housekeeper. She would entertain for him when he brought friends home, make sure the house was clean, and attend to the needs of her younger brother. Although Felicia had always been her father's favorite, she remembers thinking that a father's love was somehow more tenuous than a mother's. "With a mother you always feel secure. Somehow you just know that she loves you. With a father you always feel as if you have to prove something." While Felicia's analysis of the difference between mothers and fathers may or may not hold for others, it was certainly true for her. Felicia's father was a demanding man who would sometimes stop talking to her for days if she said or did something that displeased him. When Felicia's father began dating, she became even more uncertain of his affections. Always a disciplined and well-controlled man, Felicia's father became like an out-of-control adolescent who had just discovered the world of women. As Felicia saw her father date and then drop a succession of girlfriends, she became even more convinced that love was short-lived. Her father seemed passionate and excited about a woman one week and unable to remember her name the next.

When she left her father's home to go to college, Felicia began dating, but she was never quite sure what she should be looking for. Relationships between men and women seemed puzzling and confusing to her. She had witnessed a stable and traditional marriage between her mother and father for the first twelve years of her life. After her mother's death, however, she saw her father date a variety of women; he seemed to be more interested in sexual conquest than in forming a long-term intimate attachment.

Felicia was married briefly in her early twenties to a man who now seems like a stranger to her. The marriage ended when the young couple woke up from the days of a romantic courtship to find that they had very little in common. Felicia now concludes, "I'm not very successful in my relationships with men. I started to date late, and except for my husband, there has not been anything that has lasted more than a year. My relationships usually last three weeks to three months. I jump in completely. I'm not at all conservative with my emotions. Perhaps some of this comes from knowing that I can survive anything, but I think that I've been love-starved for such a long while that I just say, 'Let me get in and get as much as I can while I can.' " Felicia realizes that her enthusiasm often scares potential suitors away. Yet she feels unable to modulate her own responses. As she herself says, she feels like a starving woman who does not have the capacity to eat daintily. Felicia also believes that life is short. She does not feel that she has the time for a long and drawn-out courtship. She feels that one never knows when the end might come, so it is important to make the most of the time one has.

Felicia has also found herself unable to relate to many of the fantasies about romantic love held by the men with whom she has gone out. When men talk to her about "the love that will last forever," Felicia looks at them as if they are speaking a language she does not understand. "Forever" is not part of Felicia's vocabulary. She knows firsthand that love can be short and that people she cares about can die.

Those who believe that the most they can have with others are brief encounters see love as fleeting and fragile; they continue nevertheless to believe in the power and the value of loving relationships. For each of them, the pain endured when a parent died was not sufficient to frighten them away from the world of human connections forever.

Being the One to Leave First

Some individuals only feel safe to enter the rocky terrain of human relationships once they have carefully plotted an escape route for themselves. In some cases, the mere knowledge that one can leave a relationship is sufficient for an individual to feel safe enough to venture forth. In other cases, just knowing that one can leave does not suffice, and an individual has to put in place certain practical safeguards before he or she can risk connecting to another person. One way to ensure that one will not have to endure the pain of being left is to make sure that one leaves, or reserves the right to leave, first.

RUSSELL'S STORY

Russell's mother died when he was only four years old. His hardworking but stern father remarried within six months and Russell recalls little joy or happiness in his childhood. His stepmother was a submissive and quiet woman who took orders from her domineering and difficult-to-please husband. When he was not helping with the family business, Russell would escape into books and into the world of mathematical ideas and theorems. In math and science, things were clear and simple. He did not have to be confused by troubling and difficult emotions.

When Russell was twelve years old, his stepmother was diagnosed with cancer. After hearing the news, Russell remembers standing alone at the kitchen sink washing the dishes and crying to himself. In the five years between the announcement of her illness and her eventual death, Russell remembers keeping himself removed from the pain of watching his stepmother die. "Survival was everything. Life had taught me how to get along."

When he was seventeen, Russell's father died of a sudden stroke. Two months later, his stepmother died, leaving him completely orphaned and the survivor of three parental deaths before he was eighteen years old. When relatives came to tell Russell that his stepmother had died, he was packing boxes to move away from home and go to college. He remembers looking up from his packing, turning to his cousin, and saying, "Well, it's all over," and then turning back to the task of packaging up his belongings.

In addition to the literal packing of his books and records, Russell was continuing the task begun a long time before of neatly packaging his feelings. Difficult emotions were tucked away, secured, and sealed where they would not harm him again. Russell enjoyed his college years, but remembers participating in everything and committing to nothing. "I never commit fully. I always hold myself in check emotionally."

Russell dated several young women while in college and his usual style was "three dates and I'm out. I would always do or say something that would end the relationship, sometimes I would just forget to call." Nothing was worse for Russell than being told that some young woman liked him and wanted to get to know him. As soon as heard those fateful words, he made sure not to call or encounter that particular woman again. Even after he left college, Russell recalls that his most intense relationships always occurred when he knew he was leaving town. "I'd have the plane ticket in my back pocket, then I could fall in love." In those relationships, Russell felt free to have deep feelings. There was no risk, because he already knew the date and time the relationship would end. The leaving and the loss were under his control.

After a several-year courtship, which began as a long-distance relationship, Russell finally decided to marry. He and his wife have now been together for twenty-five years, yet he feels that part of him still holds back. He does not feel safe, even after almost a quarter of a century, to commit himself fully to the woman who is his wife. "I am always looking for signs that she is going to leave me. Either she will get sick, meet someone else, maybe her plane will crash. I am not going to let it hurt me again like it hurt me before."

Throughout his marriage, Russell has used both humor and intellectualization to keep himself securely distant from his wife. Even when he decided to marry, it was his intellect rather than his heart that made the decision. "I thought about the marriage as if it was a good business deal, a practical and sensible thing to do. Even though I love my wife very much I know there is a deeper level I have never reached and probably never will."

Throughout their marriage, Russell and his wife have developed the pattern of joking about how each would survive if the other died or left. Once, when Russell's wife asked him how long it would take him to start to date again if her plane crashed and she was killed, he looked at his watch and said, "I don't know. What time is your flight?" Russell maintains this sarcastic banter as part of his emotional escape route. "I keep myself safe by always seeing the other side, the funny side of things." Because he and his wife have given each other permission to fantasize about how they would cope with loss and abandonment, Russell feels that the route out is clearly marked. He knows what he would do if tragedy struck again.

The casual promiscuity that marked the sexual revolution in this country gave many people who felt the need for an escape route in a relationship a socially sanctioned rationale for why relationships should be short and sweet. The culture of the gay bar scene similarly supported the idea that sexual encounters were best when they were anonymous and without any emotional connections. For years, Victor hid his own need to be able to run away from a relationship behind the mores and values of the gay community.

Although it was his mother's death when he was ten that left Victor feeling orphaned, he, like Russell, had also lost both parents by the time he was eighteen. When he first became aware of his homosexuality in adolescence, Victor used the excuse that he did not know the rules of gay life as a reason to avoid connections with other young men. He managed to spend five years in college with only five dates, and those at the urging of friends. He kept telling himself, "I just don't know the rules of how to be a gay man." He now realizes, however, that he used this excuse to keep himself off the interpersonal playing field entirely.

When he graduated from college, Victor knew that he would be leaving town soon. He had already accepted a job in another city. Knowing that his time was short, he felt free for the first time in his life since his mother's death to allow someone to get close. He never even told the man with whom he had the relationship that he was planning to leave. "I was just here one day and gone the next. I only gave myself permission as long as I could see a clear way out."

Throughout his twenties, Victor had a series of love affairs with men from out of town. He would often wonder why when he was in a strange city he would manage to meet someone with whom he would feel an instant connection. Bells would ring and he would think, At last I have found someone I can care for. He knew, however, that the train was leaving the next morning and he would not be back in town anytime soon. At one point when a man he had seen on several occasions tried to pursue the relationship further, Victor decided that perhaps he was not gay after all and he began a series of failed relationships with women. Choosing lovers about whom he could feel little was another way Victor allowed himself to escape from the intensity of emotional connection.

In his thirties, Victor says he discovered a new way of withholding himself and not getting involved. He would be intimate but not have an orgasm. He would keep a part of himself in reserve and in that way he might feel safe enough to get close. Not surprisingly, the gay bar scene seemed made for Victor. A series of anonymous connections were ideal for someone who wanted the option of leaving on a moment's notice.

In his late thirties, Victor began to feel that something important was missing in his life. He kept thinking, I should have a lover. I should be able to make a commitment. He tried serious dating but often set up encounters so that there would be some unavoidable misunderstanding that eventually would result in a parting of the ways. Ten years ago, Victor met a man who actively pursued him, a man who tried to close off the many escape routes Victor had put in place. Once when Victor's company sent him out of town on a six-month assignment, Victor asked the man to move into his house. He reasoned that the house would be better taken care of if it had a permanent occupant. It also made economic sense for this man, who was paying rent on another apartment to live in Victor's house while Victor was away. That was ten years ago, and Victor's lover has not moved out since. His partner has redecorated the house and fully believes the relationship to be permanent. Victor, however, continues to tell himself that it is merely an economic arrangement, one that makes good business sense. Victor holds to this somewhat transparent rationalization, keeping it as an exit visa should he feel too threatened by the intimacy of a close relationship.

Seeing Only Love

For some, it is too painful and too risky to love in the shadow of loss; yet, their desire for love is overwhelming. These individuals refuse to see or be daunted by loss. They see only the love because they want to believe in the power and the triumph of loving relationships. As children left by parents they loved or had not yet had a chance to know, they imagined a romantic rendition of what love looks like. Holly's mother was widowed after only three years of marriage. Her war-hero husband left her with two small daughters and a series of fantasies about what might have been. As Holly grew up, she remembers, she heard stories about her larger-than-life father, a handsome, dashing man who was killed while fighting for his country and returned home a hero in a draped casket. Holly's mother told her that love was something magical and special and that a woman only gave her heart once. Not surprisingly, Holly's mother never remarried and lived with the fantasies of her lost husband.

When Holly went off to college and began dating, she took with her her mother's romantic notions of what relationships and marriage were like. She fell in love with a young man and, believing her mother's story that "one only falls in love once," she assumed of course that she would marry this man. After dating for a few months, he left town and did not contact her for almost a year. Holly remained convinced, however, that he would return and marry her. He was, after all, her one chance at love. Holly's story ended more happily than her mother's, and in fact her absent suitor did return and they were eventually married. Even when she and her boyfriend were separated, however, and he failed to answer her letters, Holly refused to see the possibility of loss. Love and Loss would not dance together in her life; she was convinced.

Paradoxically, many of those whose lives were marked by an absence of any affection or emotional warmth after the death of a parent became the most ardent believers in the power of love. One man whose mother died when he was seven recalls going to his father one night bereft and lonely. He sat on his father's bed and said, "Dad, I miss Mom." His father, a hardened and critical man, turned to him and said, "Too bad. Life is hard and you'd better get used to it." Another man whose mother died when he was ten recalls the barren landscape that became his home after his mother's unexpected death: "There were no hugs, no kisses. Nothing like that at all. It was just all gone."

Despite their early experiences or perhaps because of them, these two men grew up with a naive faith that love would heal the wounds of childhood. Given the absence of affection after one parent died, it might have been necessary for these individuals to continue to believe in the enduring quality of love. It is one thing to feel that love has left temporarily; it is another to believe that love is gone from one's life forever. These young boys may well have needed to continue their faith in the power of love in order to survive in a world that was temporarily loveless.

Many children after their early loss envisioned themselves to be like fairy-tale characters, temporarily frozen or asleep. Snow White lies in a glass coffin, not alive, not dead, waiting for the love of her prince to awaken her. These survivors of early loss similarly believed that despite their temporary sleep, they would eventually be awakened into a world of love and happiness.

Each of the individuals I interviewed who held to a belief in the omnipotence of love married quickly after a short court-ship when they were still quite young. All of these people continued to be married to the man or woman who had captured their heart a long time ago. One might have predicted that, given the naivete with which they entered marriage and the generally high rate of divorce, these individuals might have had troubled marriages that failed to last. Yet for each of them, the bond between love and loss had been permanently sundered. Once they were committed to loving someone, each of them banished loss from the house. They refused even to consider the possibility of untimely death, and they would never will-ingly end a relationship through separation or divorce.

These individuals boast marriages that have lasted anywhere from ten to forty years, and each spoke to me of his or her marriage in idyllic terms. One man said, "My dreams for my marriage have come true and they have been absolutely what I dreamed. My marriage is the only place in my life where I have achieved my dream world in a reality that was as good if not better than the dream." Many of these individuals were looking not only for a spouse and a companion, but for a soulmate, someone who would be able to understand the pain they had been through and to connect with the hurt child that lay within.

One man whose home became abusive and chaotic after his father's death went off to college knowing "I needed and wanted somebody." Within weeks of meeting his future wife, a student at a college five hundred miles away, he knew that he had met someone he could love. "We were both lonely people but self-reliant on the outside." Within a short time of their meeting he took her home to see his family. It was important that she know firsthand the chaos from which he had come. Unlike many adolescent love affairs, his relationship with his future wife was motivated in part by a desperate desire to be with someone who would finally see and acknowledge his pain. Although he was unable to articulate it at the time, he wanted to make sure that she knew exactly what she was "get-ting into" before he fell in love with her. He did not want to risk loving someone who might decide to leave him when she learned some secret about his past later in their relationship.

After their first summer together, he knew that he wanted to marry this young woman. However, they were both freshmen in college and marriage seemed an impossibility. During the next year, he spent many hours and long weekends hitchhiking to see the one woman he felt could understand and care for him. Their relationship alternated between intense weekends together and periods of painful separation. Loss and love were too connected for him to feel safe, and after that first year he insisted that she make a choice. He was ready for a commitment, and he wanted a similar promise from her. When she agreed, he was elated, feeling at last, "My life is my own. I'm finally away from the nightmare." After almost fifteen years of marriage he reports, "It feels like we are one in everything we do."

Herb reports feeling so lonely that he came to think of himself as "a majority of one" before he met his wife. After his mother died, Herb's father withdrew into his work and a time-consuming second marriage. Herb felt alone, without an advocate or a friend. "If I ever needed to make my case, I knew I'd have to make it on my own." From the time he began to date, Herb always wanted to make relationships into more than what they were. He knew that he was searching not only for a date but for a special friend, someone who would care about him and love him. When he drove off to college in the family car, his only gift from his withholding and stingy father, Herb felt relieved but alone. He spent most of his college years studying, working, and looking for someone to love. Shortly after he graduated from college, Herb met a young woman, herself from an abusive and chaotic family, and within two months he knew he wanted to marry her. "She had problems of her own so she was able to understand my problems. It made us closer." She was also warm, fun, and, as Herb says, "very much alive." Following his mother's death, all vitality and joy had fled from Herb's existence, and he sought in a wife a woman who would make him feel alive and loved.

Throughout their long marriage, Herb has most enjoyed watching his wife mother their three children. She is an engaged and compassionate mother, and he especially likes the fact that she will take the side of one of her children against him in a disagreement. Even though he himself may be on the losing side of an argument, he loves to see a mother who supports her children.

For some individuals, this search for "all-powerful" love can feel almost desperate. The individual believes that not only happiness, but survival itself depends on finding the needed partner. For these individuals it becomes unthinkable to consider that love, once found, might be lost.

SCOTT'S STORY

Since Scott's mother was not only loving but also very beautiful, it was easy to transform her into a fairy princess when she died quite suddenly when he was ten. Scott remembers as a child watching his very glamorous mother dress up to go out with his father. "She seemed so perfect. I guess she'll always be young and perfect in my memory." For many months after her death, Scott would dream about his mother every night. The dreams were of life as it had been before she died. He would close his eyes and be transported back in time to the wonderful everyday life he had shared with his mother. He much preferred dream time to daytime. At night he was a loved and cared-for child; during the day he was a lonely orphan. "I always knew that my mother loved me a lot. I kept that thought with me when I felt like I needed comforting."

Scott's father was overwhelmed by the task of raising three young children. For the first year after his wife's death he brought in a series of housekeepers, none very competent, some clearly too young and inexperienced to provide the mature love and caring his children needed. Within a year, Scott's father remarried. His new wife was devoted to him and to her own two children, but not at all interested in Scott and his siblings. After his stepmother appeared, Scott's own mother was never mentioned. "It was as if she vanished. There were no pictures, not a word. I was not even allowed to have my memories. It was all just buried for years." While Scott's stepmother surely did not invite him to become a son to her, he is unsure he would have agreed under any circumstances. "Everybody only has one mother. Part of me died when my own mother died. I felt more like a boarder in my father's house than like a son."

As soon as he became a teenager, Scott remembers, he thought that if only he had a girlfriend he would have someone he could love forever. Although most adolescent boys want to date as many girls as they can, Scott was searching for a wife. He wanted to find someone whom he could love and who could love him. During much of high school, he found himself to be out of sync with his peers. He was too serious for many of the girls he dated, who themselves wanted only casual romance, none being ready to commit to a lifelong relationship. Scott worried that he was too desperate, too clingy, and too needy, and that no one would ever love him. He remembers a friend of his in high school saying to him, "Scott, you will probably marry the first girl who loves you back."

When it was time for Scott to go to college, his family decided that Scott would attend the same elite, small, all-male college that had been his father's alma mater. For a boy intent on finding a wife, nothing could have been worse. For four years, Scott was miserable. Dating was difficult, and when he did meet someone he liked, he had to contend with a weeklong separation between dates. Although many of his classmates complained about the lack of women on campus, for Scott the lack of someone to care about felt like a desperate circumstance. He needed someone to love, and most importantly, he needed to know that someone loved him. He left college wondering if he was an unlovable person, someone no one would ever want to marry.

When he was twenty-two, Scott met the woman who was to become his wife. He liked the way she looked instantly, but more importantly he liked the fact that she responded to him. Within two months he knew that he wanted to marry her. His fears that he had some terrible flaw that would drive all women away from him began to disappear as this woman repeatedly assured him that she cared for him and wanted to be his wife. In ten years of marriage, he and his wife have never spent a night apart. Scott describes them as a totally devoted couple. He cannot imagine anyone with whom he would rather spend time. This is not to say that Scott and his wife do not have independent interests. Each is an active professional, both have friends and both participate in a variety of sports and hobbies. Yet each is clear that the other is the center of his or her life. "Our need for closeness is so strong that neither of us can hide it."

In his wife, Scott has finally found someone he feels comfortable and safe enough to love. "I am completely dependent on her for love. What is strange though is that I depend on her for nothing else." For the rest of his needs Scott has learned how to be a quite competent provider. He knows how to take care of himself financially and intellectually. He knows how to cook and clean and to run a household. Yet he refuses even to imagine what his life would be like if his wife were ever taken away. He will not allow loss to enter the loving world he has created.

JENNY'S STORY

Like Scott, Jenny knew that she would fully recover from her father's death only if she found someone to love. Jenny's father's death when she was only ten years old took her totally by surprise. He was a healthy, vigorous man who died in a hunting accident. In the morning he kissed her good-bye, walked out the door, and by afternoon he was dead. Jenny never got to say good-bye to her father, never had the chance to touch or hug him again.

As an only child and a pretty little girl, Jenny had enjoyed a special relationship with her father. He would take her riding and hunting with him. They would play together, and Jenny would share her secrets and her dreams for the future with her father. After her father died, Jenny kept him alive in her own mind for many years. As an only child, she had been accustomed to having imaginary playmates, made-up characters who would keep her company when her parents were busy or away. It was an easy step for Jenny to turn her father into one of these make-believe playmates. She would have long conversations with her father inside her head, telling him about her life, continuing to share her secrets and her dreams. Paradoxically, Jenny feels as if she stayed closer to her dead father than she was to her living mother. Yet a part of Jenny "shut down" after her father died. She built a wall around herself, fearing ever getting too close to anyone or ever loving anybody as much as she had loved him. Jenny knew that in order to fully heal from her loss she would need to risk loving again, but she could not imagine how that might happen.

While she was at college, Jenny met a man who had also lost his mother when he was a boy. The two felt instantly connected. Each understood the other's most secret and painful memory. Despite her immediate attraction to this man, Jenny also felt cautious and frightened. Could she take the chance of loving someone again? The two dated for almost a year before they decided to marry. A wedding was planned, and Jenny remembers the afternoon she and her fiancé went out in search of an apartment where they might live after the marriage. She came home from her afternoon out with her boyfriend feeling more depressed than she had in years. Jenny went into the bathroom and took a whole bottle of pills. She remembers that she did not want to die, she only wanted help. She was too scared of another loss to commit to her fiancé, yet equally frightened of losing him, the only man she had loved since her father. Jenny's suicide attempt enabled her to get the help she needed. She spent six months working with a psychotherapist who helped her to deal not only with her fears of intimacy but with her need finally to relinquish her special relationship with her dead father in order to commit fully to a relationship with a living man. "I was desperate to be able to fall fully in love. I knew that a wall needed to come down." Jenny's fiancé stood by her throughout her therapy, a sign of commitment and devotion, which allowed Jenny to feel more secure in her choice of this man as a life mate.

When she was in her midthirties, the mother of four and a happily married woman, Jenny's husband suffered a mild heart attack. She remembers being panicked. It was as if the past was doomed to repeat. Jenny would be widowed like her mother and once again she would feel devastated by the loss of the man she loved. The story had a different ending this time. Jenny's husband survived his heart attack, and she gained a new-found confidence in her own ability to survive unexpected and tragic events. Jenny and her husband have now been married for almost forty years, and she sees herself as living proof of the healing power of love.

Seeing Only Loss

For some individuals, the terror of being hurt in a new relationship is so great that they cannot let anyone get close enough to touch them. Repeatedly these individuals say, "I cannot bear the pain of being hurt again." They deny their need and their desire for emotional closeness, sometimes only to others, sometimes to themselves as well. For some, the denial lasts a lifetime; for others, it fades through the persistence of a loving suitor.

After the death of his mother, writer C. S. Lewis likened himself to someone who was wearing stiff clothing like a corset or even a suit of armor. He felt as if he were a lobster, tied in and constrained in his ability to feel and his capacity to love. In his autobiography, Lewis describes how he at last began to melt, to open himself up once again to the possibility of spiritual and emotional connection. For C. S. Lewis, as for many survivors who fear another loss, it took much courage and many years to feel safe enough to love again.[2]

Self-Reliance

Self-reliance is perhaps the strongest of the barriers that individuals erect to keep themselves at a distance from others: "I can do it myself, thank you very much." As long as the individual remains supremely competent, he or she does not need the help or assistance of anyone. One woman managed to drive her car, do her household chores, and attend to all of her commitments with a broken foot rather than ask anyone for any help, or more importantly, rather than allow anyone to get close enough to her emotionally to know that she needed help. Another woman commented, "I have become such a self-contained island that people would need to build a bridge in order to reach me."

ROSETTA'S STORY

Rosetta was only three years old when the call came from her father's job telling her mother that he had been killed in an accident. "I had a great sense that something was definitely wrong and that I should not bother my mother," she says. In her child's mind, Rosetta reasoned that she must be strong, not only for herself but for her weeping mother as well. When several years later Rosetta's mother married an abusive and alcoholic man, Rosetta only doubled her efforts to become self-sufficient. As long as she did not need her mother or her new father she would not risk being hurt. When her stepfather stumbled home late at night, it was Rosetta's job to creep down the long oak staircase and quickly fling open the door. Before her stepfather had a chance to hit her or to scream, she would run up the stairs into her room, hiding safely behind her bed. Rosetta was learning well the lessons of self-sufficiency.

When she was in grade school, Rosetta remembers taking great delight in making a skirt for the fifth-grade fashion show. All of the mothers watched eagerly as their daughters walked across the stage. All of the mothers except for one. Rather than expressing her disappointment at her mother's absence, Rosetta just thought, "I guess I will have to rely on myself," and the wall she had built around herself went a little higher.

Throughout high school, Rosetta was a shy and quiet girl. She did her schoolwork but had time for little else. When she was eighteen, she began to notice that she was growing into an attractive young woman and started to go out with friends and to date an occasional young man. One boy in particular was especially fond of her and began pressuring Rosetta to have a sexual relationship. She certainly did not feel safe enough to let anyone get that close to her and she repeatedly refused his overtures. The young man became angry and planned what he believed to be a suitable punishment for the unwilling Rosetta. He arranged for a friend of his to drive Rosetta home from school. This friend picked her up and the two engaged in some pleasant chitchat. He detoured, however, took Rosetta into the woods, and raped her. She was terrified, ran home, told her mother, and pressed charges against her assailant. When she arrived in court for the trial, Rosetta was appalled to find that the first young man was there to testify against her. He declared that Rosetta was a loose and unladylike young woman and had probably seduced the man who raped her. The charges were dismissed, and Rosetta left the courthouse feeling alone and unsafe. "I was out there all by myself." Rosetta resolved that the only way to survive in the world was to be strong and to need no one. For several years she worked, supported herself, and contributed money to her mother, who was now divorced from her alcoholic husband.

When she was in her midtwenties, Rosetta met a man ten years her senior who seemed mature and responsible. He came from a stable family and Rosetta reasoned that he would be able to provide some of the security and care she had not received as a girl and for which she now longed as a woman. Regrettably, Rosetta's prince changed into a toad. He was an irresponsible and callous man who spent little energy maintaining and caring for a home. Rosetta, however, asked him for little. She already believed taking care of herself was her responsibility and hers alone.

Throughout her seventeen-year marriage, Rosetta paid all of the bills, adopted a child on her own, bought a house, and became so self-sufficient and competent that her husband frequently referred to her as "the man of the house"—the strong, silent type who did not need anyone.

In her early forties, Rosetta decided that she had had enough of supporting her irresponsible husband. She filed for divorce and concluded that she would spend the rest of her life alone. She had always taken care of herself and she saw no reason to let the wall down so that someone might approach her. One day, however, at a church picnic, she met a man who was determined to get to know her. He came up to her, talked for a while, and gave her his business card. Rosetta promptly threw the card in the garbage can. Three weeks later they met again, and he said to her, "I assume you tossed my card out. You don't think you need anyone, do you?" Rosetta was intrigued by his observation, and they began the slow process of getting to know one another. Early in their relationship, Rosetta had to call to cancel a date because her car would not start in the subzero weather. Her new boyfriend told her to stay where she was, he would be right over. Before Rosetta could protest that she did not need any help, thank you, the man had hung up the phone and had begun the hour-long drive from his house to hers. Rosetta was astounded that anyone would take such trouble just to be helpful. On another occasion, she came home to find a picnic basket filled with food waiting on her doorstep. There was a little note that said simply: *I know you've been working hard—just thought you might like a little treat.* For Rosetta, this new man was like the prince who had the perseverance to cut through the brambles to get to Sleeping Beauty. The relationship is now three years old, and Rosetta is starting to believe that she does not have to be the self-reliant survivor, the woman who has to do everything on her own. Rosetta acknowledges that she has begun to lower the wall she has built up over many years. She has, however, only just begun to lower it. It has not yet been completely dismantled.

While self-reliance forms the bricks and mortar of many protective barriers, for others the wall is constructed from a breezy, casual superficiality. Although he has many friends, Jack never lets anyone get too close. He enjoys playing basketball with a group of guys. He likes to go drinking with another group of friends, but no one ever gets to know him very well. During the time I interviewed him, Jack's phone rang several times. There were several light, airy conversations and he was clearly a well-liked man. Lighthearted casualness, however, serves as Jack's defense. He has not allowed anyone to get beyond that barrier since his father's death many years ago. "I definitely think there is something about me that I hold back in relationships because of the immense loss I had. I am a very open person. I love talking to people. I've got a lot of friends, but sometimes, you know, it's like this brick wall that I reach. I can't go beyond the wall. People expect me to jump over it, go beyond it and get closer, and I just can't." Behind the world of casual banter, Jack feels safe that no one will get close enough ever to hurt him again the way he was hurt when his father died.

Others hide themselves high in a tower of cool detachment, aloof and unreachable. Liz was four when her mother died, and from that time and for many years she felt alone and disconnected. She recalls being popular through grade school and junior high school, always a class officer or a prom queen. Yet she felt connected to no one. Schooled in a Catholic educational system with reserved and austere nuns as her models, Liz reasoned that she would rather have respect than love. She placed herself somewhat above her peers as the noble and morally superior comrade. Later in her life, one of Liz's friends joked with her that she had given herself an "emotional bypass."

Although she had casual relationships with both men and women during her twenties, Liz was described by everyone as an ice maiden, aloof and untouchable. In her midthirties, Liz was finally pursued by a woman who refused to give up. She describes this woman who has now been her lover for many years as a person with a core of gentleness. This woman was determined to scale the tower even though Rapunzel refused to let down her hair. For months she sent Liz cards and flowers, undaunted by repeated rejection and good-humored throughout their difficult courtship. Although the two have now lived together for many years, Liz insists on maintaining a private space within their home. In the room she calls her own, Liz can still retreat to the tower if she feels the need. The sign on the door says: NO KNOCKING. NO INTERRUPTION.

Anger

For some, the only way to keep a safe distance from loving relationships is to adopt an angry and confrontational demeanor. If one is sufficiently prickly and hostile, one can be assured that no suitor will get close enough and no loss will ever occur. Paradoxically, in a desire to avoid losing love, these individuals abstain from loving relationships, condemning themselves to lonely and loveless lives.

For actor James Dean, the persona of the angry and brooding young man served to keep others at a distance. Dean wrote to a friend, "I see a person I would like to be very close to, then I think it would be just the same as before and they don't give a shit for me. Then I say something nasty or nothing at all and walk away."[3] Dean was safe from another devastating loss, but he was alone and lonely.

When her father died suddenly, Allison protected herself from feeling the loss by telling herself that she and her father had never had much of a relationship anyway. She protected herself from her mother's vulnerability by adopting an air of critical sarcasm toward her surviving parent. Whenever she saw her mother cry, Allison would become critical and contemptuous. It is now painful for her to remember the steady stream of putdowns she directed at her own mother. Allison's "tough-guy" persona extended to her friends as well. She was determined not to be a weak little girl, and she learned to swear and fight with the best of them. Boys in her class would frequently dare her to engage in some dangerous behavior and Allison always met the challenge. No one was going to break through her image of herself as "beyond pain." She remembers feeling superior to everyone. "I was the strong one looking down on the weak ones, constantly challenging people to acknowledge just how tough I was." Sarcasm quickly turned to meanness, and Allison gained a reputation for being a cruel little girl. "I was just doing it to protect myself."

Her tough and angry persona worked better than Allison might have imagined. Many people willingly kept their distance from one who seemed so quick to snap. As an adult, Allison has done much to soften her angry behavior. She now has a wide circle of women friends but has been unable to let down her guard in relationships with men. The caustic and angry child quickly appears when anyone gets too close. "I feel I have to keep men at arm's length because I can't let them hurt me. I'm always sure that they are going to hurt me or leave me." Allison is not surprised that it has been years since anyone has tried to reach out to her. She says, "I feel like sandpaper. I'm rough and hard to hug."

Professionally, Allison has made a career of working with seemingly incorrigible delinquents. She spends hours counseling young men and women who come into her office angry and contemptuous. "My heart goes out to them. I know how much they're hurting." Allison can understand the need these young people feel to defend themselves at all cost. She also knows, however, that anger and hatefulness are powerful defenses against intimacy. After a while they work so well that people not only stop trying to break down the barriers and reach you, they even forget that you're still on the other side.

Panic

For some individuals, relationships have become so terrifying that they feel unable to approach them at all. As much as they may want to be connected to another person, these individuals only feel terror when they think about getting close to someone else. One woman's fear of getting too close was symbolized by a dream she had repeatedly throughout her childhood and adolescence. In the dream she is sitting in a small brick house looking out of a large picture window on to a beautiful green lawn. Suddenly, a lovely ballerina appears on the grass. She is dressed in a beautiful pink tutu and is dancing magically. As the dreamer leaves the safety of her house and goes outside to approach the ballerina, the scene changes. The sky darkens and the ballerina changes into a shrieking devil. The young girl turns in terror, runs from the garden back into the house screaming and crying. The lesson that the child learned was that relationships are dangerous and one is smart to remain inside safe from harm.

For some, the terror of being in a real relationship causes them to hide behind the façade of multiple "pseudo" relationships. Bella is a beautiful and sophisticated woman and no one could say that she has not had her share of intimate encounters. Yet, since she was a nine-year-old girl and overheard her other siblings talking with certainty about the death of their mother, Bella has been unable to engage in a real relationship. Her relationships only last long enough for Bella to collect the details she will need to invent a romantic plot. With a few real-life details about her latest lover, Bella constructs the "story" of a relationship, which substitutes for a real relationship.

When you hear her talk, it sounds as if she is involved intimately with many people. Yet in truth, Bella's stories begin in
reality and grow in her imagination. She becomes preoccupied
with the details of other people's lives, details that give her the
illusion of being connected without any of the danger of really
having to know another person or allowing them to know her.

MIRANDA'S STORY

Miranda's father died when she was only two years old, and
Miranda can hardly remember a time in her life when she was
not frightened. As a young child, she would imagine that a lion
or tiger was waiting for her around every corner. Once she entered school, Miranda got in the habit of inviting a classmate
home with her to lunch every day. Her mother commented on
what a social little girl she was, but Miranda knew the real
reason for her invitations. She was afraid to walk from school
to her house by herself. She would invite anyone home. It did
not matter who the girl was, she just needed someone to keep
her company.

Behind many of her fears was Miranda's worry that her
mother, like her father, would leave her. When Miranda was
eight, her mother remarried, and despite the fact that she was
told stories of being part of a happy new family, Miranda only
remembers being afraid. While her mother was dating her stepfather, Miranda would go to the window as the couple drove
away, screaming and crying, "Please don't go. Please don't
leave me." Although her mother and stepfather tried to include
her in their life, Miranda remembers being a lonely and unhappy little girl. She was terrified of being abandoned and feeling hurt by someone for whom she cared. Yet she was afraid
to reach out and to break through her own isolation.

Over the years Miranda developed a secret world, a world in
which she could invent the person she wanted to be and the
family she wished she had. When she entered adolescence,
drugs and alcohol helped her to be even more creative in the
fantasies she constructed. Inside her own head, Miranda invented a world in which she was not an only child. She gave
herself two wonderful, fun-loving brothers and she imagined

all the good-natured fun and teasing that they would have together. "All the loneliness, all the isolation, I just eliminated it." For a while the world inside Miranda's head was sufficient to soothe her. She did not need to risk a relationship with a real person. As she got older, however, and grew into a lovely young woman, several men approached her. Each time a man would become too interested, however, Miranda says, "I screwed it up. These people would fall in love with me, then I would think something was wrong with them, then I would just run."

In her late twenties, Miranda grew tired of the pattern of ending relationships and breaking engagements. On two occasions she got to the point of actually planning a wedding before she became so frightened that she had to run away. Eventually she met a man who seemed quiet, stable, and self-possessed, a man who was not put off by her terror and her insecurity. Without any help or counseling, Miranda told herself, "You must give this a try." She took a deep breath and plunged in. She married this man, still scared of what it meant to make a commitment to another person. On her wedding night, Miranda remembers, she hid behind the bed and whimpered. She was so afraid of committing to another person and opening herself up to the vulnerability of loss.

In the first years of their marriage, Miranda went through the motions of being a wife. She had seen her mother respond appropriately to a husband and she knew how a wife should behave. She remained frightened, however, and kept herself at an emotional distance from her husband. In her early thirties, Miranda suffered a serious illness. Her husband did not panic. He stayed with her in the hospital, watching over her and comforting her throughout her ordeal. When Miranda awoke she looked at her husband with new eyes. This was a man who would not leave her. The terror of abandonment, begun when she was just a small child and her father had died, quieted as she began to believe that this man, her husband, might have the strength and the resolve to stay with her.

Finding the right balance in a relationship is a difficult task for any adult. Just how close is too close? How much distance feels like separation? Each of us must struggle with those important questions of how to be an independent person and how to be in a relationship at the same time. For the survivor of early loss, the world of relationships is both more puzzling and also more treacherous. When a parent dies young, a child's basic assumption that relationships are forever and love lasts an eternity are shattered. Perhaps those assumptions need to be shattered for all of us; they are in fact an unrealistic basis on which to build a relationship. Without those fantasies of permanence and security, however, many of us might feel too frightened to take the risk and allow another person to get close. Survivors of early loss enter into relationships with childish fantasies disabused. They know that relationships are not permanent. Some of them choose to venture forth; others stay behind, safe but alone.

CHAPTER 7

◡

Parenting

PARENTING POSES PROBLEMS FOR SOME survivors of early loss for an obvious and quite practical reason. When the same-sexed parent dies, we lose our primary model for how to be a parent. As we parent our own children, it is not uncommon to hear the voices of our mothers and fathers echoing in the distance. Even when we try to do otherwise, we often find it difficult to parent differently than we were parented ourselves. When a fatherless man or a motherless woman listens for the echoes from the past, he or she hears only silence.

Many of the people I interviewed expressed bafflement and confusion at the role of parent. Even those who chose to have children did so with the knowledge that they were exploring uncharted territory. The closer their adult family resembled the family of childhood, the more uncertain they felt. For example, a fatherless man felt more lost in parenting a son than a daughter. Whenever one could ask, "How can I do what was not done for me?" parenting became more complex and more difficult.

For other survivors of early loss, the role of parent was troubling for a more subtle psychological reason. These individuals felt frozen in the parent-child relationship as perpetual children. Despite being chronological adults, many individuals felt that at some deep interior place they remained emotional children. When they heard the word *parent*, they could not help but think, not of themselves, but of some long-lost mother or father: "How can I be a parent when that is Dad's job or Mom's responsibility?" Even though many of these individuals did actually become parents, they often found the adult role of parent challenged by their own frozen-in-time memories of themselves as children.

Just as individuals who have not suffered early loss approach the task of parenting in a variety of ways, so too do those who have experienced early death. Some decide to remain childless; others proceed, continually asking themselves whether or not they can do what was not done for them. Can someone who was not parented well become a successful parent? Still others find that they have great difficulty responding to their children as separate and unique individuals. The memories of that earlier parent/child relationship haunt the new relationship in powerful ways. Sometimes a child appears to be a reincarnation of one's own younger self. Sometimes the child seems to be a stand-in for the lost parent.

In other cases, individuals parent with a style and an intent informed by their own earlier experiences. These men and women learned lessons in their grief and early childhood experiences, lessons that have directed the way they now parent their own children. Finally, some individuals see parenting as the final repair in their own process of mourning and recovery from the loss experienced in childhood. Becoming a parent completes the cycle of human growth in a way that is not only healing but joyful. The birth of their own children becomes the ultimate triumph of life over death.

Childless by Choice

Those survivors of early loss who decide not to have children do so for a variety of reasons. Perhaps the most obvious is the fear of repeating the loss they had suffered as children. These individuals were concerned both about losing a child to early death and about their own possible death, which would leave a child orphaned. One man said, "I could never deal with the death of a child. I had trouble when my dog died." Another commented, "I had a lousy childhood after my mother died. I would not want to burden a child with my death." One woman, who saw her powerful and robust father dwindle to a 125-pound skeleton, commented, "I carried the possibility of a very mean, genetic illness. I would not want to pass that along to my child. I could not bear to witness that kind of death again."

Fearing both the loss of a child and their own untimely death, these individuals choose to remain childless. For others, childhood is associated with vulnerability and dependency, and they cannot bear to experience such helplessness again. As children, they felt powerless and panicked when death took a parent away. As adults, they now look at the dependency and vulnerability of even healthy and happy children and recoil in fear and disgust. Never again do they want to be so close to the powerless and trusting dependency of childhood.

After Cynthia's father died, she felt panicked. His death was sudden and unexpected, and she had been his favorite and beloved daughter. Her mother was overwhelmed by the responsibilities of widowhood and could not comfort Cynthia's vulnerability and anxiety. When Cynthia felt needy, her mother sent her off to her room or gave her a tranquilizer. Cynthia learned to hide and hate her own dependent self. As an adult, she is defiantly self-reliant, and while she has been successful and competent in her adult life, she allows herself little room for neediness or vulnerability. Cynthia cannot imagine having to contend with the dependency of a child. Seeing such vulnerability would remind her of the vulnerable child that she was, a child she has safely and securely put away.

In recent years, Cynthia has allowed herself to have a cat. As she says, "My cat is independent enough so that I can tolerate his wanting to sit next to me. He doesn't sit on me, though, just beside me." Occasionally when her cat whines and meows, Cynthia is able to provide some soothing and comfort, soothing that she herself did not receive as a child. Yet she can only provide that kind of comfort in private, and she says quite candidly she is sure that if she ever did have a child, she would only be able to be nurturing and tender in a private space. She feels she will never be able to tolerate public vulnerability and dependency.

Another woman who spent years taking care of her invalid mother says quite simply, "I've had enough of dependency. I raised my mother. I don't need another child."

For still other individuals, the decision to remain childless stems from a perception that one has no aptitude for being a parent. Brian, whose father died when he was only three, says, "I've never been very motivated to have children. I feel comfortable and natural not being a father. It seems right somehow. It's symmetric. I don't have a father and I'm not a father. I'm sort of unto myself at both ends of the spectrum." Brian is very devoted to his niece and nephew, and spends many hours every week playing with them and taking them places. He takes his role as an uncle very seriously. After a long day together when the little boy or girl accidentally calls him Dad, Brian hears that word with a mixture of pleasure and confusion. "I just don't understand what it means to be dad. I'm just someone who loves them."

In his career, Brian manages a large organization. Occasionally when he walks into the office, one of the administrative staff will comment, "The father is here." "They say that because I'm the boss, but it always makes me uncomfortable. I never think of myself in that role." Brian recalls being invited to a Father's Day celebration at the home of one of his friends. Although he did not think about it before he accepted the invitation, he felt uneasy when he arrived at the family gathering. "I realized that I had never celebrated Father's Day in my whole life. For me it is a holiday with no meaning and no relevance."

Jerome, whose father died when he was one year old, remembers never being able to use the word *Dad*: "*Dad* was not part of my vocabulary." Throughout his twenties and thirties, this man continued to assume that one day he would have a child. However, he took no steps to make that childish notion a reality. In his late thirties he became a scoutmaster and became involved with young boys, many of them fatherless, who were looking not only for a scouting experience but also a connection to an older man. He enjoyed that experience, and while working with some of the boys met a woman with two sons who eventually became his wife. He remembers feeling pleased at the prospect of entering into a ready-made family. His wife's two children do not call him Dad. They call him Mr. Jerome. He reports, "I want to be a model for them, to encourage them and support them. I'm not sure what else 'fathering' might entail."

Parenting without a Model

When a child is an infant or young toddler at the time a parent dies, especially a same-sexed parent, as an adult he or she really has no idea how to be a father or a mother to a child. When, however, the parent dies during a child's adolescence or late childhood years, the child has had at least some experience with a sustaining and caretaking parent. This model, however short-lived it may have been, can still be used to allow the man or woman to take on the role of parent. One woman whose mother died when she was fourteen remembers thinking, I will be fine until my daughter reaches fourteen. I had a mother for those first years and I will know what to do. But I'm curious as hell about what it's going to be like when she reaches fourteen because I'm going to really be on my own then. Clearly this woman believes that the early mothering she received has been internalized in a way that would serve her well with a young and developing child. It is a teenaged daughter who seems a mystery to her. She mused further, "At least I won't do what so many people do, which is to repeat the mistakes of the parent." Then she paused and said, "Of course, I could make the worst mistake, that is, to die on her."

Another woman who also lost her mother was afraid at the prospect of having a daughter. She was a girl without a mother and she could not imagine how she could then mother a daughter of her own. In fact, the most problematic scenario seems to occur when a child loses a parent of the same sex and then has a child of that same sex. One believes, rightly or wrongly, that there is something very special about fathering boys that a boy can only learn from his own father, or something about mothering a daughter that can only be learned from a girl's own mother.

Fran, whose mother died when she was twelve, recounts, "I was afraid to have children because I felt like I did not have a role model. I didn't know what it was like to be a mother because I didn't have one. And then when I was pregnant I very much wanted a boy. I thought I could learn as I went along. You don't need history because boys are different." Fran found that she had no trouble mothering her son until he reached adolescence, the time during which she herself was motherless. Her son's rebellious acting out seemed confusing to her. She had not gone through a similar phase with her stern and disinterested stepmother. After some advice from a family counselor, Fran allowed herself to rely on her own common sense and on the good relationship she had established with her son. When she realized that she did indeed have the skill to mother him through adolescence, she was able to dispel some of her anxiety and provide him with the support he needed.

Despite attempts to unlearn many of the painful lessons of childhood and try as we might to do otherwise, we often parent our children in just the same way we were parented. Those who were disciplined sternly find themselves disciplining their own children with words that might well have been uttered by their own parents. One man who was nurtured and guided by one mentor after another after his father's untimely death repeated the style of mentorship that had been so sustaining for him with his own children and with others throughout his life.

LUKE'S STORY

Luke was only four years old when his father died in a car accident. All he remembers is that his father went to work one foggy morning and never came home. Luke has few other memories of his father, and in particular he has no memory of being nurtured and cared for by his dad. Because his mother chose not to remarry, Luke also missed the experience of growing up with a stepfather who might have served as a father substitute. Yet Luke likes to think of the small town where he was raised as one large extended family. "Everyone there knew me. I considered almost everyone a friend."

Luke's early boyhood and adolescence were peopled by powerful and kind mentors. As a young boy, he became the special charge of a dedicated scoutmaster. Luke wanted very much to please this man, consequently he participated in all the scouting activities and earned the rank of Eagle Scout. "I did everything you could do and I learned a lot." Luke's scoutmaster began his own career in scouting as a young man in his twenties; he continued to work with this same group of boys through the ten years of his own marriage and early fatherhood. Consequently, this man was part of Luke's life for almost a decade, and Luke counts his scoutmaster as one of the most powerful and positive influences on his own development.

Luke also remembers a close relationship with the father of a good friend of his. Luke would join this boy and his father on fishing and camping trips, and was frequently invited to their home for dinner or an afternoon of watching television. Luke remembers feeling privileged to be included in the family life of this happy and intact family. As he was talking about this man, a successful builder, during the interview, Luke stopped the conversation for a minute and looked introspective. Luke had an "aha" experience when he realized for the first time that his own career as an architect might well have been inspired by the example of this competent and successful father.

In high school, Luke remembers a science teacher who took him under his wing. This man would work as a teacher during the year and as a carpenter in the summer, and Luke spent two summers apprenticed to him. While they worked together on a project, Luke's teacher would talk about his own experiences as a boy and about how he made the decision to become a teacher. At times, the man would just think out loud, allowing Luke to listen and ask questions. More than any practical skills he taught or any advice he gave, this teacher shared the texture of a father-son relationship with Luke. Their summers together had a comfortable and secure rhythm that Luke came to value and that he has remembered decades later.

The relationship that Luke had with these men was a characteristic mentor-disciple relationship. They were older and wiser, and had information to impart to Luke, who was a ready and earnest pupil. Luke listened to what they had to say, took in their guidance and counsel, and never challenged their authority. The disciple does not rebel against the mentor, unlike the son, who does rebel against the father. The disciple's role is to be dutiful, compliant, and grateful; Luke played his part exquisitely. As an adult, Luke has sometimes wondered if these early relationships trained him to be perhaps a bit "too" compliant. He knows that throughout his life pleasing people has been an important motivator for him.

Luke's early experiences caused him to develop a philosophy based on what he called "the power of sufficiency." While it might be nice to be indulged, one only needs what is absolutely necessary in order to survive. The many mentors who guided Luke through childhood and adolescence were "sufficient" to help him grow into successful adulthood. Luke knew firsthand that while it might have been wonderful to have a father of his own, he had survived on a leaner diet. As an adult, Luke has let the law of sufficiency guide his actions. Although he has been very successful in his career, he never reaches for more than he needs. Given his professional reputation, Luke could command huge consulting fees, but he feels satisfied with earning a sufficient income to care for himself and his family.

When Luke became a parent, he used his own experiences with being mentored as a guide for how to be a father. Luke assumed that his children would respond to him in the same open and grateful way he had responded to those who had provided counsel to him. However, this turned out not to be the case. The older his children became, the more they challenged their father's authority and did contrary things just so they could feel independent. The more they rebelled, the more inadequate Luke's own early experience was as a model for how to parent.

Adolescent children who have been raised in a secure and comfortable home naturally rebel against their parents. They create themselves by butting up against the secure barrier presented by their mothers and fathers. When Luke's children began to rebel, he was baffled. He did not understand what he had done wrong. In his own experience, he had no firsthand knowledge of adolescent rebellion, and the behavior of his sons seemed baffling and inexplicable. Luke had an especially difficult time with his oldest son, a bright young man who decided to leave college after one year to go off and write poetry while working part time as a bartender. Luke, who had been so grateful for the opportunities given to him, could not understand how his son would walk away from the chance for a rigorous and secure education.

At one point, Luke's son spent months hanging around the house, reading, and as Luke says, "annoying" his mother. Luke came home from a business trip and said to his son, "You have one week to find a job. If you do not find a job you will have to leave the house." His son looked at him, perplexed. Many of the son's peers were living similarly at the homes of their parents and no father had laid down such an ultimatum. Luke's son could not believe that his father was serious. Yet Luke had no idea how to engage his son and to open a dialogue between the two of them about his son's behavior. Eventually Luke's son returned to college and continued along the usual path of adolescent and young adult development. Yet Luke remains confused by his son's rebellious and, to Luke, purposeless behavior.

During the course of raising his children, Luke has found ways to replicate the mentor relationship that he knew so well and that he enjoyed. He and his wife took in a fourteen-year-old foster son whose own father had been unable to care for him. This son has behaved in ways Luke understands. He has been a dutiful learner and a grateful family member. He and Luke are very close and, not surprisingly, he wants to follow in Luke's footsteps professionally.

Throughout the years, Luke and his wife have provided support and a home for twenty-six exchange students, each of whom has resided with the family for six months or more. This large pool of surrogate children remains connected to Luke and his wife. All send the usual Christmas and birthday cards and letters, but, more significantly, many of these men and women now come to visit and share with Luke and his wife the stories of their own families and their adult successes.

Luke is a partner in a large consulting firm, and throughout his career he has mentored many young associates in the firm. He is known as someone whose door is always open and who is always willing to give time, advice, and counsel. Recently, Luke has encouraged the senior partners in his firm to participate in a program for enriching the lives of inner-city children. Each summer the firm will invite several promising high school students to learn and work for two months. Luke is excited about this program because once again it gives him the opportunity to function in the parental role that feels most comfortable for him, that of mentor. Luke says quite candidly, "I may have worked successfully with other kids throughout my life. I don't know that I've been much of a success with my own children." While Luke may be somewhat hard on himself, he is reading accurately the difference between a parent and a mentor. Luke grew in the supportive relationship that developed between himself and a series of men who were only temporary guides in his life. Luke learned that one must be "a good boy, a receptive student," in order to receive the continued attention of a mentor. Luke had no experience with having a father who is there even when one is bad, even when one rebels or is defiant. Luke assumed that his own children would behave as he had behaved, forgetting, however, that they acted with the secure belief that their father would always be there for them.

A Confused Parent/Child Drama

From the time a child is first born, friends, relatives, and parents are quick to see resemblances between the child and someone from another generation. Parents naturally see themselves in their young offspring or they are quick to reminisce about a long gone aunt, uncle, or grandparent when a particular skill, talent, or in some cases, disagreeable trait makes itself known.

Early loss freezes images in time. Even when we become chronological adults, we often retain a vivid image of ourselves as children. Looking at one's own young son or daughter, it may be easy to see the face of one's childhood staring back. When this happens, a survivor of early loss risks treating a child as a reincarnation of his or her own childish self. Similarly, as a child grows into young adulthood, that child may well remind the survivor of a lost parent. When the distinction between past and present is blurred, one is unable to see a current child as a separate and unique individual. The child exists, perhaps only for a short time, as a stand-in for someone long gone.

In a number of interviews, men and women talked about their children as living replicas of their own childish selves. They felt tenderness and compassion for their children, feelings they must have harbored for the frightened children they had been years ago when they witnessed the deaths of their own parents. These individuals sought to provide their children with what had been missing for them long ago.

Miranda remembers the early loss of her father and her painful childhood with visible distress. In recounting the story of her first experience with overnight camp, Miranda captured her own sense of abandonment and fear as a growing child. She was first sent to sleep-away camp when she was only four years old. Her mother was newly widowed and eager to reestablish her own social life and find a replacement husband and father. Miranda was sent to camp for eight weeks and poignantly remembers a time when the group went on a treasure hunt. Miranda became separated from the other children. Lost, confused, and with a four-year-old's sense of direction, she walked to the top of a hill and looked out over empty space. She remembers that she was scared and crying. This memory of camp captures her feeling of her entire childhood. She was alone on top of a mountain and all she could see in front of her was empty space.

Throughout her childhood and adolescence, Miranda made up stories, invented a life that was richer and more comforting than the one she lived. As the mother of a young daughter, Miranda is determined to give her child a very different experience. "She won't have to make up stories because her life is going to be wonderful. My daughter will have an enchanted childhood." Remembering how lonely she felt, Miranda says, "I want my daughter to be surrounded by kids. I don't care if they are brothers and sisters. They can be neighbors or friends.

I want the house to be the kind of house where kids feel happy and comfortable. I want her to be confident and I want her to be everything that I wasn't."

While one can certainly recognize in Miranda's determination a mother's desire to provide her daughter with a healthy and rich experience, one also hears an urgent need in Miranda's determination. Her daughter's childhood will not only be comfortable and warm, it will be perfect. It has to be perfect. It is to make up for the childhood that Miranda missed. Because she herself has no memories of her father, Miranda is determined that her daughter will have rich and wonderful memories of growing up. Miranda carefully orchestrates events designed with posterity in mind. When a successful play day is completed, Miranda thinks to herself, This will be a memory. My daughter will have this forever. Miranda says that she is able to count the number of times her mother hugged her on only one hand. She is determined that her daughter will not have a similar experience: "I probably smother my daughter. I am all over her." Once again, Miranda is nurturing not only her real daughter, but also the lost and needy child she was when her own father died.

Ted's friends teasingly tell him that he is the most loving parent they have ever seen. He is determined that his young daughter will feel cherished and loved. Ted was only an infant when his father died and his cold and independent mother withdrew into the security of her active career. Ted grew up feeling not only that he was unloved, but also that he was unlovable. He is determined that his daughter will have none of those painful feelings. He frequently tells his daughter how much he adores her and loves her. Every night after work he spends several hours playing with his young child. He has constructed a series of stories and fantasies in which his daughter is the heroine, the most important person in the world, and he delights in telling his daughter these stories, which make her feel special and cherished.

Ted, who has no memories at all of his father, is determined that his daughter will have special memories, reminiscences she can treasure throughout her life. Once again, one gets the feeling that Ted's determination is not only born out of the sense of good parenting, but also arises from his own need to repair the damage he experienced as a lonely and unloved child.

When Tessa's son was first born, she looked at the tiny infant and thought, He will have a normal life. Tessa's own childhood was far from normal. Her mother died when she was an infant. She lost her father at the age of fourteen, after which Tessa lived with two different sets of relatives. First an aunt and uncle took her in and told her that she was welcome to stay provided they did not need the spare room for anyone else. After just a short time, Tessa lost her room when the couple's adult daughter decided to move back home. Tessa slept on the porch for a while, but when this proved unsatisfactory she was moved to the home of her grandmother. Tessa stayed there until she completed high school, but her grandmother's home was far from a "normal one." Tessa had an uncle who also lived at her grandmother's house and who suffered from a serious mental illness, which required frequent hospitalization. Tessa remembers one night when he ran around the house screaming and brandishing a knife before the police came and took him away.

When Tessa left the home of her grandmother and went off to college, all she remembers is that she desperately wanted a "normal" life. Tessa, however, had no idea really what normal meant. She imagined the family life she watched on television. Growing up in the 1950s, Tessa was brought up on *Father Knows Best* and *The Donna Reed Show,* programs with happy two-parent families where love flowed abundantly and problems were solved within the space of half an hour.

Tessa married the first man who showed any real interest in her. Love was not a necessary ingredient in her formula for normalcy. She needed a husband, a home, and children. Love was something Tessa did not really understand. When her first child was born, she thought not only that he would have a normal life, but that he would make her life normal. She thought, He will have a nice home, nice friends, and milk and cookies when he comes back from school. "I needed him more than he needed me," she now says. Tessa's decision to have a second child was motivated more by her desire to provide her son with a sibling than it was to have another baby. Growing up alone,

Tessa reports, "I was more than an only child. I was an only person." She was determined to repair her own isolation and loneliness through the life of her son. He would have a companion, never feeling as she did, so alone and frightened.

Tessa's son grew up sensitive to his mother's needs, and she reports now that, perhaps to his detriment, he followed her plan to be a "normal and perfect" boy. Tessa, who has gained considerable insight into her own early mothering over the years, now feels that she treated her first child merely as an extension of herself. She was desperately trying to repair her own damaged childhood through the life and experiences of her young son.

While it is easy to see how an adult parent might mistake a child for his or her own young self, it is a bit more complicated to understand how some survivors of early loss look at their children and see not themselves, but see instead the parent who died long ago. This association is often triggered by a particular behavior or circumstance, which causes the survivor to link child and parent via a connection that is emotionally real but factually mistaken.

After Margie's father committed suicide she worked very hard to be the good and perfect girl. She did not want to draw any attention to herself or to bring any additional shame on her family. When Margie's son was born, she idealized him immediately. "He was the most wonderful, perfect child. He just seemed special to me, not a real boy, but something ideal." As he was growing up, Margie often worried that something would happen to her perfect son. If he was late coming home, she would immediately think that perhaps he had been in an accident or been injured somehow.

Margie's warm and loving connection to her son continued until he reached adolescence. Then his risky, arrogant rebellion felt to her like a repeat of her father's callous and self-indulgent suicide. By taking his life, Margie's father had deprived her of a normal childhood. He had abandoned her and left her feeling ashamed of her family. Margie was confronted with all of the same feelings as her son struggled with being a teenager. Once, as they were driving in a car, she lashed out at him: "I worked so hard at not letting people hurt me, keeping them at a distance, and the only two people who have been able to hurt me are my father and you." Margie was shocked by the power and venom of her own words and realized at that moment that she was not seeing her son for who he was, but was, rather, venting at last her rage at her father. Margie saw a counselor and sorted through her tangled feelings about both her father and her son. She now feels she is better able to see her son for who he is: a young man trying to be an adult, not an ideal version of the father she lost. Still, it is difficult for her not to worry that this son will be taken away from her just as her father was. When her son seems moody or irritable, she worries that perhaps he is hiding some big problem, something she has missed that might push him over the edge.

Ron never thought of his daughter as being anything like his mother. In fact, Ron could not remember the mother who died suddenly when he was only thirteen. After her death, he consciously blocked out any memories of the woman who had been at the center of his family's life. What he did remember, however, was that he could not mourn for his mother because his father was in such deep despair and needed him as a companion.

One day, Ron's twenty-year-old daughter called from across the country to announce to her mother and father that she had gotten married. Ron, who had believed himself to have a close and special relationship with his daughter, felt stunned. While any parent might be shocked, disappointed, and upset to hear of an unplanned and sudden marriage, Ron felt his own reaction to be extreme: "It was like a death, the same emotion as when you are not expecting something and then there is a total change. It was as if she had been completely removed from my life. I knew it related back to the death of my mother."

In an instant, Ron's daughter and mother became merged as the same person, a beloved woman who was suddenly leaving him with no warning and no regard. For several months Ron felt unable to regain his footing and to resume anything resembling his normal life. "I felt adrift, unmotivated, just like when my mother died. My mother's death denied me a chance to be a part of her life in an ongoing way. All of the ceremonies and rituals were gone. My daughter did the same thing." Ron had looked forward to walking his daughter down the aisle, to participating in a rite of passage that connects one generation to the next. His daughter, like his mother in the past, denied him the chance to be part of those things that make a family a family.

Ron is well aware that he is reacting to his daughter with emotions buried long ago in the past, yet he feels unable to do otherwise. He is terrified that he will do to his daughter what he did to his mother: cut her out of his life completely. "When the pain is too great, I know I have the capacity to block something out completely." Ron is afraid that in an attempt to protect himself from unmourned pain, he will bury his daughter alive. "I keep telling myself I must move on. If I don't get past this, the feelings will destroy me."

In talking about his daughter in the course of the interview, Ron became clear that in order to maintain any kind of relationship with his adult daughter, he needed to be able to see her as separate from his mother. His daughter, unlike his mother, did not die. Ron believed, however, that she had chosen in a thoughtless and self-centered way to get married without informing her family. Yet she did not desire to end her relationship with her mother and father. Like so many young adults, she was struggling with issues of autonomy and separation, trying to balance becoming her own person with staying in contact with her family. Ron's mother had died, lost and gone forever. His daughter had merely made a choice of which he disapproved.

By the end of the interview, Ron seemed clearer about the distinction, and he resolved to take the advice already given him by many friends: to call his daughter and make a trip to see her. For Ron, it was the suddenness of his daughter's announcement, an announcement that said "she was separate and on her own," that sent him reeling back into the past, overwhelmed by feelings he thought he had long since buried. Had she not made such an abrupt announcement, it is unlikely that Ron would have ever confused his daughter and his mother. But for Ron, sudden loss means only one thing. It means death, and Ron had no other symbolic language with which he could understand his daughter's behavior. In most cases, confusing a child with a lost parent or a lost image of the self is short-lived. As circumstances change, as the child grows, the temporary coalescence of images disappears. When images are merged, however, the adult survivor is unable to see his or her child as a separate person. The child exists only as a reminder of the past.

Applying Lessons Learned in the Past

Being raised without the support and guidance of two parents often causes a child to learn how to survive on his or her own. At times those lessons prove invaluable, and some men and women reach adulthood convinced that the lessons they learned as a result of trauma are lessons worth passing on to their own children. Often these lessons have to do with the value of independence, self-reliance, and truthfulness.

When her father committed suicide, Sally was left with a series of puzzling questions as to why this man she had loved so well had chosen to leave her behind. Although she rationally knew that she was in no way the cause of her father's death, she often wondered if perhaps something she had done or said had displeased him so that he chose to take his own life. As a mother, Sally is firmly convinced that children need accurate information. They should never be allowed to guess how an adult is feeling or what he or she is thinking. Consequently, Sally takes great care to inform her children of why she is doing what she is doing. If she is angry or irritable, she tells them why so they are not left to guess and perhaps inaccurately conclude that their mother's mood is their responsibility.

Keith, on the other hand, considers himself a self-educated man. He grew up with little parental guidance, and when his father died when Keith was only twelve, any chance for a strong father disappeared. Keith educated himself by reading and gaining as much life experience as he possibly could. When he had two sons of his own, Keith was determined that they would grow to be independent young men. After a bitter divorce, Keith became the sole parent for his two young sons. He was more determined than ever that they should grow up confident in their own ability to care for themselves. Keith often thought, If I can just get these boys to age sixteen then they won't need me and they'll be okay. He consciously taught his sons to cook, to sew, to box, to defend themselves, and to be young men who could survive in the world. Having grown up as an only child, Keith was well aware of the need for a trusted companion. Consequently, he encouraged his sons to become friends and supports for one another. He repeatedly told them, "Depend on each other. Don't depend on me," and gave them opportunities to enjoy each other's company and to develop a brotherly bond.

When his sons were teenagers, Keith decided to send them to boarding school. It was hard for him because he enjoyed being a parent and greatly missed his sons when they were gone. However, he was convinced that the best lesson he could give his boys was to teach them how to survive on their own. He wanted his sons to love him, but he did not want them to feel dependent on their only parent.

Throughout their childhood and adolescence, Keith provided his sons with a variety of experiences that many would label storybook adventures. They climbed mountains, camped in the wilderness, and rode rapids in a canoe. He wanted them to learn to take risks but not to be foolhardy. He himself had engaged in dangerous and risky behavior as an adolescent because he had no one guide him or to set limits on his behavior. Keith was determined that his sons would learn the difference between a reasonable risk and dangerous behavior. In remembering his own childhood, Keith assessed what skills had allowed him to survive in circumstances that might have destroyed others. He wanted to teach his own sons those same skills and provide them with rich experiences so that if fate chose to be unkind to them, they would not be unprepared.

Although not well parented themselves, these individuals are behaving as supportive parents. They are taking the experiences of their own childhood and using those experiences to evolve a set of principles that now guide their own parenting. They are not trying to compensate for what they did not get. Rather, they are trying to share those lessons of childhood that were so valuable in their own stories of survival.

Sam, who grew up watching his mother abuse her younger children, struggled throughout his adolescence with questions of good and evil. He needed a moral code to help guide his own decision-making and to free himself from the guilt and blame for the terrible abuse he was forced to witness. Sam is convinced that the moral education he gave himself saved him from going insane in a confusing and unreal household. As a parent, Sam has been careful to provide moral guidance for his sons. He does so in a gentle and thoughtful way by telling his sons stories at night that contain some moral or message. Sam is a creative storyteller and some of the parables he writes himself. Others he has culled from his own vast knowledge of world religion and folklore. Sam is convinced that with a strong sense of right and wrong, his sons will not feel lost when they have to make important decisions.

Despite their desire to prepare their children for eventual independence, each of the parents who sought to teach important lessons was aware that untimely death could derail the best-made plans. Each imagined a particular age at which a child could survive without their parental guidance. "If I can just get my son to age twelve or my daughter to age fourteen then I know they will be all right." The age chosen was always three or four years older than they themselves had been when death took a parent away. Not surprisingly, survivors of early loss *always* felt their parent had died too soon—whether the death had occurred when they were six or sixteen—and they imagined that just "a few more" years would have made a big difference. It was these "few more" years that they now wanted for their own children.

Parenting and Personal Repair

For some individuals, the act of becoming a parent represents the final stage in completing their own healing from their own early loss of a parent. As one man said, "What was broken was made whole again. The father/son relationship was restored, and now I was the father and I knew I could do it this time." For this man, years of being inappropriately thrust into an adult role as a child left him feeling inadequate and fraudulent. Finally becoming a father allowed him to feel like a competent man and to put aside forever the image of the irresponsible boy. "When my son was born I thought, You brought him into the world, now you take care of him. That saved my life. I finally grew up." Others find in the role of parent an opportunity to give and receive unambivalent love, an opportunity that had not been present since death intruded on their lives years ago.

Jenny in particular felt as if she had closed down after her father's death. Love had been put away and stored in some inaccessible place after her father died suddenly. Jenny knew that she would need to love again in order to become a whole person, and although she felt partially healed in her decision to marry and to make a commitment to her husband, she felt more fully repaired after she became a mother. "Being a mother is learning to expand love. It was a risk I needed to take. I created a family and created a space for myself."

For others, having children is more than just being a parent. It is creating a family; creating a warm, loving space in which growth and development can occur. When Jonah's mother died, he lost not only his supportive parent, he lost all semblance of happy family life. Jonah was determined that in his own marriage and fatherhood, he would once again enjoy the comforts of a home. After his mother's death, Jonah's family home became a place from which he and his sister wanted only to escape. In his marriage, Jonah created a home where people wanted to come, an open, warm environment where his sons and daughters entertained their friends comfortably and with ease. "Being a father has been an incredible joy. I have been able to watch someone else's growth and take pleasure in that." Joy left Jonah's life with his mother's death, and for him the creation of a family in which joy was a welcomed guest marked an act of genuine healing from the pain and despair of his own early loss.

The task of parenting children seems enormous for all of us. How do you love without smothering? How do you guide without controlling? How do you discipline without abusing?

Is it ever really possible to see this person who is in many ways a replication of yourself as a separate and unique individual? The struggles of raising the next generation are the struggles of the human race. They become even more complicated when a mother or father has lost a parent in childhood. That person brings to motherhood or fatherhood not only the usual expectations, dreams, and fears, but also a host of fantasies born from the experiences of an orphaned child.

Despite the difficulties they face, children who lose parents can become adults who raise healthy and successful sons and daughters. I know this firsthand. My own mother lost her father when she was only seven. She was raised by her immigrant mother who loved her dearly but who relied on my mother for support and companionship.

Although she married early, my mother came to motherhood late. I think she felt she was not quite "cut out" for motherhood. Yet she raised three daughters with love and courage.

I know there were times when she looked at us and remembered her own childhood. I think she felt cheated. But that never stopped her from giving us all she could. There were times when I could feel her fears about being abandoned again. They were so ever present that I sometimes imagined them to be my own. Her anxieties did not stop her from encouraging our independence. She watched with pride as each of us left home to attend college and find our own place in the world. Having lost a father may have made it harder for my mother to be a parent, but it certainly did not make it impossible—three healthy and loving daughters are proof enough.

CHAPTER 8

～

Death, Mortality, and Vitality

So many obvious and practical things change in a child's world when a parent dies young. Less immediately apparent is the change that occurs in the child's relationship to "inevitable death." The Grim Reaper, the Gay Deceiver, the draining sands in an hourglass, all assume a personal, perhaps too personal, relevance. Death ceases to be a stranger, and for some, it becomes the enemy that stalks them throughout their lives.

Before children have any direct encounter with death, they imagine that death is optional, something they choose or perhaps decide to pass. I remember sitting in a restaurant with my five-year-old niece as she scanned a series of portraits that rimmed the walls of the eatery. The portraits were of Renaissance philosophers. My niece asked me who these people were and if they were still alive. I told her, in language she could understand, that they had died a long time ago. She pondered for a while and asked me about her own death. I told her that she did not need to worry, death would not come for her for a very long time. She thought again and said to me, "I don't think I want it to come at all. I don't think I am going to die." For her, death was still optional, as much of a choice as whether to have ice cream or cake for dessert.

When a parent dies young, children are confronted abruptly with the reality that death is not optional; it is not something in which they can choose or not choose to participate. This too-early encounter with the reality of death and mortality changes a child. A seventeenth-century maxim proclaims that "Death and the sun are not to be looked at steadily."[1] When a child looks steadily on the aura of death, his or her world is altered. For some, this encounter with death leads to a lifelong preoccupation with mortality and finality.

Edgar Allan Poe, who was orphaned before the age of three, spent a lifetime creating poems and stories that repeatedly asked the question, Do the dead remain dead?[2] Poe was obsessed with coming to know the dead intimately. Who are they? Where do they go? Can they return to us? In many of his poems, Poe wrote from the perspective of the one who had died, trying to enter into the mind of the deceased and to understand the mental state of the dead.

Poe both longed for and feared a reunion with his dead mother. He imagined that to be with her again would be blissful, but to be reunited meant that he himself would die. In one of his poems Poe wrote:

> I could not love except where Death
> Was mingling his with Beauty's breath.[3]

Early death and loss defined what became the central preoccupation of Poe's artistic quest: both to understand and to master the complex interplay between death and life.

Few survivors of early loss mix their yearning for answers with the creative brilliance of Edgar Allan Poe. Many, however, share Poe's fear of death. Some individuals told me that a day does not pass when they do not think about their own death or the death of someone they love. These survivors of early loss are almost always anxious that death will pay them another unwanted visit.

For others, early loss leaves them not with a fear of death but rather with an awareness of the reality of death and of their own mortality. These individuals often believe that they, like their parents, will die young, and this belief—taken as fact, not felt as fear—guides the choices and the decisions they make about how to live their lives. In ancient Rome, Caesar would often be accompanied by a slave whose job it was to whisper in his ear, "You too are mortal." For some survivors of early loss the whisper of mortality is never far off.

For others, life and death do not exist as separate and distinct states. Rather, life is mingled with a kind of death. These survivors experience what social historian Robert Lifton has called "death in life," a form of "walking death" that allows them to merge elements of life with images of death.[4] By living as if they are only half alive, these individuals identify with the dead on one hand and "play possum" on the other. If they are weakened and deenergized, perhaps they can fool Death into leaving them alone.

Finally, there are those who use their early encounter with death to develop a worldview that accepts the inevitability of an ending. These individuals live their lives fully, cherish their worldly experiences, but feel prepared to accept Death more as a peaceful sleep or a long awaited reunion than as a Grim Reaper.

The Fear of Death

For some individuals, the early death of a mother or father leaves them quite literally quaking at the prospect of their own early demise. These individuals think about their own death or about the death of a loved companion on an almost daily basis. This preoccupation with death limits their ability to engage in or enjoy life fully.

ALLAN'S STORY

Watching his father's death from heart disease, Allan became convinced that he, like his father, would die young. When AIDS came along, Allan, a gay man in his thirties, thought, That will be my disease. Allan, however, has been tested repeatedly for HIV and continues to test negative. Despite his apparent good health, Allan continues to be convinced that an early death will be his fate.

Because his father died at the age of forty, Allan hopes that if he can magically stop the progress of time, perhaps he can fool death; the Grim Reaper might well pass him by, mistaking him for a younger man. Consequently, Allan tries to look young and act boyish. "I am always happy when people tell me that I look younger than my age. I'd like to stop time. I don't want to take my father's place. I don't want to die." Allan's pervasive anxiety about death was shared by his mother, who worried constantly about her frail and incapacitated husband. "I grew up with the feeling that the wolf was always at the door. One could never get too far from the specter of death."

As a young man living in a large urban gay community, Allan is amazed "that I have no friends who have been sick. It's as if I don't want to be near someone who might be dying. I keep my distance. I'm very careful about making friends." Allan is aware that he sometimes appears cold and unfeeling to his acquaintances, but he does not want to hear people's stories of illness and death. Recently, Allan met a man from another city with whom he wanted to begin a relationship. "Once I heard that he was sick I began to pull away. I told myself it was because he was from out of town." In fact Allan knows that his desire to distance himself from this man was because he felt scared and anxious to be near someone who might be dying. "I didn't know what to say. I didn't even know what to feel."

Recently, a friend of Allan's told him that she had been diagnosed with cancer. He remembers panicking on the phone as she conveyed the information. He became almost deaf to her words. "I wasn't sure what she was saying. I kept thinking, Oh my God. Oh my God." Although Allan is an intelligent and insightful man, he could not make sense of his friend's communication. He had to ask her several times exactly what was wrong and what her treatment might entail. When Allan failed to hear from his friend for two weeks, he was convinced that she was dead, and became afraid to pick up the phone, call, and find out. This friend has recently invited Allan to come and visit her for a long weekend over the summer. Allan wants to visit his friend, in part because he wants to see her and in part because he knows he must stare down this personal demon. Allan has reached a point in his life where he can no longer run from his fear of death. He asks himself, however, "How can I get close to this woman? Is there any place for me in her life? Does she even have a life? Do I want her in my life?" Allan is aware that he is phobic about the prospect of death and has sought counseling to help him deal with his pervasive death anxiety.

Allan's inability to separate himself completely from someone who might be dying or sick hearkens back to his inability to experience himself as separate from his dying father. He says, "My father and I were merged. My whole family became occupied with his life. I always felt like I had his life." Allan must learn that each person finally has his or her own death. Death is not an experience that we share, but rather an experience that comes to each individual only once. In order to feel more at ease in his own life, Allan needs to stop living in the shadow of his father's death.

For other survivors of early loss, the fear of death makes itself felt, not as a fear for themselves, but rather as a fear of death for a loved one. Janice, whose father's early death left her mother an unhappy widow, is terrified that her husband will also die young, leaving her as her mother was left. Janice adored her father and always wanted to marry "someone just like Dad." She sought a man who was bright, funny, ambitious, and hardworking, all of the things she so admired in her father. Now Janice fears that being "like Dad" might be a curse rather than a blessing. "I worry so much that my husband will die like my father and then I will end up like my mother."

Janice's fears are not entirely unfounded. Her husband has a history of heart disease in his family, and he himself has some early signs of coronary artery disease. Yet Janice knows that her fears are not solely based on her husband's medical history. She is convinced that the happy life she has made for herself will be taken away from her just as her idyllic childhood vanished when her father died. "My life is just too good to last forever. I had an idyllic childhood and all of a sudden it was gone. This life is too good. I'm afraid death will get me again."

Janice's fear of death makes her unable to enjoy her life fully. She is so worried about her husband's early death that she finds herself preoccupied and anxious when they are together and enjoying themselves. Although he is generally easygoing, Janice's husband has begun to become annoyed with her constant nagging and worrying. Her obsession with his early death makes him uncomfortable and also prevents them from enjoying the time they do have. Yet Janice feels, "I have this great life. I wish I could just enjoy it. I try. I say to myself, 'Just live each day to the fullest,' but then I start to worry."

Fully believing in her own early widowhood, Janice has taken steps to ensure that "even if I am left like my mother, I won't be my mother." She has maintained her maiden name and has pursued an independent career. Although she and her husband are a close couple and enjoy a circle of mutual friends, Janice has been conscious to maintain a network of separate friends and separate interests. She maintains a "fallback" life that she has not shared with her husband and to which she could easily return once her husband is gone. In her own mind, Janice has imagined how she would meet her financial obligations and raise her three children without a husband to help. As much as she tries to live in the present, Janice feels burdened by a past that she is convinced foreshadows the future.

Not all survivors who fear death appear anxious. Some engage in dangerous and at times life-threatening behavior in order to prove to themselves and demonstrate to others that they are "above" a fear of death. Actor James Dean adopted a fearless, cavalier attitude toward death. He continually mocked death, almost playing a game of tag with the Grim Reaper, daring the specter to come and get him. Once, while posing for a photographic essay, Dean requested that the photographer take his picture while Dean lay in a coffin.[5] This irreverent behavior was typical for the actor who personified the "rebel." But it also addressed Dean's challenge to cruel death, which had robbed him of a much-loved mother.

For others, the fear of death translates into a push for immortality. One may not be able to live forever *in fact,* but historical immortality offers some small measure of victory over the finality of death. If one can write a great book, build a monument, win a war, or accomplish something outstanding, then at least one's name and one's accomplishments will live on. As long as there was one reader left on earth to read his books, Sartre believed he would cheat "inevitable death."[6] His immortality was not his alone, but was linked to the survival of the race.

One rarely thinks of Abraham Lincoln and Adolf Hitler as bedfellows, yet both men shared an overwhelming fear of death and a lifelong desire to be remembered forever in the annals of history and in the minds of men and women.

When Hitler was asked by the Nazi Party archives for a memoir, he began his story, "I was orphaned with no father or mother at seventeen. . . ."[7] Throughout his life, Hitler was obsessed with the idea that time was short and that he did not have long enough to live. Every day, the man who came to control the lives of millions began his morning with a child's game. Hitler would race the clock to see how long it would take him to dress for his appointments. He was constantly trying to beat the record of the day before. Hitler took his game quite seriously, a man obsessed with trying to master time. Repeatedly, Hitler commented, "I shall become the greatest man in history. I have to gain immortality even if the whole German nation perishes in the process."[8] To the horror of the world, Adolf Hitler was successful in his quest for immortality.

Abraham Lincoln began staring at the face of death when he was only nine years old and his mother died. In the next several years he experienced the deaths of two more beloved women: his older sister Sarah and his dear friend Ann Rutledge. Lincoln suffered from melancholy throughout his life and seemed unable to recover fully from the deaths of these three women.[9] In his early thirties, Lincoln suffered a bout of depression so severe that his friends feared for his life. Several friends took turns staying with Lincoln, removing all razors, knives, and pistols from his reach.

Lincoln's favorite poem, one he committed to memory, was entitled "Mortality." In the poem, life was likened to a swift, fleeting meteor, a fast-flying cloud, a flash of lightning, and a break in the wave.[10] Lincoln was all too aware of how quickly life passed and how fragile was the structure on which a child builds his world. Lincoln wrote to his friends not only of his preoccupation with death, but also of his desire for immortality. He wanted to live on in the minds of others, to survive "by proxy."[11] Lincoln believed that the key to immortality was to connect his name with the great events of his day, and to link the name Lincoln with something that would benefit all of humanity.[12]

Like Hitler, Lincoln believed that by doing something great he could cheat death. For Lincoln, memory was an in-between state, a perpetual limbo bridging life and death.[13] By doing something truly outstanding, Lincoln believed he would "live forever" as a memory in the minds of men and women.

Mortality: An Early Death

Early loss does not always lead to a fear of death and final endings. It does, however, make a young man or woman aware of issues of mortality. When one has survived early loss, one cannot help but think about one's own life in a different way. Death, and in particular one's own early death, is taken as a "given." Just as one takes for granted other essentials of life, one is aware of the ever-present shadow of death. Author Ben Hecht writes, "I can recall the hour in which I lost my immortality, in which I tried on my shroud for the first time and saw how it became me. . . . The knowledge of my dying came to me when my mother died. There was more than sorrow involved. Her vanished voice echoes in my head and the love she bore me struggled painfully to stay alive around me. But my heart did not claw at the empty space where she stood and demand her return. I accepted death for both of us. I went and returned dry-eyed from the burial, but I brought death back with me. I had been to the edge of the world and looked over its last foot of territory into nothingness."[14] Although he was an adult when his mother died, Hecht's eloquent passage describes the moment of awareness when one knows not only that life in general is finite, but, more significantly, that one's own life will come to an end.

The texture and rhythm of life is different for someone who assumes that he or she will die young. If life is only expected to last for thirty or forty years, then one reaches midlife in one's twenties. The stages of life are altered and one carries what Robert Lifton has labeled in the survivors of the Hiroshima bombing as "a legacy of lethal impairment."[15] The individual lives with an internal time bomb, slowly but inexorably ticking toward an early end.

For some, the expectation of early death removes the need to plan. Why plan for a future one will not live to enjoy?

One woman who was convinced that her early death would occur before she graduated from high school made no plans for a life past age eighteen. "I excelled at school, but I did not have a lot of friends. I didn't date. It was weird. It's almost as if I was waiting to die. I made no plans to go to college until I absolutely had to. I thought, Oh, my God, I'm not dead yet. I'd better do something."

Another woman is convinced that she remained in bad relationships for a long time because she did not think it was worth the effort to try to change her life. "My mother had died young. Her mother had died young. I was sure that I was doomed. I think I let my twenties get eaten up because I didn't think it mattered. I don't think I put a lot of value on my life and the things I wanted. I didn't really even want to believe in those things because I thought I could not have them." There was no reason to put effort into nurturing a loving relationship. She was convinced that the fast-ticking clock would cheat her of any future happiness.

One man was convinced that his belief in an early death gave him permission to avoid any responsibility for his behavior as an adult. The consequences of his actions mattered little because he was certain he would not live either to reap the benefits or to shoulder the blame for his actions: "My failure to complete things reflected the lack of real concern for how things were going to turn out because I didn't think I was going to be there anyway."

Baseball player Mickey Mantle, who was hospitalized for his addiction to alcohol, commented that he lived a dissipated life because he was fully convinced that he would die young and therefore would not have to contend with the consequences of his own irresponsible and self-destructive behavior.

For still others, the belief in an early death is sufficient motivation in and of itself to live a full life. If death is going to come too soon, one has an obligation to do as much as possible as quickly as possible. Lee, another man I interviewed, not only assumes that he will die the same way his father did, but he is actively planning for his own early death. Lee's father died of a rare but lethal genetic illness, which strikes men in their extended family. "I try to take advantage of everything. I take the trips I want to take now. I don't believe in waiting for the future." Lee's family comes from Central Africa, and he is determined to take his young daughter to the birthplace of his ancestors. Although his daughter is only a toddler, Lee plans to take the trip soon. He does not feel that he has the luxury of waiting several years.

Lee has purchased a large life insurance policy that would handsomely take care of both his wife and his child. With their future secure, Lee feels free to enjoy his income now. He sees no reason to deny himself little luxuries or to worry about eating an extra dessert. Lee feels in a hurry to live as much of his life as he can before death takes him away.

Lee's sense of his own mortality has changed the way he views time. Lee never thinks about any commitment or responsibility beyond three years' duration. "I assume I can commit for three years, nothing longer. I don't want anyone to be dependent on my survival because I can't promise that I will be around for very long." When he has successfully reached another three-year marker, Lee plans once again for the next three years, never allowing himself to imagine a future that extends beyond thirty-six months at a time.

Sometimes issues about mortality only become conscious when one reaches the age at which a parent died. This recognition, known as "comparative death timing," is often fraught with anxiety.[16] The age at which a mother or father died serves as a milestone that many fear will mark the end of their own journey. Many people who have not yet reached that age actively fear its arrival. One man declared, "I will just be so happy when I pass age forty-six." Others who have successfully passed that fateful age find themselves oddly confused about what to do next. What does it mean, in Jean-Paul Sartre's words, "to become a man older than one's father"?[17]

One man who had just passed the age of his mother's death commented, "I feel as if my life is completed. I could die now. Perhaps I should be looking for a new life. I don't know what to do, and it's the first time in my life I have felt like that." He had unconsciously assumed that his life, like his mother's, would end at age forty-eight. When age forty-eight came and went, and he found himself not only alive but active and at the height of his career, he was puzzled. Fate had played a strange, albeit welcome, trick on him. He now had to plan for a future he had never anticipated. He also had to change his personal sense of identity, allowing himself to think of being first a middle-aged and eventually an old man.

Another man felt both exhilarated and confused to be older than his father: "At first I just felt astounded. How could I be older than my own father? He seemed so much older than me." On the one hand, he felt unable to become excited about the future, feeling as if he had given up on the remaining part of his life. At other times, he felt exhilarated. At last he was truly free to be his own man, unencumbered by any legacy of his father's life. Sartre, who insisted that he saw his father's early death as a blessing, proclaimed that "family life is a gallery of mirrors; the child, the man, the dotard are reflections which change places. In them he [a man] sees his future. . . ."[18] Once this man reached the age of his father's death, the mirror ceased to contain a vital image. He now saw only his own reflection and was intrigued at the possibility of creating himself.

Tracy lived counting to the age of thirty-seven. "I did not want to get breast cancer. Now I am thirty-nine and I beat my mother by two years. I'm beginning to think, Maybe I'm not going to be my mother." Tracy spent much of her early adulthood waiting to be age thirty-seven, waiting to die. "I set no goals for myself. I just thought, Here is life, I might as well take it as it comes." Although she is a brilliant and creative woman, Tracy allowed herself to fall into a comfortable but unchallenging career and to accept a safe but passionless marriage. Once she passed the milestone age of thirty-seven, Tracy began to think that perhaps she was going to have her own life. "If I'm going to live, I might as well start taking some control over what happens to me." Tracy has entered counseling and has begun asserting her own needs and desires in her relationship. Although she has successfully mothered one child, she is excited about becoming pregnant again. Now that she feels alive herself, she feels better able to nurture new life. Rather than feeling confused as she moves past the age of her mother's death, Tracy at last feels a sense of authority and ownership in her life.

Attacks on Vitality

Some individuals continue to live their lives for many, many years after experiencing an early loss, but with diminished vitality and life energy. It is as if the only way they can allow themselves to live is to be not fully alive, what Robert Lifton has called "death in life," a syndrome in which one's waking life takes on an eerie resemblance to the nonexistence of the dead.[19]

There are several complicated psychological causes to explain the experience of "half living." In some cases, it results from a misguided identification with the dead parent. To be dead, after all, is to be permanently stilled. The child who feels bonded to a parent who died young might well imagine that he or she must walk through life in slow motion. Russell Baker recalls his own response to seeing his lifeless father laid out in a coffin: "I gazed at the motionless hand laid across his chest, thinking no one can lie so still for so long without moving a finger. I waited for the closed eyelids to flutter, for his chest to move in a slight sigh to capture a fresh breath of air. Nothing. His motionlessness was majestic and terrifying. I wanted to be away from that room and never see him like that again."[20] For the young Baker, his father was in a state of suspended animation. The six-year-old child did not understand the permanence of death. He only knew that his father was in a motionless, strangely still state.

For some, the image of life without movement becomes a psychological image that inspires adult living. One woman, in talking about her own life energy, recalled, "My passion was something that had just been in storage for years and years." The life force that had animated her had been buried with her mother.

Others feel only half alive because they appear to have been drained by their association with the dead. There are many folk myths about the "homeless dead" who have often died young and who now wander the earth and drink the vital blood of the living.[21] Jocelyn, whose childhood and young adulthood were marked by multiple losses, feels sapped by having witnessed so much death. She often feels as if she is the only one left standing after a disaster. Every time Jocelyn has made an attempt to live her own life, to enjoy her womanhood, or to pursue some interest, another dying relative materializes to demand her attention and to sap her lifeblood. A woman in her forties, Jocelyn no longer has the energy to pursue any of her own goals. She walks through life numbed, not merely pained and burdened by the losses she has sustained, but clearly weakened by them. The deaths that Jocelyn has experienced have never been sudden. When someone has died it has been a long and painful affair. Jocelyn has witnessed life energy slowly drain away from people she loves. Her own life energy has become similarly depleted as each new death leaves her in a more weakened state.

Other survivors of early loss believe that they will betray the dead by living their own lives with vitality. Active living involves change and evolution. When one changes, one inevitably leaves the past behind. Some survivors fear that their own forward movement is an abandonment of the dead. In some cases, the desire not to move beyond those who have died takes the form of freezing the past. A strange kind of mummification occurs as the survivor and his or her family preserve a room or a home exactly as it was when the dead mother or father was an occupant. Some survivors of early loss recall how the objects on a desk remained untouched for decades, almost as if the dead parent had just walked to the corner and was expected to return momentarily.

Others manifest their fear of moving forward in more subtle ways. One man recounted how he dreads any type of transition; even a movement to something positive and more profitable makes him uncomfortable. Any change disturbs the past, making him feel farther and farther from his lost father. Still others experience their active living as an affront to the dead. Some survivors of the Nazi Holocaust report that they are almost ashamed to live with gusto and passion.[22] The dead seem to be the only pure ones, and the survivor feels that living actively is an insult to those who have died. The most extreme example of this phenomenon is "survivor guilt," in which the survivor actually feels guilty for being alive.[23] It is as if the Angel of Death could have chosen anyone, and the survivor continued to live at the expense of the dead parent. I remember reading a chilling anecdote written after the death of David Kennedy, one of the sons of Robert Kennedy. Shortly before his assassination, Robert Kennedy and his son were swimming in the ocean. The boy got in trouble in some deep water and was rescued by his father. When his father was killed, not long after this incident, the boy tragically concluded that Death had wanted a Kennedy and, being cheated of him, had taken his father instead. For years David Kennedy battled a serious drug addiction before dying of an overdose in his twenties. Although we will never know, it may well be that he felt he was finally paying an old debt to Death.

Bertolt Brecht writes eloquently in a passage inscribed on the wall of the Holocaust Museum in Washington, D.C., about his own survivorship of the Holocaust: "I know of course it's simply luck that I've survived so many friends. But last night in a dream I heard those friends say of me 'survival of the fittest' and I hated myself." The guilty survivor sees his or her continued life as an affront to the dead, a betrayal of those who were less fortunate.

CARLA'S STORY

Carla's father died of heart failure when she was seventeen, but for years she watched as the disease that eventually took his life slowly sapped her father's life energy. The father she remembers from childhood was gregarious, wild, funny, and full of life. Over the years, however, his very aliveness became com promised by the heart disease that eventually killed him. Carla also witnessed her mother become old before her time. "I can't believe it when I look at the pictures of my mother. She lost so much of her attractiveness, working so hard to make life bearable for my father." During her early thirties, Carla's mother devoted herself to the care of her ailing husband. She was determined that no undue stress would shorten his life more than necessary. She also prepared for her own eventual and inevitable widowhood by taking classes and embarking on a career. As Carla was growing up, the family needed to curtail its social life in order to accommodate her father's diminished health. By the time he died, one of his only remaining pleasures was going out to dinner with his large family.

On the night of his death, the family went to a favorite restaurant for a big meal. Although they had shared such an evening many times in the past, Carla's mother was overwhelmed with guilt when, returning from the restaurant, her husband collapsed with a fatal heart attack. Carla's mother blamed herself for her husband's death. She felt as if she had failed in her assignment to protect him from too much fun and too much aliveness. Although she gathered her children to her and pledged that they would all form a bond with one another and survive their shared loss, Carla's mother was less than successful in her own adjustment. She worked hard during the day supporting her children, but at night she was unable to cope with her grief and her despair. Her nights were filled with crying and drinking, and Carla remembers hearing her mother wail into the night, lost and frightened about the future.

Carla was a junior in high school when her father died, and it was soon time for her to leave home and attend college. She was anxious about leaving her mother and her siblings behind. She compromised with herself and chose to go to a university close to home. An hour's commute would allow her to return home on the weekends and continue to attend to her mother's needs. Despite her compromise, Carla felt guilty for getting on with her life. Compared to her martyred mother, she seemed to herself to be an unloving daughter. Carla's mother was unable to live fully and well without her husband. Yet Carla wanted to go to college and to have a life of her own. "How could I function so well while my mother seemed so bereft?"

Carla's mother continued to deteriorate until Carla's younger brother began to have serious problems at school, drinking and engaging in dangerous and wild behavior. His dysfunction proved sufficient motivation for Carla's mother to reorganize her life. Once again, she became the caretaking woman she had been for years with her sick husband. She helped her son through a difficult time and began to move forward in her own life. Carla recalls that about this time her mother's career began to take off. Her mother had opened a small business, which was highly successful, and Carla saw her mother gain self-confidence and once again begin to look like the attractive young woman she had been many years before.

As Carla saw her mother regain some sense of aliveness and engagement in the world, she was elated. Inside she cried, "Hallelujah!" If her mother could be happy then there was hope for her too. She might have a right to a life of her own. Carla's survival without guilt was short-lived, however. Twelve years after her husband's early death, just months after her last child graduated from college, Carla's mother became seriously ill with a deadly cancer that took her life within nine months. Carla's mother's illness coincided with Carla's own marriage and last year of graduate education. Once again Carla was faced with the dilemma, Am I allowed to have my own life when someone I love is dying? Once again Carla attempted to fashion a compromise. She would spend the week with her husband and attend classes, and on the weekends she would be by her mother's side. Once again, Carla felt guilty with her compromise. This time, however, her siblings and relatives fueled her guilt. They repeatedly told her that her own life could wait and that her responsibility as a "good daughter" was to nurse her mother in the final months of life.

Toward the end of her mother's illness, Carla's mother became so weakened that nurses were needed to provide in-home care. Carla remembers thinking, If I were really a good daughter, I would be here. We wouldn't need to hire nurses. My mother would be cared for by her own child. Since her mother's death, Carla has been so overwhelmed by her guilt that she has been unable to enjoy her own life. She believes that she "chose" to live rather than to suspend her life in order to be with her mother, and that choice now haunts her. Carla feels unable to take pleasure in things. She keeps thinking, Why should I be able to do this? My mother can't do it. At times she makes a magical compromise with herself: "If I think of my mother twelve times during the evening, then I can go to the party. Or, if I don't let myself have any fun, then I am allowed to go to the fair." It seems that if Carla is only half alive then maybe she will be able to endure her own survivorship without unbearable guilt.

Carla finds herself getting angry with older men and women for no obvious reason. She believes that she is angry with these people just because they are alive. How dare they live and enjoy life when both her mother and father are dead? Twice, when given a chance to opt for her own life in the face of death, Carla has chosen selfishly, or so she now believes. She has opted for herself and for her own life. After her father's death, she chose not to remain in perpetual mourning. She was a young woman, and she wanted the normal life of a young woman. As a newly married young professional, she chose not to suspend her life in order to sit by her mother's bedside. Each time she chose to take care of herself and her own needs, Carla, rather than feeling empowered and strong, felt unworthy and guilty. She wonders if she will ever be able to move beyond the weight of the guilt she now feels for having chosen to survive.

Other survivors avoid living full and active lives, not out of guilt but out of fear. To live fully means to know not only life's joys, but its pains and disappointments as well. These individuals are so afraid of sustaining additional losses and enduring more suffering that they choose to sit on the sidelines and watch life be played by others. They may not score any touchdowns, but at least they do not break any bones or lose any points. C. S. Lewis talks of his own constriction during much of his adolescence and early adulthood as being a self-imposed armor designed primarily to allow him to stay safe from life's tragedies.[24]

In the fairy tale *Through the Mickle Woods,* a king in mourning for his queen embarks on a journey.[25] The king is instructed to listen to the tales told by a bear in a dark cave. One of the stories is about a man who lives alone in the woods. He never sows his seeds in the spring because he fears the drought. He never travels because he worries that his ship might sink. One day, he encounters a small bird and begins to engage the bird in a discussion about his own fears. He asks the bird if she is not afraid of the wind. The bird replies, "Of course I am." He then asks her if she is afraid of fire, and once again she answers in the affirmative. Finally, he asks her why, if she is afraid of the wind and the fire, she still flies. There are things in life, she tells him, that she would not miss: the beautiful morning, the fledglings in the spring.[26] If she did not risk the wind and fire in order to fly high, she would not have the things she loves about life. The bird tells the man, moreover, that both joy and sorrow are necessary for her song. Unlike the man, who lives locked away accompanied only by his fears, the bird takes risks because she wants to live life.

For some, the fear is more explicit than just the pain and loss of living. The fear is specifically a fear of dying; to begin to live is to allow the possibility that one will die. A seventeenth-century verse concludes with the line "He that begins to live, begins to die."[27] To engage life in its fullest, to be open to all that life has to offer, is to acknowledge the reality and the inevitability of death. For some individuals, "underliving"—the life that is not really life—is an attempt to fool the Angel of Death. Just as the ancient Israelites smeared their door frames with blood so that the Angel of Death would pass over their homes, these survivors play possum so as to fool the Angel of Death. "There is no reason for anyone to kill me if I have already killed myself," they say to themselves. The Angel of death has better prey than to pick someone who is already dead.

TONY'S STORY

After his father's death, Tony's mother turned his father's office into a museum. Files remained in the drawer exactly as

Tony's father had left them. His pipes stood neatly arranged in the pipe stand. The office remained untouched for almost thirty-five years. Even more tragically, the house in which Tony, his sisters, and his mother continued to live became lifeless. Tony's family stopped participating in the world; they never went to a park or a movie, nothing that was "just fun" was a part of the routine of their lives. Tony's mother would frequently say, "If your father were alive, he'd teach you how to live." She attended to the needs of her children as far as food, clothing, and shelter were concerned, "but beyond that," says Tony, "she did not have a clue."

Tony found some solace in the church school he attended. In contrast to his home, church and school seemed palpably alive. But the teachings of the church did not encourage him to be a passionate little boy. Tony remembers wanting to emulate all of the little saints, the perfect people who had been taken young and untainted to God. When Tony would recite the prayer to our Father in heaven, he would think, I have two fathers in heaven: God my father, and my very own father who is there waiting for me. In his fantasies, Tony would frequently refer to himself as Saint Tony. Even as a young boy, Tony became aware of the confusion that was building inside of him. The most alive people he knew were dead. The people he lived with on earth seemed like the walking dead. Tony felt so tied to his mother and her lifeless life that if he went more than half an hour away from her home he would have an asthma attack and need to be brought back. Tony's forays into the world were limited by his pathological attachment to his mother and the mausoleum in which she lived.

As he became a teenager, Tony became increasingly aware that "I don't know how to live. I don't know how to have a good time. I don't know how to have fun with people." Tony realized that he could hide from life by working all the time. As a teenager he was admired for being a determined entrepreneur. He worked three jobs simultaneously and attended church regularly. He was the most pious boy he knew. In his adolescence, Tony became aware that he was gay. Yet sexuality of any type seemed unimportant to Tony compared to his more overriding concern: "How can I dare to be alive?"

Tony's mother had convinced him that life was dangerous, that the best way to continue breathing was to conserve your energy and not live much. As a late adolescent, Tony read biographies voraciously. He was an ardent reader, but more importantly, he was desperate for an example of how to live a life. He reasoned that his father had been a vital and alive man, yet his father had died. Being alive then must not be very safe. Whenever Tony felt a surge of passion or positive life energy, he became frightened, and quickly returned to playing possum in the role of Saint Tony.

When he left home to go to college, Tony was terrified that he did not know how to function. The world of college offered Tony an artificial infusion of liveliness. Drugs and alcohol were one way a deadened boy could feel alive. Not surprisingly, amphetamines became Tony's drug of choice. With speed in his veins he could feel alive even when there was terror in his heart. Tony recalls going home for vacations during college and watching his mother's reaction to his addiction. She had no problem when Tony was drinking and was dulled by the effects of alcohol. She was terrified, however, when Tony appeared sparkly and alive under the influence of speed. "My mother could not handle it when I seemed jazzy even if my aliveness came from chemicals."

In his late twenties, Tony joined Alcoholics Anonymous, and in the twelve-step recovery program he began to gain control over his addiction. Yet for Tony, sobriety was a mixed blessing. His first thought when he no longer took drugs was, Oh God, it's over. I'm closed off again.

Tony has remained a committed participant in twelve-step programs for more than twenty years. He realizes that at times he hides within these programs, following the script of recovery rather than actively engaging his life. While he has had a few long-term relationships, Tony has been celibate for the last several years. "AIDS gave me an excuse for staying away from sex. I'm chronically afraid of catching death." The AIDS epidemic has also caused Tony to confront the specter of death, which took his father away and terrified him for so many years. Tony believes that he has probably buried close to three hundred friends and acquaintances. Death has knocked so consistently and loudly at Tony's door that he has been forced to hear the knock. "At last I had to confront my grief and mourn for my father. Through that, I think I have become more alive than at any other time in my life." Tony's aliveness has allowed him to recapture some of the joy he felt as a boy when he was first introduced to the spiritual world of the church. While his early passion for religion might well have stemmed from his fear of dying, Tony's current faith seems more real and more deeply felt.

C. S. Lewis, who like Tony walked for years in the shadow of death, felt intense joy as he began once again to feel his feelings. For Lewis, joy led him to spirituality and to Christianity, but first, he merely experienced the excitement of his own aliveness. "There was a transitional moment of delicious uneasiness and then—instantaneously—the long inhibition was over, the dry desert lay behind, I was off once more into the land of longing, my heart at once broken and exalted as it had never been since the old days. . . ."[28]

Early loss may deprive some people of vital life energy. As with Tony, enthusiasm, vitality, and engagement fade in the wake of an early death. Others, however, feel inspired by early loss to live their lives to the fullest. Eleanor Roosevelt declared that one must never, regardless of the circumstances, turn one's back on life.[29] Roosevelt experienced many losses in her life, yet she remained committed to living fully and vitally.

After her mother's early death, America's "Material Girl," Madonna, came to believe that life was too short to wait for what you want. She says, "I want everything there is in life and love."[30] Some survivors feel similarly, believing that the only lesson to be learned from premature death is that you must live life fully. One man commented, "My only regrets are that I did not go more places or do more things when I was younger and could stay up all night." One cannot get too much of life, and the only regret is to have not lived fully.

Another woman recalls her father saying to her before he died, "People's passions are what you will remember about them. You must be passionate about something in order to survive." She has taken her father's words to heart and lives her life with energy and enthusiasm. "There is no time for not doing what you really want to do," she says.

Charles believes he is living as his mother would have wanted him to when he says, "I'm not going to spend my time worrying about what might happen or focusing on the bad. I just try to enjoy myself." The day after he learned of his mother's death, Charles joined a group of friends to play baseball. He remembers thinking that his mother would have approved of his decision. She was a fun-loving and somewhat mischievous woman who enjoyed the short life she had. Charles and his wife work hard, but they also play hard as well. Both have many hobbies and interests, some of which they share, some of which they do separately, but they are always on the go. Charles declares, "We never run out of money. We only run out of time."

He gets angry when he encounters friends who fail to appreciate the good things in their lives and only find something to complain about. "Most people can't enjoy life for what it is. Let me give you an example. I'll be playing golf with somebody and he is a good golfer but he is having a bad day and he starts to complain. I want to grab him by the neck and say, 'You stupid idiot, you're playing golf. There are no bombs dropping on your head; nobody is jumping out of the bushes to hurt you. You're playing golf and you're moaning. I can't stand that.' " Charles feels committed to enjoying himself not only for himself but also because he truly believes that to enjoy his life is the best way to honor his mother. "The only legacy you have to leave is that you loved your life and that you had the best time you could have."

Vitality is what distinguishes the living from the dead. When one is vital, one is actively engaged in one's life, committed to participating in the world fully. For some individuals, early loss infuses them with a determination to live life with gusto and enthusiasm.

Death Is Nothing to Fear

Some individuals who have experienced early loss insist that "though they walk through the valley of the shadow of death, they fear no evil." In some cases, these individuals have come to believe that they have a friend on the other side. Death is not to be feared because it holds a reunion with the parent lost long ago. One man fondly recalls a song he used to sing in church as a boy: "When I get to heaven I'll meet my mother." He remembers that he took comfort in this song because he understood its message quite literally and believed then as he believes now, that when he finally dies he will be reunited with his mother and at last have a chance to know the woman who was taken from him when he was just a boy.

For some individuals, an anticipated reunion with the dead parent slips into a longing that begets suicide. One woman whose father had himself committed suicide felt no fear of dying because she was convinced that in death she would finally get to know her father. As a girl she would often ask for information about her enigmatic parent. Her father was described as "brilliant but troubled," and other than this cryptic epitaph, few people had any details about the man who had hung himself in the basement.

In her early twenties, this woman made an unsuccessful suicide attempt. "The overriding feeling I had which gave me the courage to do it was that I wanted to be with him finally. I wanted to go where he was so I could just know him; that was in my head the entire day before I did it." Paradoxically, she now believes that this aborted attempt actually did allow her to know her father. "I am the only one of my brothers or sisters who has ever been suicidal, so I understand what he did in a way that I don't think you can unless you have been suicidal yourself." She has made no subsequent suicide attempts, yet she continues to insist that she has no fear of death because when she does finally die, she will be reunited with her father.

For many who have lived a long life, an acceptance of the inevitability of death comes in their seventies or eighties. One looks back over years of struggles and accomplishments and feels satisfied with the result. If, however, because a parent died young, an individual only expects to live to forty or fifty, he or she might arrive at this last stage of life prematurely. As a man or woman still in midlife, the individual might come to an acceptance of death after what is believed to have been a full life.

Several individuals who were in their late forties and early fifties expressed a strong sense that they would accept death if it came. One woman asserted, "I feel like I have lived through the major events of a life. I've had children, been a good mother, had good and bad relationships, been professionally successful, and I have dealt with loss. There is nothing left now to do but just enjoy the rest of my life." Although she was barely fifty, she felt that she had tasted life fully. She had seen both her mother and father die young and felt ready to accept death if it came her way.

Another man maintained, "If there is a tragedy in dying it is in dying too young. I feel like I have already lived a pretty full life. I don't want to die, don't get me wrong, but I have the sense that death is a part of life. It is there, you accept it." This man, also in his fifties, had had a successful career and raised four children. Many people his age would be looking forward to a long and rich retirement. As the son of a man who had died quite young, however, he felt that he had already had more than his share of living.

Another man who suffered a heart attack in his thirties also expressed an acceptance of death as part of the natural rhythm of life. "I'm not afraid of dying. In fact I've had to face it fairly realistically. I feel comfortable with the reality of it. It's not that I am ready to die, I just don't have any fear of it. I'd like to hang around and see a couple of grandchildren and have a few more enjoyable years. But it wouldn't really bother me if I couldn't because my life hasn't been that bad, that short, or that unfilled."

Jean-Paul Sartre, in commenting on the death of a young colleague, maintained that every life is complete at its end.[31] A full life has a beginning, a middle, and an end. It does not have a preset duration. When it reaches the end, it is complete. Some individuals who had experienced early loss felt that same sense of completion in contemplating their own lives and their own longevity. Although they were all, by modern standards, individuals who might expect to live many more years, those who had come to accept death had somewhat precociously reached this final stage of adult development, "the stage of integrity" in which one comes to see one's life as an integral whole, meaningful and sensible in itself.[32]

Folklore and fairy tales are filled with images of death, usually depicted as an old, decrepit, deceitful monster. Yet no life passes without making the acquaintance of death. There is a Buddhist parable in which a woman runs to the Buddha after the death of her young son. She is weeping and bereft and pleads with the master to restore her son to life. The Buddha tells her that he will gladly help her but first she must obtain four pomegranate seeds from a home that has not known death. Initially she is elated and proceeds to scour the town in search of a family free of death where she might obtain what she needs. Of course, she is unsuccessful—no home has not known death—and in time she comes to realize the wisdom of the Buddha's lesson: the person does not exist who has been untouched by death.

Yet for most people, death does not make an appearance until an individual has enjoyed a full life. We are spared having to deal with loss and tragedy until we are better able to handle the trauma of death. When people meet death in childhood, it marks them. Often, they change the way they understand their own lives, the way they perceive time, and the way they move through the life cycle. They also alter their view of death itself. Death is no longer a mere character in a story but a very real presence that has robbed them of something precious and dear.

To say that one is marked by early loss may sound dramatic and perhaps extreme. Survivors of early loss do not "look different" from the rest of us. Their loss is invisible and unseen by most of us. Yet it was surprising how many people I interviewed had come to love and share their lives with another survivor of early loss. It was as if each did indeed bear a mark, perhaps only visible to another survivor, but a mark nonetheless, recognizable and clear to one who had been through the same experience. In Ben Hecht's words, these were all people who had been "to the edge of the world and looked over its last foot of territory into nothingness."

PART III

The Next Step

CHAPTER 9

~

Acts of Repair

AFTER THE EARLY DEATH OF a mother or father, the world at first seems shattered. For some, time and the loving concern of other caretakers help to heal the profound emptiness and the terrifying insecurity death leaves behind. For others, the wounds persist into adulthood, and the job of repairing the emotional damage caused by early and unexpected death becomes one of the principal challenges of adult life.

The repair that one seeks following the early loss of a parent is not like the repair that occurs when we drive our car into the shop, have a fan belt changed, and then drive away with the car "as good as new." C. S. Lewis likened the repair one experiences after grief to a man learning to walk after a leg has been amputated.[1] The amputee may get along quite well, may even become facile and agile on crutches or on a carefully designed artificial limb. But the amputee must accommodate to permanent loss. He or she will never walk as before; repair does not mean a return to the way things were.

The repair that follows early loss, like all human growth, requires a creative act. The survivor must make the best possible use of whatever personal and interpersonal resources survive the trauma of loss—a lively intelligence, a sense of humor, a compassionate voice. Sometimes the repair is modest: a small part of what was damaged is fixed or altered through

a special encounter later in life. These modest repairs often in-
volve delayed mourning and a release of feelings that have
been locked away for many years. At other times, repair is
more all-encompassing. The individual engages in a creative
act or a life project that seems directly related to the loss and
represents an attempt to master the experience of early
trauma. Less frequently, repair entails a re-creation of the self.
The damage the young boy or girl experienced at the time of
loss was so profound that only a dramatic act, designed to re-
make the self, can constitute repair sufficient to allow the individual to lead a fulfilling life.

Modest Repair/Delayed Mourning

Circumstances often make it difficult if not impossible for a
child to mourn at the time a death actually occurs. Ted was
only two months old when his father died, and it was not until
he became a young boy that he even realized he was missing a
father, at which time he began to ask questions about the father he never knew. The older he became and the more he in-
teracted with other young men, the more aware Ted grew of
the loss he had sustained. In his early thirties, Ted sought counseling because he felt unable to shake off a pervasive sense of
sorrow and unfulfilled longing. The therapy focused on the
loss of Ted's father, and the therapist asked him if he had ever
mourned for his dad. Ted realized that since the death had occurred so long ago and at a time when he himself would have
been unable to participate in any rituals of mourning, he had
never formally grieved for his father. The therapist suggested
that Ted take time off from work and mourn the death of his
dad. At first, Ted seemed somewhat perplexed by this suggestion and protested that he had too much work to do. The therapist reminded him that if Ted's father, like the mothers and
fathers of so many of his peers, were to die now, Ted would
not hesitate to take time off.

At his therapist's suggestion, Ted took off two days from
work in the middle of a week. He went to a synagogue and sat
alone. Although Ted himself was not religious, he had always

been told that his father had been a spiritual and religious man. Ted also chose a synagogue because he wanted a place of sanctuary, a place that was quiet and that would allow him not only the physical but also the psychological space in which to mourn.

After his visit to the temple, Ted spent the rest of his day walking and thinking. When he came home, he wrote a long letter to his father. In the letter, Ted introduced himself to the man he had never known. He told his father what he had been doing with his life, recounting his experiences, his triumphs, and his disappointments. He also told his father that he missed him and he wished his father had been there for him when he was growing up. Ted recalls that he felt "very, very good afterward."

This act of formal mourning allowed Ted to fill some of the emptiness he had carried following his father's death. Ted had not only been cheated of a father, but he had been cheated of the chance to mourn for that father. The therapist's exercise could not give Ted back the father he had never had. It could, however, allow Ted the chance to mourn, a chance available to men and women who lose parents in adulthood. Several years later when he married, Ted named his only child for his father, continuing not only his tenuous connection to his roots, but also continuing part of the traditional mourning within the Jewish religion, namely to honor the dead by naming a child for one who has passed away.

Sometimes a child is denied the opportunity to mourn because of the responses of the surviving parent. Scott's father's quick remarriage to a woman who did not want to hear of her predecessor deprived Scott and his sisters of a chance to mourn for their mother. Although he adored his mother and recalls her as a loving, nurturing woman, Scott has no recollection of crying for his mother after her death. She was rarely spoken of during the years of Scott's childhood and adolescence. As an adult, however, Scott believes he finally cried for his mother when a family pet died. "A few years ago my wife and I had a cat, a great cat, a cat named Sam. We had the cat for a couple of years. The cat followed me around. He worshipped me. It was great. I would sit there and the cat would sit there with me and stare at me. The cat loved me so much. She [Scott used the feminine pronoun by mistake] died of cancer and I cried for days and days because there was nothing I could do. It was such a helpless feeling and God it was just a cat and I was a grown adult. I can't imagine how it must have felt when I was a kid." Much of Scott's response to the death of his cat seems to be connected to the loss of his mother. The cat was more than a pet; it was an adoring, loving parent. The cat would sit and watch Scott, and Scott was comforted by just being near his pet. Scott's mother, like his cat, died of cancer, and as a young boy, Scott was as helpless to care for his beloved mother as he was to save the life of his cat.

In some cases, the child's own personality makes complete mourning impossible. The child resolves to be strong and stoic, determined to put away immature tears and feelings of vulnerability. One woman recounts how she cried uncontrollably at the funeral of her father. She was only eleven years old, but she remembers feeling terribly embarrassed by her public display of emotion. She vowed at the funeral that she would never cry again. She recalls hiding behind the hedges on her way home from school so friends and neighbors would not stop her and ask her how she was doing. She did not want to risk feeling vulnerable and breaking her pledge that she would cry no more.

When this woman was twenty-one and had been without tears for ten years, she had a dream. In the dream, her father returned to her. She looked at him, aware that he was dead but also aware that he was present and talking to her. She spoke with him in the dream, and when she awoke she cried and cried. Since she had the dream, which helped her to repair her own self-imposed moratorium on feeling, crying has never been a problem for her. It was as if her father returned to free her from her pledge and to allow her to feel her feelings once again.

Another woman whose father died just as she was entering her teenage years felt she needed to deny her grief so that she could appear tough and strong. Crying about one's father did not seem like the "cool thing to do," and she remembers hiding her feelings behind an air of bravado and humor. At her father's funeral, she felt completely disconnected. She did not cry and she remembers being excluded from the rest of the family, who were actively weeping and grieving. After the funeral, when people returned to the family home, she left and went off to a park by herself, wanting distance from the ritual of mourning but also wanting to assert her own independence from the weeping that was going on.

Several years later when an uncle of hers died, this woman was able to allow herself to feel the grief that had been locked away during much of her adolescence. "I remember just falling apart. It was the first time I allowed myself. I didn't even see my uncle. It was like my father all over again. I finally could see all the grief around me. I really loved my uncle but this time I realized I really loved my father too." Her need to maintain her teenage bravado was no longer present, and this time she was able to experience her genuine feelings at the loss not only of her uncle but of her father as well.

Delayed mourning allows the individual to release feelings that have been repressed and denied. In many cases the feelings are triggered by another loss or death. Despite the fact that the impetus for the present grief is a loss separate and distinct from the one sustained in childhood, most mourners realized that they were really grieving for a long dead and deeply missed parent.

Mastery via Creativity and Work

Art has been called our chief means of breaking bread with the dead.[2] For many individuals, creative work becomes a way of making sense not only of an early loss but also of their feelings following that loss. Certainly creativity is multidetermined and it would be wrong to suggest that early loss is the primary driving force for creativity in the lives of artistic geniuses. However, loss seems to be a factor in the form one's creative expression takes. "Indeed, the creative product may reflect the mourning process in theme, style, form, content, and may itself stand as a memorial."[3] An individual's literary, artistic, or philosophical talent mixes with the need to "infuse life into dead fragments and re-create life" to produce the work of genius.[4]

Author Virginia Woolf recognized that her own desire to write was tied to a need to master the trauma she experienced following the death of her mother. When something bad would happen, Woolf would try to explain it, and that would blunt what she called "the sledge hammer force of the blow."[5] Throughout her life, Woolf responded to tragedy by writing down and explaining what had happened, first to herself, then to others. "It is not, as I thought as a child, simply a blow from an enemy hidden behind the cotton wool of daily life; it is or will become a revelation of some order; it is a token of some real thing behind appearances; and I make it real by putting it into words. It is only by putting it into words that I make it whole; this wholeness means that it has lost its power to hurt me. . . ."[6] Woolf masters and controls tragedy by explaining it, and as a writer, her medium for explanation is the written word.

For much of her life, Woolf was haunted by the image of her mother. "I could hear her voice, see her, imagine what she would do or say as I went about my day's doings. She was one of the invisible presences who after all play so important a part in every life."[7]

In her midforties, as she was going for a walk and composing a new book, an idea came to Virginia Woolf in a rush. The idea became the book *To the Lighthouse,* a book that Woolf wrote quickly and that finally allowed her to break her obsession with the image of her mother. Woolf says, ". . . when it was written, I ceased to be obsessed by my mother. I no longer hear her voice; I do not see her. . . . I expressed some very long felt and deeply felt emotion. And in expressing it I explained it and then laid it to rest."[8]

To the Lighthouse is the story of the life and death of Mrs. Ramsay. The first part of the book recounts the events in a day in the life of the Ramsay family. Mrs. Ramsay is the focus of the family, and one knows that knowledge and wisdom are stored in her heart. The young painter Lilly Briscoe, who seems to represent Woolf herself, is enamored of Mrs. Ramsay, enamored of her solidity and her presence. Lilly likens Mrs. Ramsay to a dome-shaped hive, an image reminiscent of the great cathedral space that Woolf felt had been occupied by her mother in her own childhood.

The first part of the book concludes with a dinner party where Mrs. Ramsay muses about her life: "They would, she thought, going on again, how ever long they lived, come back to this night; this moon; this wind; this house: and to her too. It flattered her, where she was most susceptible to flattery, to think how, wound about in their hearts, however long they lived she would be woven."[9]

The second part of the book, entitled "Time Passes," begins with the family's return to their summer home following the death of Mrs. Ramsay. The desolation of loss is captured beautifully in Woolf's description of the house: "The house was left; the house was deserted. It was left like a shell on a sandhill to fill with dry salt grain now that life had left it."[10]

In the final section of the book, the painter Lilly Briscoe, now a woman of forty-four, the same age as Woolf when she wrote *To the Lighthouse,* finally completes a painting she had begun of Mrs. Ramsay. The completed painting allows Lilly to put to rest a memory she had carried for many years: "She had borne it in her mind all these years. It seemed as if the solution had come to her: she knew now what she wanted to do."[11] As she paints her picture, Lilly is aware of how angry she is with Mrs. Ramsay: "With the brush slightly trembling in her fingers she looked at the hedge, the step, the wall. It was all Mrs. Ramsay's doing. She was dead. Here was Lilly, at forty-four wasting her time, unable to do a thing, standing there playing at painting, playing at the one thing one did not play at, and it was all Mrs. Ramsay's fault. She was dead. The step where she used to sit was empty. She was dead. But why repeat this over and over again? Why be always trying to bring up some feeling she had not got? There was a kind of blasphemy in it. It was all dry: all withered: all spent."[12]

As she completes her painting, Lilly Briscoe does recapture the feeling buried deep inside her. She shouts out Mrs. Ramsay's name: "Mrs. Ramsay, Mrs. Ramsay," and the tears run down her face. When she finishes her painting, her creative work, Lilly Briscoe says simply, "It is finished,"[13] referring perhaps not only to the painting on the canvas but to her own mourning, finished at last with the creative act. So too did Virginia Woolf complete her own mourning by writing *To the Lighthouse.*

It would be unfair to compare the creative efforts of others to a literary master like Virginia Woolf. However, several of the people with whom I spoke did attempt to gain control over the terror of loss through the creative process. One woman who is a successful painter described two projects that were clearly linked to the death of her father. Early in her career, she did a photographic essay using prints from the time period 1914–1925. The essay was an attempt to capture the mood and spirit of that particular time in American history. "My father was born in 1914 and I have always wondered if the project was some attempt to understand the time he was born in and the world at that time. I wanted to recapture what was important to him." This early project was her attempt to forge a personal link with the father she barely knew.

Later in her career, her art became more political, and she has turned her attention to the struggles of women and the passion and beauty of a woman's body. Her paintings are not merely done with oil on canvas or charcoal and ink. She uses blood in the construction of her images: "I paint with menstrual blood. It is blood transformed to be an image of life instead of death." This woman's father died of a rare blood disease, which required that he have frequent transfusions in the months before his death. These transfusions were performed in the home. When her father finally died, he bled to death through his mouth and rectum. For this young girl, blood became the vehicle of death. She must have been terrified by the vision of her bloody father being carried to the ambulance. As an adult, she has taken the image of blood and used it as something creative rather than something associated with death. By working with blood, she has taken this death image and tamed it.

Another man, who became a successful artist and architect, recalls the way he experienced the night of his mother's death. The sudden announcement came at 11 P.M., waking the sleeping children and gathering them to the kitchen table to hear that their mother had died suddenly. He recalls that he had no immediate response to the announcement. Instead he focused his attention on the room. "I remember every aspect of the space; everything about it; the lighting, the shadows, everything." As a boy of only thirteen, his artist's eye allowed him to gain control over the traumatic announcement of his mother's death.

Because his father's grief was overwhelming, this man never had a chance to mourn openly for his mother. When his father died ten years later, he was once again denied the chance to grieve. His father died carrying old grievances against his own devoutly Catholic family, and he demanded that his funeral be without any of the rituals of the Church. There was to be no service, no wake, no hearse carrying him to the cemetery. His body was to be delivered to the cemetery in a plain pine box, laid in the ground, and only then could mourners arrive. The family honored his wishes but this stark and barren burial once again deprived the son of the space and opportunity to mourn.

As an artist and an architect, this man has spent his life designing spaces where people will feel comfortable and at home. When he designs a personal residence, he spends hours, sometimes days, interviewing the family members. He wants to know them, to understand not only their particular needs, but also their personalities so that he might build a home for them that will be emotionally open and nurturing.

During his long career, he has also designed a number of community parks and public spaces where people might come together for a festival, a concert, or some group activity. Once again, before designing these spaces, he talks with the people who will use them. He is able to feel great empathy for the needs of his clients and has devoted his life to creating spaces where people can feel their feelings and be at home in both a literal and a psychological sense. It is both ironic and fitting that he creates for others what was denied to him as a boy.

All people who seek to master the trauma of early loss do not become artists or architects or designers. There are many ways in which via one's life work, one can creatively master past loss. Some who choose to be healers bring to their work a heightened sense of empathy for the pain and distress of others.

Lois Akner, a social worker who runs groups for adults whose parents have recently died, has written a thoughtful and helpful book entitled *How to Survive the Loss of a Parent.* Akner works with adult survivors of loss, bringing to her work the special empathy of one who knows loss firsthand. Her own father died when she was only six, and she says, "For a very long time, I believed that the only major thing that ever happened in our family was my father's death. It influenced what I did; it excused what I couldn't do. Everything else seemed to be viewed through the lens of that event."[14] Akner's life work has been inspired by her own early experiences.

Similarly, Judith Wallerstein, whose landmark study of the impact of divorce on the lives of survivors has changed the way we think about divorce, came to her own calling via an experience of loss in childhood. Wallerstein writes in the preface of her book *Second Chances,* "My father died of cancer when I was eight years old, leaving my mother at the age of twenty-nine with two children, several years of college education, little money, and few marketable skills. No doubt my lifelong professional interest in helping children, especially those suffering loss and separation, has its roots in my own continued mourning for my father and in my compassion for my mother's gallant struggles to protect my younger brother and me from the economic and personal hardships that she faced daily."[15] Wallerstein might not have been as sensitive to the enduring impact of family breakup if she had not learned firsthand what it means to be a survivor of loss.

One woman grew up viewing death as a cruel trickster. Her mother died when she was only five months old, her father died years later when she was barely a teenager. These early deaths were followed in adulthood by the illness of her husband, the stabbing death of an aunt who had helped to raise her, and the suicide of another aunt. Although she wanted to be able to see death as peaceful sleep, for her, death was indeed a Grim Reaper, a cruel presence that snatched life away prematurely. After years of raising her children, this woman returned to graduate school and obtained a degree in gerontology. She now works as a counselor in an old-age home, and she says, "I love my job. People in the home die of 'natural causes,' most of them after a long and productive life." She told me the story of a client of hers who had just recently died. She had grown quite close to this woman yet felt no pain or sadness when the woman passed away. Her client was ninety-six and died one night in her sleep. By her work, this woman had managed finally to transform for herself the image of death. She has come to know death as a benign presence, coming quietly and peacefully at the end of a long life.

Another woman whose father died in a plane crash became an aerospace engineer. As she told me of her profession, she was almost embarrassed: "It's so obvious." Yet, from the time of her father's tragic death she was intent on understanding what had happened. As a child she had turned to religion for an explanation. "My father never went to church but I started after my father died. I started walking myself to church. I got up Sundays, walked a mile to church, and then walked home, but it didn't help so I abandoned God and church and almost became an atheist." As a young woman, she turned to science for an explanation of what had happened to her father. "I was intent on learning how planes worked. I wanted to understand what went wrong. It helps me to understand physically just what happened." In her professional life, she is the designer, the engineer, the one in control, deciding how things will be built. She is no longer the helpless victim, waiting on the ground for the plane to land.

A career, a life's work or a passion, sometimes allows one as an adult the opportunity to gain mastery and control over the tragic events that seemed so confusing and inexplicable in childhood.

Re-creating the Self

Imagine that you are given the task of reassembling an object from several broken fragments. Not a difficult assignment if you know how the final object should appear. If, however, you have no idea whether you are working with fragments of a vase, a skull, or a toy, you have no idea where to begin. You may well construct some object, yet it may be far from the original.

Children take the fragments of their lives left after early loss has shattered their experience and attempt to reconstruct a meaningful whole. In most cases, although they do not create the self as it might have looked had death not intervened, they do manage to build a self that is sufficient to meet the challenges of adult life. In a few cases, the self that emerges following early loss is too fragile and too unstable to withstand the rigors of growing up. In these cases, the individual may need to re-create the self as an adult. A few of the stories I heard were just such, total reconstructions of the self. In each case, the process of reconstruction was so unique and so personal that it is difficult to generalize from one person's experience to the next. Yet each of these stories represented struggles of monumental will, energy, and spirit. The individual literally brought forth a new self, created in part from necessity, in part from opportunity, and in part from determination and a will to survive. Each of these stories is a triumph of the human spirit.

SHAWNA'S STORY

Shawna was orphaned at the age of two when her single-parent mother died suddenly of a stroke. She was then placed with a cousin, who promised to raise her as if Shawna were her own daughter. Yet Shawna always felt that there was an enormous difference between "being a daughter and being like a daughter." "We were two people living in the same house but I would not call us a family." Shawna remembers hearing repeatedly, "This is not your home. You are only here because I say so."

Shawna grew up painfully aware that she was missing someone in her life who would love her unconditionally, no matter what she did. Learning well the lesson that she could break no rules if she wanted to continue to have a home, Shawna grew up to be a very good girl. Shawna's cousin would often become angry at any small infraction of the rules. She would yell at Shawna, and if in anger Shawna made the mistake of yelling back, her cousin would hit her with an electrical cord she had removed from a toaster just for the purpose of keeping Shawna in line.

Once Shawna tried to run away and go to the home of another cousin. Unwelcome there, she returned to the only home she knew. Shawna learned a bitter lesson. There was no fairy godmother who would rescue her from life with her abusive cousin. She was completely on her own, and if she was to be saved she would have to save herself.

By the time she was fourteen, Shawna had also learned that if she wanted any material things, she would need to buy them or get them for herself. She saved her money and hunted for bargains. Even necessities like underwear and shoes were her responsibility. Shawna had no one on whom she could depend, and she needed to be her own caretaker in every respect.

Shawna was a good student in school and teachers usually liked her. She remembers one teacher in particular who spent extra time tutoring her and eventually began inviting Shawna to come and spend time at her own home. Although Shawna longed for a normal home and a family of her own, she was reluctant to accept her teacher's offer. Although she felt no love for her cousin, Shawna at least knew what she had at her cousin's house. She was unwilling to trade a known evil for an unknown situation that merely promised to be good. Shawna was a girl who had little faith in the promises others made. Years of disappointment had taught her that it was risky and pointless to trust other people.

By the time she was a senior in high school, Shawna was suspicious, emotionally distant, and often alone. She did not feel safe enough to reach out to anyone. "I didn't take any risks. People needed to hang in with me for a long time before I would even give them a chance." Although she could not articulate what was missing from her life, Shawna knew that something she needed desperately in order to grow and survive was absent.

When she was eighteen, Shawna met a woman from her church, a woman who was in her early fifties, about the age Shawna's mother would have been if she had lived. The woman remembered Shawna's mother from years ago and also recalled Shawna as a little girl. At first, Shawna was skeptical of this woman's offers of friendship. When the woman approached her after the Sunday service, Shawna would either look away or mumble something hostile. She was both angry and frightened. This woman was not put off by Shawna's angry response. She continued to approach the girl for many months until finally Shawna allowed herself to be open to this woman's kindness. "She and I created a bond. I call her my mother to this day and I call her husband my father because I needed to find a family. I really needed that. I needed a hug sometimes. I needed somebody to just pat me on the shoulder. I couldn't grow up without that." Shawna needed acceptance and unconditional love, and this woman was able to provide that for her for many years.

At first their relationship resembled that between a mother and a young child. This woman would take Shawna shopping for clothes and Shawna would respond like a little girl, as if she could not pick out her own shoes or her own dresses. She would let this woman tell her what looked nice and offer her advice, not only advice as to how a young woman should dress, but also guidance as to how a young woman should behave. Shawna tagged along after her "new friend" like a little duck paddling after its mother. "I loved letting her care for me," she says. Shawna and her adopted mother went places together, but most importantly they just spent time near each other. Shawna loved "hanging out" with her mom. She would often sit and just watch with a mixture of affection and curiosity as this woman would read the newspaper or drink her coffee. "Once I was able to be a child, get that love, be taken care of, I think then I started to grow up right there in her house. I could see myself getting mature." Shawna never actually moved in with this woman and her family, but she spent all of her time after school or work in her adopted mother's home. Her cousin was only too glad to get Shawna out from underfoot and never questioned her relationship with this woman.

When she went off to college, Shawna did not act like the other young freshmen. Instead of spending time at the student union after classes were over, Shawna, who was a day student, would come home to her adopted mother's house; they would then resume the routine that had started in high school. Shawna would tag along with her friend as the woman went about her daily chores. Sometimes they would sit and watch television together. Shawna felt like a child in elementary school who comes home and has milk and cookies with her mom after a day away at school. She remembers being aware that she was more like a girl of eight or nine than a young woman of nineteen. Yet Shawna knew she was getting something very important from this woman, something that she needed desperately if she was ever to grow into a woman herself.

Throughout this period, separations from her adoptive mother were always difficult for Shawna. Whenever the woman would go on vacation with her own family, Shawna would panic. Her first thought was always that something terrible would happen and that her second mother would be taken away from her forever. Realizing that Shawna was like a dependent and helpless child even though she was chronologically an adult woman, her adopted mother offered her the reassurances and comfort Shawna needed in order to endure increasingly long separations. Shawna was growing just like a child, learning how to be away from her mother.

After she graduated from college, Shawna received a management position with a large and successful company. Although she had the technical skills to do the job, Shawna still felt like a girl of twelve rather than like a woman in her twenties. She remembers being awed and frightened when she was handed the roster with the names of her supervisees. How could she possibly be supervising someone else when she herself did not quite "feel grown"? After her first days at work, Shawna would come home and ask her adopted mother for advice on how to handle problems in the office. This woman, continuing her function of mother, would guide Shawna through the problems she was having with her employees. Shawna's confidence grew and eventually she came to trust that she could handle the circumstances at work without her mother's help.

In her midtwenties, Shawna, like all growing children, began to rebel against her mother. She can laugh now at some of her adolescent behavior, behavior that marked her first real separation from the woman who had quite literally raised her to adulthood. Like any mother and daughter, they struggled over issues of autonomy. Shawna was convinced that her mother would not like her friends. Her mother felt that Shawna was growing too independent. Eventually the two, like most mothers and daughters, resolved their differences. They continue to respect one another, yet they acknowledge that the lifestyle of a sixty-year-old is quite different from that of a woman in her twenties. Shawna feels convinced that she could not have grown into adulthood without the help of this woman. "The person I am today I owe to her. She took an emotionally stunted girl and helped her grow into a woman."

It is rare that one has the opportunity to be reparented to the extent that Shawna was. It is also rare, however, that one has as little nurturing and guidance as Shawna experienced growing up. Shawna knew that the relationships she might find in adulthood would not be sufficient to help her to grow up given the damage from her early loss. She needed quite literally to create the home environment of a young girl who is raised by a loving mother.

Shawna's story has some similarities to the complicated relationship that author C. S. Lewis developed with Mrs. Moore, his long-time companion. When Lewis, who had lost his mother in boyhood, was in college, he and his roommate made a pledge to one another that if either were to be killed in the war, the survivor would look after the family of the man who had been killed. Lewis survived the war but his roommate did not, and his pledge resulted in his inheriting a mother. For thirty years, C. S. Lewis lived as the companion of a woman he called mother and who in turn called him son. Although Lewis was a creative writer and a renowned scholar, his relationship to Mrs. Moore was very ordinary. The two spent time engaged in routine domestic tasks. Lewis would hang curtains and go shopping with his adopted mother. Although his colleagues often questioned this somewhat unusual relationship, Lewis never complained about it and remained devoted to Mrs. Moore until her death.[16]

In one of his books, Lewis described "a great lady" not un-like Mrs. Moore, and he says about this character, "In her they [all the beasts and birds who came to live near her] became themselves."[17] Mrs. Moore functioned for Lewis like the mother he had lost, providing the nurturing ground on which he could grow into himself. The task of parents, after all, is to help us become that which we have the capacity to be.

TANYA'S STORY

Although she was sixteen when her father died, Tanya was eleven when he was first diagnosed with cancer. Despite the fact that his illness required repeated treatments and occasion-ally prevented him from working, Tanya's family never dis-cussed the cancer that was killing her father. Her mother's only acknowledgement of her father's illness was to take him one Sunday afternoon to view the cemetery plot where he would eventually rest. To Tanya, her mother seemed more like a real estate agent showing property than a wife who was about to lose her husband.

Although she has few memories of her family's response to her father's illness, Tanya remembers vividly the last attack, which eventually took his life. "In the fall of my eleventh-grade year I was doing my homework upstairs in our living room one night and my mother came to the stairs and yelled for me to come down. It was late, maybe eleven o'clock. She said, 'Come down quick. Your father is having trouble breathing.' She told me to stand there and watch him, just stand there. So I stood at the door of their bedroom. He was in the bed. I stood there while my mother went to the kitchen to call an ambulance. When I think about it now I feel terrible. I hate it that I didn't go over to him. I don't think I even spoke to him. I just stood at the door. The thing I hate the most about his death and his being sick is that he had to do it so completely alone."

When Tanya's father finally died, her mother moved quickly to erase any traces of her husband from the family home. "The day after my father died it was as if he had never lived. My mother gave his clothes away on the afternoon of the funeral." In the years following her father's death, Tanya recalls that her family talked about him so little that any memories she had quickly faded. In Virginia Woolf's *To the Lighthouse,* the family returns to the home they had shared in happier times to find that only fragments of the past remain. The inexorable movement of time has dulled things, changed things, and left behind only token memories.[18]

Tanya remembers the day of her father's funeral, when four of her girlfriends came over supposedly to comfort her. The teenagers tried to amuse their friend. They told her that above all else she should not cry. Their mission was not to help her grieve but rather to facilitate her denial.

For many years, Tanya lived with deep regret about the circumstances surrounding her father's death. She mourned for her father, but more significantly, she hated herself for the way she had behaved in the final years of his life. She wished that she had been able to offer him the comfort he so obviously needed. In her own mind, Tanya evolved a personal set of commandments for how one should treat a loved one who is sick. Like the Judeo-Christian decalogue, Tanya's commandments begin with a series of "Thou shalt not"s: Thou shalt not abandon someone who is dying. Thou shalt not deny the illness. Thou shalt not impose your own vision of death on someone else. Her commandments conclude with two positive prescriptions: Thou shalt remember the deceased, and Thou shalt make space for a child to grieve.

Life rarely presents one with a chance to replay the past, a chance to go back and relive an experience, doing it differently this time. For Tanya, however, the illness of her lover in adulthood allowed her the opportunity to re-create the circumstances of her father's death. In her late twenties, Tanya, a lesbian, met a woman with whom she was intrigued. The two began dating and quickly the friendship developed into a serious and intense romance. Tanya began to think that she had at last met the person with whom she could spend her life. Shortly after returning from a vacation to the beach, Tanya's lover discovered a lump in her breast. The woman was diagnosed as having breast cancer and surgery was recommended. Tanya's first response was to panic. "I grew up with this thing looming over me and now I was in it again." Tanya remembered her own first commandment: Thou shalt not abandon someone who is dying. She never seriously considered breaking off the relationship just because her lover was sick. "I was crazy about her and I never thought of ending it." Throughout the illness, Tanya and her lover openly discussed the cancer. When she was a child, Tanya had experienced the pain of denial as her family colluded in pretending that her father was not sick. Tanya's second commandment was "Do not deny."

Tanya's lover recovered successfully from surgery and her prognosis was excellent. Several years after the cancer was first discovered she was pronounced "cured." At this point, the couple made a decision to adopt a child. Several years after the birth of their daughter, Tanya's lover's cancer reappeared. This time the prognosis was not favorable. Tanya's daughter repeatedly asked what was wrong that her mommy needed to go to the hospital so often. The couple decided that they would explain cancer to the child in language that she could understand. They told her that cancer was "confused cells" and that "Mommy was sick." When the six-year-old girl asked if her mother was going to die, Tanya's lover responded, "I hope not." The couple also decided not to shield their daughter from the obvious physical changes that occurred as the result of chemotherapy. Tanya's daughter saw her mommy's bald head and felt comfortable helping her mom adjust the wig she wore in public.

Tanya was determined not to impose some "right way" to die on her lover. The dying woman would be allowed to meet death on her own terms, even if that was uncomfortable for Tanya. Moreover, Tanya felt that it was imperative that their daughter find some way to be included in the death of her mother. Tanya's daughter saw her sick mommy every day in the last weeks of her illness. When she was told finally that her mommy had died, Tanya's daughter asked, "Can I see her, please?" She was allowed to see her mother's lifeless body, and after a few moments she turned away. She had many questions for Tanya, questions that Tanya would answer again and again over the next several months.

Just as Tanya had allowed her lover to die in her own way, she has allowed her daughter to grieve in a way that fits the little girl's personality. Tanya's daughter is a sensible and pragmatic child who likes to know the reasons for things. Occasionally, Tanya will cry openly in front of her reserved and less emotional daughter. At those times, Tanya's daughter has held her hand and said to her mother, "Mom, some people don't cry even when they are sad."

Following her final commandment, Tanya has pledged that she and her daughter will remember the woman who died. Tanya has set up a small table in her home on which she has pictures of her lover. The table is set at eye level for a child so that her daughter can go and look at the pictures whenever she chooses. Each year, Tanya and her daughter hold a small memorial service for Tanya's lover. They tell stories and they remember the woman they both loved.

Recently, Tanya was at a party and met a woman to whom she was attracted. The two spent time talking and Tanya discovered that this woman suffered from a chronic and potentially fatal illness. Tanya smiled to herself and walked away. She thought, I've done this once. I don't need to do it again.

While it would be incorrect to characterize Tanya's relationship with her lover as primarily an attempt to repair her own damaged history surrounding her father's death, Tanya's second encounter with death did indeed repair something that had been broken for a long time. Tanya's self-hate and self-doubt, generated by her critical judgment of how she had behaved as a girl, was now gone. What was broken had truly been fixed.

BRENT'S STORY

After his father's death, Brent became the man of the house. He was only twelve years old, but he assumed the role of head of the house. Brent helped his mother with routine activities like shopping and paying bills, and he also provided support and care for his brothers. Occasionally Brent felt overwhelmed; he was after all, only a boy. But most of the time, he felt proud of himself, proud that he was able to step in and take his father's place.

Brent's fragile attempt to be a man shattered, however, when his mother experienced a recurrence of her cancer. As she became increasingly ill, she required more care and she turned to Brent for the emotional and physical help she needed. Here, Brent failed miserably. He was frightened and disgusted by his mother's "decaying body." He did not know how to soothe her anxiety. He felt overwhelmed at the task of having to bathe and dress his own mother. Brent tried to maintain his pseudo-adulthood, but deep inside he felt himself to be a fraud. He knew he was a scared little boy just pretending to be grown up.

Whenever he had the chance, Brent would stay out late with his friends. The responsibilities that waited for him at home felt overwhelming. Because he had once performed so well at being a "little man," Brent's relatives were angered when he fell down on the job. They repeatedly criticized him for being irresponsible and selfish: couldn't he see that his mother needed him at home?

Throughout his teenage years when Brent was beginning to develop a sense of himself as an autonomous person, a powerful negative image was forming inside. Brent thought of himself as an irresponsible fraud and he began to loathe himself. He would tell himself, "You're a fake. Everything you do is just pretend. Deep inside you're nothing at all." When he looks back on those years, Brent recounts sadly, "All I can remember of that time are my failures."

When he went off to college, Brent took with him his deep belief that he was a phony. "I kept thinking, I am a fake and I will be found out." Consequently, Brent decided that his best strategy was to dance as fast as he could, keep moving, and not let anybody get too close or expect anything from him. "If people build expectations of you, then you will be forced to perform. If you are forced to perform, then you will be found out."

Brent seemed to have many friends, yet he knew that all of these relationships were superficial. He could not let anyone get close enough to learn his secret. Although he was an intelligent young man and had been accepted into a good college, Brent spent his college years settling for an acceptable C. He says, "The name of my story was 'I can't do it. I am in over my head. I won't even try.' " As long as professors and peers had no expectations, Brent could not fail. Everyone assumed he was just a charming guy satisfied with getting by.

Brent spent much of his early adulthood running from one relationship to the next, traveling all over the world, and trying on a variety of careers. Brent would allow himself to commit to nothing and to no one, because he was convinced that if he tried he would fail. After all, he was the man "who wasn't there" when his mother needed him.

In his late thirties, Brent married, finally finding a woman who could see past his public bravado and reach the vulnerable child who was trapped inside. His marriage presented Brent with the first opportunity to repair the self-hate he had carried since childhood. Early in their marriage, Brent's wife developed a serious but mysterious illness from which she suffered for many months before recovering. She was weak, feverish, and chilled, yet doctors could find no easy explanation for her symptoms. "I wanted to run, but this time I did not. I came home every night. I listened to her fears. I held her. I was a good guy. I was responsible. I wanted to be responsible this time. It was my choice and I felt good about it." At one point, Brent's wife said to him, "I wouldn't blame you if you went out and had a good time. I know it can't be very much fun staying here with me." Brent realized that the worst thing that he could do for himself was go out and have fun. "I needed to come home and be a man and this time it was surprisingly easy to do." Brent was no longer a boy pretending to be a man; this time he was a man acting responsibly toward a woman he loved. This time Brent had the maturity and the experience to be there with someone who was sick.

After years of floundering professionally, Brent went to graduate school and obtained a degree in social work. He worked as a general counselor, not specializing in a particular type of therapy or working with any special group. "Then AIDS came along and I said to myself, 'This is it. This is my work. I have something to give.' " When Brent sat with a young man who was suffering with AIDS, he could understand the man's fear and helplessness. He could empathize with his client's inability to accept the dramatic changes that were happening inside his body. As Brent sat with his patient, he remembered his mother and the terrible physical decay that had preceded her death. He remembered her fear and her confusion. This time he did not run away. He used his memories of the past to help him be there for his patient in a caring and humane way.

Brent now runs a clinic that provides a range of services to AIDS patients. Not only do Brent and his staff provide counseling, but they also help people with AIDS obtain needed medical and social services. "This is my life's work. The hand was dealt from the beginning. Now I know how to play it and I think I am a whole person because of it. People come to me with their lives and I can help them. People turn to me and say, 'I don't know where I would be without you.' I finally know who I am." The boy who was a fraud has become the man with something to offer. This time, Brent is not playing at being an adult. The experiences of his childhood have equipped him to be a genuine and caring companion to those who are dying.

In Richard Rhodes's words, one can never repair the hole in the world left when a parent dies.[19] However, one can fill in some of the edges. Many individuals are given the opportunity in adulthood to repair some of the effects of the trauma they experienced years ago.

At times the repair is effected by only a modest event. A long buried emotion is felt at last. At other times, repair requires a more far-reaching experience—a relationship that allows old wounds to be healed. For some, repair becomes a life's mission. The artist, the healer, or the writer who turns his or her own private attempt to fill the void into a creative act shares his or her repair with others. Richard Rhodes struggled with the terrifying insecurity he felt after his mother's death in the books he wrote. "Each of my books felt different to write. Each is set in a different milieu and tells a different story, in a different voice, in a different prose still. Yet I see now that they're all repetitions. They all repeat the same story. Each focuses on one or several men of character who confront violence, resist it or endure it, and discover beyond its inhumanity a narrow margin of hope."[20]

Occasionally an individual is lucky and life presents him or her with a chance to "do it" differently, a chance to play the tape of the past one more time and to make significant changes. When I used the word *luck* with one of the people I interviewed, he corrected me: "There is no such thing as luck. Luck happens when preparation and opportunity collide." People prepare to be lucky when they struggle with the aftereffects of early loss.

CHAPTER 10

∿

Unwanted Legacies

THE MORE PEOPLE I INTERVIEWED for this book, the more I became convinced that theirs were powerful stories of triumph over loss. These were not lives characterized by damage and defined by pathology. And yet, I could not ignore that there were some who struggled less successfully with demons from the past, and a greater number who had to fight sporadic battles with feelings of emptiness and insecurity throughout their lives.

In her poem entitled "Self Portrait I," Danish poet Tove Ditlevsen describes the person she has become as a result of the early deaths of both her mother and father:

> I can not:
> cook
> wear a hat
> make people comfortable
> wear jewelry
> arrange flowers
> remember appointments
> thank others for gifts
> tip correctly
> keep a man
> show interest
> at meetings for parents.

I can not
stop:
smoking
drinking
eating chocolate
stealing umbrellas
oversleeping
forgetting to remember
birthdays
and to clean my nails.
Telling people
what they want to hear
giving away secrets
liking
strange places
and psychopaths.

I can:
be alone
wash dishes
read books
form sentences
listen
and be happy
without guilt.[1]

Although Ditlevsen lived courageously and productively for many years, she eventually took her own life. Her poem is a record not only of what she was able to do but, more important, of all the things she felt she could not do: the permanent and unwanted legacy of her early loss.

All of the long-term destructive effects of early death derive from a child's attempt to master his or her experience of absolute catastrophe and the feelings of profound emptiness and insecurity that follow. At first this may seem paradoxical. How can an attempt to master something painful lead to a negative outcome? Imagine for a moment, however, trying to swat a fly with a hammer. You may successfully kill the fly, but you destroy the furniture in the process.

Problematic attempts at mastery fall into three broad categories: *emotional numbing, recurrent anxiety and depression,* and the development of *destructive explanatory myths or metaphors.* In the first case, the individual feels so overwhelmed by painful and chaotic feelings that survival demands those feelings be blocked out. Some consciously develop an air of detachment toward their own lives, never feeling either pain or joy very deeply again. Others blot out memories of the past in an attempt to remove the source of their pain. And still others use drugs and alcohol to achieve oblivion. In each case of numbing, however, the individual believes that to feel the pain of emptiness and the chaos of insecurity would be intolerable.

For those who live with recurrent anxiety and depression, the peace they desire seems out of reach. Regardless of how hard they try, they seem unable to prevent anxiety and depression from breaking through their defenses. Even when they feel happy and free of despair, they are often uneasy, fearful of the next time they will be flooded by feelings from the past.

Some construct a story or employ a metaphor to help them find their way out of the chaos that follows early loss. In some cases, these explanations are relatively benign and become incorporated into one's personal mythology. In other cases, the story that serves to explain is also destructive. The child uses an image—often one of blame—which then interferes with the leading of a full life.

Varieties of Numbing

When she was taken to the bedside of her dead mother, Virginia Woolf remembers saying to herself, "I feel nothing whatever."[2] Her conscious deadening of her own response was a defense that Woolf used throughout her life to control whatever felt painful and overwhelming. Woolf was conscious and aware that she was stifling her own feelings by exerting enormous control and force of will to prevent herself from experiencing pain.

Charles Darwin, whose mother died when he was eight, used less conscious strategies of numbing to dull his own anguish.

Darwin used a combination of forgetfulness, hard work, and emotional distancing to bury the feelings he could not master or control. Darwin's biographer John Bowlby suggests that Darwin's family encouraged him to forget his mother by never mentioning her name or discussing her death.[3] Later in his life, Darwin wrote, "When my mother died I was eight and a half years old, and Catherine [his sister] one year less, yet she remembers all particulars and events of each day, whilst I scarcely recollect anything . . . except being sent for, the memory of going into her room, my father meeting me—crying afterwards. I recollect my mother's gown and scarcely anything of her appearance, except one or two walks with her. I have no distinct remembrance of any conversation, and those only of a very trivial nature."[4] The tonic of forgetfulness had indeed worked its magic when years later Darwin wrote to a friend whose wife had died, "Never in my life having lost one near relation, I dare say I cannot imagine how severe grief such as yours must be."[5]

For Charles Darwin, the primary route to forgetfulness and to the dulling of his own pain and anxiety was work and more work. Despite his obvious success, at points in his life when Darwin felt insecure, he would repeat to himself the words: "I have worked as hard as I could, and no man can do more than this."[6] Work was his salvation and the primary means of distracting himself from the emotional pain of the early death of his mother.

When Darwin finally made the decision to marry, he weighed the pros and cons as might a dispassionate scientist. Feelings and emotions, long numbed in Darwin's psyche, were not a factor in his decision to wed. Despite his not wanting to live his life as what he called "a neutered bee," Darwin worried that marriage would entail expense, anxiety about children, quarreling, and most certainly, loss of time for his work.[7] Darwin eventually chose to marry, and found great comfort in his relationship to his wife, a nurturing woman to whom he came to refer as "Mammy."

Throughout his life, Darwin feared that his anxieties would become uncontrollable and that even his compulsive work habits would be unable to contain them. Despite his attempts to numb himself, Darwin suffered from a lifelong struggle with serious gastrointestinal ailments, many of which appeared to be psychosomatic in origin. He believed that his weak constitution was inherited from his mother and would eventually cause his own death. His recurrent stomach pains may well have been the reflection of buried feelings gurgling to the surface.[8]

Donna, one of the women I interviewed, spent most of her childhood caring for her invalid mother. She felt that if she had not been able to numb herself, she would not have been able to survive: "My whole life was focused on her (my mother). I had no chance to focus on myself or to think at all about my future. I just grew up too fast." In high school she recalls that friends complimented her for being so "laid-back and easy-going." She may well have appeared calm to outsiders, but inside she felt as if she was living in a trance. "In truth I had no energy to worry about anything." She was not calm as her classmates imagined; instead she was drained and numb.

Despite all of the energy it took to control her feelings, Donna did well in school, especially in math and science, subjects she could master while maintaining her air of emotional distance. She could excel without having a personal response. "Whenever I felt something, especially the anger, I just blocked it out. I was able to do that at a very young age. I hid the fact that the family wasn't normal and I pretended to myself that I was just growing up like everybody else. I was a pretty good actor and I could block the feelings that I had. Sometimes I think I acted so well I almost fooled myself."

Throughout her adolescence, Donna developed a style of never expressing any feelings. She wanted to be free of the pain, but she had another reason for banishing her feelings. Emotions seemed pointless to her. There was no one there who could hear her concerns, so why express them at all? In late adolescence, Donna found that taking drugs and drinking wine could help the process of numbing. She went through a period of several years during which she used chemicals to help her "not feel" her feelings.

Numbing, while useful in helping her to survive many of the stresses of childhood, has proven to be an unwanted legacy for Donna as she enters adulthood. In the last several years,

Donna has developed a chronic illness that demands she accurately read the responses of her own body. Her illness can only be managed if she modulates her day-to-day behavior in response to subtle cues that emanate from inside her body—cues that she must acknowledge and label correctly. At first, Donna found that she read herself poorly. She could not tell when she was feeling ill until she was so sick that she had to miss weeks of work. She had learned so well to be oblivious to the feelings that came from inside herself that she could not help ignoring them even when it meant seriously compromising her own health. Initially, Donna tried to learn about the nuances of her physical responses on her own. Eventually, she had to seek the assistance of a behavioral counselor to help her begin to recognize and acknowledge her own body's internal language.

Donna is now learning a whole new vocabulary, a language of feelings and sensations that she had successfully numbed in girlhood. As she finds herself, in C. S. Lewis's words, "melting like a snow man,"[9] she is also discovering a whole range of other feelings that have been frozen for years. Donna is learning how to recognize her annoyance and frustration with others and to set limits on the demands her friends and colleagues make of her. In the past, it never even occurred to Donna that she might have legitimate feelings about requests others made of her. If someone made a request, she just assumed that she had to do their bidding and ignore or suppress how she really felt.

As she begins to attend to her own responses, Donna is allowing herself a much broader range of expression. She is also learning how to have open disagreements and even fights with her husband. "I am learning that my feelings matter. I can say how I feel and it doesn't have to turn into a disaster." Had it not been for her potentially life-threatening illness, Donna might have gone through her entire life numbed and closed off to the feelings she held inside. Just as she chose to survive as a girl by moving out of her father's house and finally opting for her own life over the life of her mother, Donna now once again has chosen her own survival. She has learned to feel, because to do otherwise would mean to risk her very existence.

For some individuals, numbing assumes the form of what they call "callousness or cold realism." They are unable to allow themselves the luxury of having tender or soft feelings for anyone. Several people described what they termed their own impatience at the weakness or vulnerabilities of others. They felt intolerant of what often appeared to be the trivial complaints of their friends. When people related to me what they considered "trivial," their assessments were sometimes accurate. At other times, however, they labeled as "trivial" what many of us might consider quite serious—divorce, illness, the loss of a job. Yet, these individuals felt themselves unable or unwilling to "be bothered" with other people's problems.

One man described how he consciously distanced himself from people who either might need extra support or have plans to move to another city. He felt unable and unwilling to invest emotional energy in anyone who might be a source of future pain for him. Another man marveled at his own ability to turn his back on acquaintances who moved away or were merely out of sight for a time: "Gone is gone. I have no time for people who are not in my life." At times he worried that he might prematurely push someone away. Yet mostly he saw his own distancing as a necessary protection against future and further pain. Still another man felt somewhat uneasy about what friends had termed his "callousness." He remarked, "I guess my edges are just a bit sharper." People sometimes saw him as tactless when, for example, he correctly labelled the seriousness of certain life-and-death situations. "Death is a reality. We are all going to die. It's not something we can pretend isn't going to happen." Although his need to keep people at a distance and his somewhat tactless style caused friends to see him as cold, inside he felt himself to be soft and vulnerable. "People don't know it, but I spend time worrying about my cat." His tender side remains hidden from even those to whom he is most close, hidden because he cannot bear the pain of further hurt and disappointment.

One particular form psychic numbing takes is substance abuse. When an individual is unable to dull the pain of loss simply by forgetting, compulsive activity, or emotional distancing, he or she finds that the oblivion is brought on only by alcohol or other drugs.

HUGH'S STORY

Although he was already seventeen and almost prepared to leave for college when his mother died, Hugh found himself unable to recover from the impact of her death. In part, his difficulty stemmed from his complete inability to process his final visit with his mother. "I went to visit her at the hospital. I can still remember walking into the room. It must have been about eight o'clock at night. She was in bed and her food tray was propped up against her throat and it had hardly been touched. I could tell that she was unable to eat. She was just completely wasted away. I haven't seen other cancer patients, but I have seen enough AIDS patients and I know it's the same thing. I came up very close to her and at first I was angry because no one was in there feeding her. I remember trying to control my anger and I offered to give her some food. She just shook her head no. Then she asked me if I had had my dinner. I told her that I had not and then she tried to feed me. Oh, God, I cannot even think what that felt like. I felt so sad for myself. My mother who was just about dead and couldn't feed herself was trying to pick up a few lousy peas on a fork and feed me. I didn't know what to do. At that point my mother died for me. It made all the feelings real." After years of thinking about that event, Hugh is aware of how complicated his feelings were. He felt not only anger and sadness, but shame as well. He also felt a profound and almost suffocating connection with his mother. At that moment, it was not clear to him who was dying, his mother or himself.

After his mother died a few days later, Hugh remembers going to the home of a friend whose parents were casual about the use of alcohol. Hugh began drinking and stayed at his friend's house well into the night, seeking the oblivion that would come from being drunk. "What I wanted was to make a bubble around myself if only for a few minutes. I felt like I was drowning in the feelings and I just wanted them to go away. I didn't want to pass out. I just wanted to stop feeling."

With six younger siblings at home, Hugh quickly assumed the role of the responsible oldest child. He became the one who took care of everyone else's feelings and had no room to feel his own. In college, Hugh firmly established his pattern of drinking in order to dull his feelings: "I went to college and then I really started drinking a lot. I would be studying with a bottle of scotch next to my bed and I would drink until I would pass out. I just wanted to get enough emptiness so that I could go to sleep because I was still feeling the weight of her death and I didn't know how to let go of it. It was always there, like an extra twenty pounds sitting on my shoulder all the time."

Almost a year to the day after his mother's death, Hugh collapsed in class, suffering from stomach pains. He was taken to the infirmary and his ulcerlike symptoms were diagnosed as being stress related. No one asked him about his drinking, and no one suggested that Hugh needed help in overcoming the grief he was still feeling about his mother's death. By the time he was in his third year of college, Hugh rarely felt the pain from which he was running. He managed to numb himself successfully with a combination of alcohol and now marijuana. Hugh would think about his mother often, but was free of the worst pain because he was drunk or high most of the time. Occasionally, he would consciously decide that it was better to feel just a little of the pain than to be perpetually numb. At those times he would take himself to the cemetery or sit alone at the back of a church. The numbness would lift and he would feel the pain again. At those moments, Hugh would know that he was alive. But he was only able to tolerate his own feelings for a short time, and he would quickly return to his drug-induced escape.

When he graduated from college, Hugh went to work for an aggressive sales firm that encouraged its young employees to be upbeat, eager, and energetic. Drugs and alcohol were accepted as a necessary part of the business culture. Hugh already knew how to drink and smoke marijuana, and it was easy to add cocaine and speed to his personal cocktail. "Once in a while I would let my world settle down and I would accidentally be with myself without any outside stimulus; then I would think of my mother and I would be sad."

Several times while he was in his twenties, Hugh moved to a different city. Each new city gave him a chance to reinvent himself. The drinking and drug use always came along as part of his repertoire. Hugh firmly believed that without chemicals to dull his feelings he would be unable to survive. Occasionally, Hugh would become aware that the primary feeling he was trying to control was anger. The refrain "Why, why, why did this happen to me?" would run through his mind before he silenced the words with another drink.

Almost fifteen years after his mother's death and the beginning of his alcohol and drug use, Hugh received his first citation for driving while intoxicated. He was sentenced by the court to six months in a rehabilitation program and required to attend four meetings of Alcoholics Anonymous. Hugh participated in the rehabilitation program, watching the films designed to educate him about the impact of heavy drinking. He also made an effort, as he says, to "control his drinking" during that time. However, Hugh resisted attending the meetings of Alcoholics Anonymous. Five months into his sentence he still had not attended a single meeting. Yet the judge had warned him that if he did not appear in court with four signed slips verifying that he had attended meetings he would need to repeat his time in the rehabilitation program. With only a few weeks remaining, Hugh went to a meeting with an old drinking buddy of his. He went to the AA meeting intending only to meet the letter of the law laid down by the court. As he listened to the speakers, other recovering alcoholics, many of them spoke of experiences and feelings he shared. He was both moved and comforted by what he heard. That was almost twelve years ago, and Hugh has been attending meetings of Alcoholics Anonymous ever since.

Almost six months into his recovery program, Hugh was out for dinner with his sponsor from Alcoholics Anonymous. This man's own lover had just died of AIDS. "I remember when I fell apart; when it overwhelmed me and finally hit me. It must have been triggered by his lover's dying. I was overwhelmed with the feelings. They came up out of my gut and just washed over me. There was tremendous release. Instead of the cold feelings from the past, I felt the hot feeling of pain. Why did it happen to me? Why did it happen to me? The feelings gushed off of my shoulders and out of my heart, and I kept asking why again and again. Someone at the table, not my sponsor but another man, turned to me and said, 'Hugh, it was not about you. It was about her. It was about her life and her dying. It wasn't about you at all.' That started a way of thinking about her death which I have worked with for years now. It did not mean that my feelings were not real, but the dying was not about me. I only have to die once. When it gets to be about me I'll know it, then I'll be center stage and I'll deal with things then. When I was sixteen years old, I didn't know that. I thought her dying was about me." Hugh's beginning sobriety and the wisdom of the man at his dinner table allowed him to begin to separate his image of himself from the memory of his dying mother. The confusion that had formed in Hugh's mind in the hospital room many, many years ago began to clear. Hugh could now mourn for his mother and separate himself from her. He did not need to mourn for himself. He had not yet died.

In the course of his recovery and in witnessing the deaths of several friends over the last ten years, Hugh has come to gain a new understanding of the role one person plays in the death of another. "You can bring your love and you can serve as a witness. If you can't bring those things to someone's deathbed, then you have no business being in the room, because otherwise it becomes about you and your fear." Hugh was unable to be present for his mother when she was dying. He then hid from his overwhelming feelings in a fog of alcoholic oblivion. Through a slow process of recovery, Hugh has not only shed his addiction, but also gained a wisdom and calm about the process of dying.

Chemical dependence and substance addiction are such obviously self-destructive means for achieving relief from psychic pain that one must always wonder if the severely addicted individual is not also suicidal, consciously or otherwise. For Vincent, his almost thirty-year addiction to drugs was mingled with a conscious flirtation with death. After his mother's death when he was eight years old, Vincent often fantasized about a reunion with his perfect mother. Death seemed to be one easy way to join at last the mother he so desperately missed. Vincent was convinced that his life would have been different if his mother had lived, and he often felt angry when he visited friends in the neighborhood who seemed to have the ideal two-parent family out of which he had been cheated. An unfulfilled longing took root in Vincent's psyche and became one of the primary dynamics in his many-year addiction.

The world and its rules had cheated Vincent of a mother and as a result he resolved that he would pay no allegiance to the rules that men made for other men. As early as junior high school, Vincent began flaunting authority whenever he came up against it. Initially, his rebellion took the form of truancy from school. He would frequently think to himself, No one cares for me, and consequently no one has a right to control me or tell me what to do. As he grew into adolescence, Vincent had a series of minor run-ins with the law. Each time, however, he was let off with a stern reprimand. He would often think to himself, Thanks, Mom, and he was convinced that the watchful eye of his mother was guarding him from more serious harm. Minor infractions of the rules quickly escalated, and Vincent was expelled from high school with only months to go before graduation. He eventually received his high school diploma, but not in time to graduate with his class. The usual rites of passage marked by the senior prom and graduation from high school were denied to Vincent.

Once free of the constraints of school, Vincent eagerly went out into the world, desiring to find a job and to become more independent. In the work world, he once again confronted rules and regulations that felt constricting. He would push the limit in terms of attendance at work, frequently coming in late, but not late enough so that he would be fired. He would drive fast, often drinking while he was driving, and would think to himself, What is the limit here? Let me see how far I can push it.

Vincent lost his first job for drinking on the job site. He recalls now that he had an "angry man" inside himself whom he carried around with him wherever he went. Finding himself unemployed, Vincent decided to enroll in college. He reasoned that if he had an education he would be freer to set his own rules and be less bound by the dictates of others. Initially he did well in school, but college introduced Vincent to a new world of drugs and fast living. Vincent began by using drugs but eventually started to sell them as well. Vincent would try any drug offered to him. He began with marijuana and quickly escalated to heroin and cocaine. With the drugs as with everything else, Vincent would push his own limits, seeing how much he could take before he lost control. He was aware even then that he did not care if one of his experimentations lead to an overdose and death.

By the time he was in his early twenties, Vincent was addicted to heroin and dealing drugs in a dangerous community. When I asked him how he managed to survive without being shot or killed, he told me that he had acquired a reputation for being a wild and crazy man. "There were a couple of times when someone pulled a gun on me and I would stare at them and dare them to shoot. The word got out that I was kind of crazy." Vincent truly did not care if he died, so he risked being outrageous and confrontational, daring others to put him out of his misery.

Through his midtwenties, Vincent continued his drug use and his flirtation with death. He also managed to marry a woman who reminded him very much of his mother. For a while Vincent felt safe and somewhat calmed by his new relationship. Yet he was unable to control his addiction. After several years of their arguing about his drug use and after he was arrested for the possession of heroin, Vincent's wife asked him to leave. Once rejected by this surrogate mother, Vincent quickly self-destructed. Within two weeks, he had committed two robberies and was arrested and sentenced to three years in jail. While in prison, Vincent spent his time reading, studying, and recriminating himself. How could he have been so stupid? How could he have allowed his life to get so out of control? Vincent was not out of jail more than six weeks, however, when he was using drugs again. Once again he was arrested and this time he returned to jail for another five years.

Released for a second time, Vincent attempted to find a job and to put the pieces of his life back together, but escape through drugs and alcohol was now such a well-worn path for Vincent that he felt unable to resist. Several lost jobs and an eviction from his apartment led to eventual homelessness. Vincent found himself living on the streets, scrounging for food and drugs. One night when he was sleeping at a shelter for homeless men, Vincent heard an announcement over the public address system for a Narcotics Anonymous meeting that was being held in the recreation room downstairs. "I need to go. I need to go," kept running through his head. Two days later Vincent attended his first Narcotics Anonymous meeting and he has been attending regularly ever since.

At his first meeting, Vincent recalls breaking down and crying. "I tried not to be vulnerable to my feelings for such a long time." Vincent recalls crying again on the one-year anniversary of his sobriety when his own son talked about what it had been like to have Vincent for a father. It has now been seven years since Vincent attended his first meeting. He has returned to college and now works as an addiction counselor. He said, at first somewhat tentatively, "I think I enjoy my life. No, I do enjoy my life." Vincent believes deeply that he was spared by the grace of God so that he might help others to recover from the addiction that nearly killed him.

For both Hugh and Vincent, years of addiction and psychic numbing were followed by an almost miraculous conversion experience and then a long, slow road of recovery. Certainly there are others, not interviewed for this book, who never found the path back. Those individuals are permanent casualties of the unwanted legacy of early loss.

Depression and Anxiety

Conventional wisdom says that loss in childhood leads to depression in adulthood. Many scientific researchers have investigated the relationship between early loss and adult depression, but the path from one to the other remains unclear. Many factors influence the impact an early loss might have, including the relationship to the deceased, the personality of the child, and the quality of family life after the death. Researcher John

Bowlby concluded that "childhood bereavement plays a causal role in *only a small* minority of cases of mental illness."[10]

Regardless of what experts say about the strength of the connection between loss and depression, many survivors are convinced that their childhood experience of loss figured prominently in their lifelong struggle with depression. To them, the despair and emptiness they felt as children never went away. As they grew into adults, those feelings resurfaced as hopelessness, existential angst, and boredom, and in extreme cases as suicidality.

Actor James Dean wrote to a friend: "I am sad most of the time. Awful lonely too. (I hope you're dying) BECAUSE I AM."[11] Although Dean's own untimely death was most likely an accident, many believed that his dangerous behavior with cars and motorcycles was a form of suicidality and that he never recovered from the despair he felt over the loss of his mother.

Abraham Lincoln saw his frequent bouts of depression early in his life as being connected with his unresolved mourning for his mother. Lincoln was convinced that any woman he loved would die prematurely. His decision to break off his engagement with Mary Owens in 1836 was connected to his belief that he might bring death to a woman he loved. Prior to ending their relationship, Lincoln struggled with depressive ruminations and obsessive thoughts. Eventually he severed the engagement, writing to Mary Owens that he wished her "a long life and a merry one."[12]

In some cases, depressive symptoms seem so severe that they lead to hospitalization or suicide. Author William Styron, who wrote eloquently of his depression in his book *Darkness Visible*, attributed his lifelong depressive illness to the early death of his mother. "Loss in all its manifestations is the touchstone of depression—in the progress of the disease and, most likely, in its origin."[13] Styron believed that his mother's death when he was thirteen figured "as a probable genesis of my own disorder."[14]

When he was in the throes of a depressive episode, Styron felt his life to be dominated by loss: the loss of things, of time, and of people close to him. Although he was hospitalized only once for his depression, Styron came to believe that depression "had clung close to the outer edges of my life for many years."[15] Once he acknowledged how ever-present depression had been in his life, Styron realized that suicide and death had been themes in several of his books.

Styron's hospitalization was precipitated by a suicide attempt. Feeling that he could no longer endure what he called the "despair beyond despair,"[16] Styron began to make preparations to take his own life. On the night of his intended suicide, Styron was watching a movie. The musical score included a song Styron's mother used to sing. Hearing the song, Styron felt something that had been absent from his life—pleasure. And that moment of pleasure reminded him of all the pleasures he would lose if he killed himself. Styron later speculated that his own decision to live "may have been belated homage to my mother,"[17] whose loss drove him to despair but whose remembered voice may have called him to life.

Others have lost the battle with depression and committed suicide. Poets Sylvia Plath and John Berryman, both survivors of the early death of fathers, saw their early losses as important in their lifelong depressions and eventual suicides. Because of the pain that she suffered over the loss of her father, Plath likened herself to a Holocaust survivor, "an honorary Jew," having earned her place by the pain she had endured.[18]

In his epic poem "Dream Songs," John Berryman writes about a character named Henry, a middle-aged white male who has suffered an irreversible loss. Berryman tells the reader that Henry is not the poet himself, although his character sounds pointedly autobiographical. Throughout the many dream songs that make up this epic poem, Berryman refers to the suicide of Henry's father and to Henry's struggle with depression and despair. At one point, the poet says that nothing in all the great cities of the world can make up for "the horror of unlove,"[19] and at another point he writes, "Grief is fatiguing."[20] The character, Henry, is drained by a lifelong struggle with depression, anger, and loneliness. "*Father*," writes Berryman, "is the loneliest word."[21]

In one of the final dream songs, Berryman describes vividly the self-loathing the depressed person often feels before a successful suicide. Berryman, like Plath, eventually took his own life.

> Henry, monstrous bug, laid himself down
> on the machine in the penal colony
> without a single regret.
> He was *all* regret, swallowing his own vomit,
> disappointing people, letting everyone down
> in the forests of the soul.[22]

Although many of the people I interviewed talked about feelings of emptiness, sadness, and longing, none described the kind of depressive anguish experienced by William Styron or John Berryman. One woman, Rebecca, did undergo a psychiatric hospitalization for depressive symptoms later in her life. Rebecca's mother had died when Rebecca was only six, and the child was left in the care of a distant and withdrawn father and a self-involved and callous stepmother. Throughout her childhood, she remembers thinking, "Nothing in this world comes close to being cherished by two parents."

Rebecca first experienced depression after her first child was born. She felt overwhelmed at the task of being a mother both because she had no model for how to mother and because she felt that she had no one to help her. At the time of her daughter's birth, Rebecca recalls feeling exhausted and anxious. However, she was successful at taking care of this child, and she experienced no repetition of this early depression with the births of her other children. Her own memories of raising her children are that she loved them, cared for them, and provided as best she could. Her children have different memories, however. They tell Rebecca that living with her was like living with a Holocaust survivor. They often felt that their mother was so overwhelmed by her loss and the pain of her childhood that she could focus on little else. They recall that Rebecca talked often about the loss of her mother. Rebecca has no such recollections and when she asks her husband and friends, she gets confirmation of her own view of reality. Yet, she must face the fact that her children saw it differently. It may have been that she only talked occasionally of her own depression and loss but for her small children, her infrequent reminiscences seemed overwhelming.

On the fortieth anniversary of her mother's death, Rebecca became inconsolable. She began weeping and shaking, and her despair was so profound that she entered a hospital for psychiatric treatment. During her seven-week hospitalization, she remembers weeping openly for her mother. In particular, she remembers a psychodrama exercise in which her leader asked her to imagine that she was seated in the same room with someone who had died long ago. She was then told to say out loud to this imaginary figure words that had been held inside but never uttered out loud. Rebecca cried out loud and sobbed over and over again, "I miss you. I miss you."

Following her hospitalization, Rebecca initiated several attempts to reconnect with surviving members of her mother's family. She has since attended several family reunions at which she feels welcomed and accepted by this large group of people who "look like her." Rebecca has also begun going to the cemetery on holidays and special occasions to honor her mother. She feels as if she is "righting a wrong and restoring something that was taken away long ago."

While most survivors who experience psychic distress label it as depression, others are left not with depression, but with profound anxiety. For these individuals, the world seems changeable and unpredictable, and they fear that even that which seems most secure could be taken away on a moment's notice.

After her father's death when she was only twelve, Clare came to see the world as an insecure and unsafe place. "I started to think that things could be swept away tomorrow." In reality, much was swept away after Clare's father died. Clare's mother became anxious about the family finances and sold the big house in which Clare had grown up. There was no realistic basis for her mother's anxiety—the family's finances were quite secure—yet that anxiety dominated Clare's experience immediately following her father's death.

During the time her mother was building a new home in a less expensive suburb, Clare and her mother shared a small apartment together. Clare remembers feeling ashamed about the little apartment in which she and her mother now lived.

She also remembers feeling stunned by the enormity of the change that had overtaken her in such a short time. It seemed to Clare as if her whole world had altered overnight. She went from being a loved daughter in a secure and stable two-parent home, a child of the privileged class, to being alone with her insecure and anxious mother, living in what seemed to her to be a shabby and run-down apartment.

Throughout high school and college, Clare continued to worry that anything about which she cared deeply would be taken away. She not only could not trust her possessions or her relationships, but she also could not trust her own mood. A happy girl could turn into a sad and despairing girl at a moment's notice.

In her early twenties, Clare fell in love for the first time. Regrettably, her lover was someone who needed to keep their relationship a secret. Throughout an affair that lasted for several years, Clare continually worried that her lover would decide one day that the relationship was no longer possible. Just as love had been snatched away by death when Clare was a girl, she now feared that the whim of her lover would snatch love away once again.

Clare's pervasive anxiety about the world has had several unwanted consequences in her adult life. Her anxiety prevents her from enjoying many of the pleasures that are hers. Clare recently moved into a new and lovely home, which she designed and helped to build, yet she is afraid to enjoy fully the pleasures of her new home. Clare feels, "If I enjoy it too much, it will probably be taken away."

Clare's anxiety about the future also caused her to remain in an unsatisfying marriage for almost twenty years with a man who functioned primarily as a security blanket. Clare's husband was neither passionate nor engaged in life, but he was stable and predictable, and when she married him she longed for a sense of security, which had been so lacking in her early life. It never occurred to Clare that she could be involved with someone who was both lively *and* stable. In the past, if Clare was forced to choose between passion and safety, there would have been no choice; she would always opt for security because without that she became too overwhelmed by her own anxiety and her fears about the future.

In recent years, Clare has taken a risk by becoming involved with a lover who is much more emotional and tempestuous. In this new relationship, Clare has allowed herself to take the emotional risk she had avoided for years. She has even dared to believe that her new relationship does not necessarily need to end just because she enjoys it and cherishes it.

Clare knows that her anxiety comes from her early loss of her father, and most of the time she regrets that she is unable to experience enjoyment unaccompanied by worry. Occasionally, she rationalizes that there is a positive side to her insecurity: because Clare does not believe in the certainty of a tomorrow, she tries to live her life fully today.

Destructive Metaphors

Language is a powerful tool that helps frame the experience of early loss. Children use words to help them make sense of what has happened to them: "Death is like a long nap." "Death is a trip to a faraway place." "A bad guy came and took my mommy. That's why she died." At times, the language chosen has unfortunate consequences. Certain metaphors or images, central to helping the bereaved child understand the loss, persist as unwanted legacies into adulthood.

One of the ways we think about loss is in the language of crime and victimization. Linguistically, the words *bereave* and *rob* even come from the same root.[23] In this metaphor, death involves a victim—the bereaved child, a lost treasure—the beloved parent, and a thief, the faceless specter of death who takes life away. The child feels robbed or cheated by untimely death, robbed of the relationship and robbed of the parent who is now gone. When one thinks of a death as a robbery, one feels not only victimized, but cheated and angry as well. Questions of "Why me?" predominate, and one feels envy and even ill will toward those who seem untouched by death.

Sally was well aware that after her father's suicide, her mother felt both deprived and cheated. Sally's mother worked the evening shift on a dull and tedious job to insure that her children would have the things they needed. Sally remembers that her mother preferred to shop at the very best stores even though the family had little money. Her mother would use the layaway plan in order to buy her children quality items, trying to make sure they did not feel poor just because they had no father. Nevertheless, Sally continued to feel her own "less than" status, compounded by her mother's sense of shame and inferiority.

As she was growing up, Sally remembers specifically being envious of the other children who had fathers. One time in particular, she remembers feeling alienated from her classmates when the art teacher asked them to make an ashtray for their fathers as a Father's Day gift. Sally recalls her pain as she had to explain to the teacher that she had no father. She sat down and began to make her ashtray for an uncle who lived in another city, pretending that the uncle was a special favorite and that he would enjoy her present.

As she recalls her childhood, Sally says, "I had a sense of being a deprived child. I felt envious of everyone, yet if I got anything, I felt so guilty for having more than someone who was starving that I could not enjoy it." Throughout her adolescence, Sally recalls being obsessed by the plight of the "havenots." She was aware of her own kinship to those who seemed deprived. "I saw myself as one of those unfortunates, and I had a strong identification with the underdog.

In college, Sally recalls being especially envious of classmates who seemed "like Daddy's little girls." To Sally, these young women appeared to be "spoiled princesses." Yet despite her envy or perhaps because of it, Sally was very aware that people described her relationship to her own father in just those same terms. She was his "special little girl" and might well have been spoiled and indulged by him had he lived. Sally feels that her father's early death robbed her of the opportunity to enjoy the privileges and the comforts other girls seemed to take for granted.

As she told her story to me, Sally felt bad and was visibly shaken by how envious she sounded. Yet, she felt unable to contain the strong sense of deprivation that pervaded her life.

Sally described several encounters with her husband's wealthy family in which she could not keep her envy at bay. Sally and her husband are often treated to opulent getaways when they are invited to join her in-laws for a weekend. Rather than being able to enjoy a life of privilege, if only temporarily, Sally feels blocked by her envy and her sense of how unfair it all is. While she is with her in-laws, Sally often thinks to herself, somewhat contemptuously, that if she had so much money she would not indulge herself as her relatives do. Instead, she would become a patron of the poor, giving much of what she had to those who were less fortunate than she.

Sally's envy is not limited to her wealthy relatives. "I have a chip on my shoulder because I must make do. When I see friends with nicer houses, I think, Why not me?" The same lament of "Why me?" that haunted Sally as a girl when she lost her father continues to haunt her now as an adult woman. When she thinks about her ongoing struggle with envy, Sally's greatest anxiety derives from her knowledge that she turns her envying eye on the lives of her own children: "My daughters already have more than I had when I was a girl." Sally feels envious not only of her daughters' carefree childhoods but, more important, of the fact that they are able to enjoy the love and attention of two parents.

Sally realizes that in order to enjoy her own adult life, she needs to curb the raging river of envy that has run through her experience. Seeing the loss of her father as a robbery in which she was the helpless victim makes it difficult for Sally to move beyond her anger and her envy. Death, unlike a robbery, is a natural event. It is not a crime; there is no perpetrator, no villain who deserves to be punished, no wrong that must be righted. The metaphor of robbery makes it difficult for Sally to come to terms with her loss. She keeps looking for a criminal whose punishment will somehow right the wrongs she experienced in childhood.

Some survivors of early loss carry the burden of a destructive metaphor in which they are cast as dangerous and deadly perpetrators. Metaphors of toxicity, in which the individual believes him- or herself to be evil, dangerous, or violent, may limit an individual to a life of loneliness or to a self-imposed banishment to the world of abusive relationships. If you believe yourself to be toxic for other people, then you have only two choices: either you avoid human contact, protecting others by staying away, or else you decide that you can only live in a world where others are also toxic and bad. If your lovers and friends are dangerous people, then you do not need to worry that you might harm or destroy them; they are powerful villains themselves.

Allison recalls having no relationship at all with her father. She remembers him as a scary, hot-tempered man whose frequent outbursts frightened her. Her other siblings have tender memories of time they spent alone with a gentler dad. Allison has no such fond recollections. Even as a child, she felt that she and her father were not well matched, and she deeply believed that her father did not like her.

When Allison's father died, it was easy for her to block her feelings of grief by adopting a tough-girl persona. While her angry defenses may have protected her from feeling sad and from feeling the loss of a father whose love she had never known, those same defenses isolated her from the rest of her family. Allison's mother and her siblings not only shared fond memories of her father, but they also mourned openly and together for him. Allison felt like an outsider, different from the rest of the family, alone and bitter. Her openly critical attitude toward her mother further estranged Allison from the rest of the family. Allison remembers the mixed feelings she had when her mother told her, "You are too aggressive, too opinionated, and too challenging." In part, her mother's accusations made Allison feel superior; in part, however, they also made her feel different and unacceptable.

The image Allison carried of herself was that she was "like sandpaper," an annoying, grating child, unloved by her father and unable to get along with her mother. When Allison left home to go to college, she continued to see herself as an angry outsider. Over the years, Allison has softened her persona somewhat. She now feels that she is able to approach other people and to offer herself as a friend. She is most comfortable in relationships with other women. She has never been able to have a successful relationship with a man. "I feel defective. I think to myself, If my own father didn't like me, how is any man going to like me."

Recently, Allison placed an ad in the personal section of her local newspaper. She received many interesting responses. However, they all sit in a pile on her living room floor. Allison has been unable to answer any of the responses she received; sadly, Allison is frightened to take a risk. She is convinced that these men who express an interest in her ad would be uninterested when they meet the "real Allison."

If Allison's father had lived, the two might well have discovered that they had more in common than she has come to believe. Allison's challenging and brusque demeanor sounds similar to her father's gruff manner. Had father and daughter had more time, they might have been able to forge a bond that would have allowed Allison to feel both lovable and loved. When Allison was a girl, she was too frightened to challenge her father, to engage him the way she subsequently tried to engage her more timid mother. If her father had lived, the two would certainly have fought, but they might have gained respect for each other's energy and passion.

Throughout her adult life, Allison has traveled widely, mostly alone, usually to far-off places, searching for adventure and pushing herself to experience new things. One of Allison's favorite places is Japan, and she has decorated her apartment with many of the Japanese artifacts she collected in her travels. Prominently displayed in her living room is a small Shinto shrine. On the altar, Allison has amassed several personal items, small tokens that are meaningful to her. Among the items displayed is a photograph, a photograph of Allison as a child seated happily on her father's lap. Allison became very emotional during the interview as she showed me her one photo of her and her father together. It was clearly important for Allison to honor and remember this image of her and her father connected by a loving embrace.

The metaphor of toxicity has left Allison a lonely woman. She feels that she is too rough, too abrasive, and too hard to be loved by a man. Although she still longs for an intimate connection, Allison often feels that it may be too late for her;

the negative image she carries of herself is so ingrained and so central to who she is that it may not be changeable.

For Jane, the image of herself as toxic has consigned her to a series of abusive relationships. Years of being criticized and abused by her mother after her father's suicide convinced Jane that she was a toxic person. Her mother may have been angry and out of control when she shouted the fateful words, "You should never have been born," but for Jane, those words struck a chord deep inside her. As an adult woman, Jane has been involved with a number of men who are either self-destructive or highly abusive. Jane reasons that she is safe from her own evil core with these men because there is no way she can possibly hurt them. "The one thing that all of my boyfriends have in common is that they are all incredibly strong. None of them is vulnerable. I just couldn't bear it if I hurt someone, and I don't trust that I will be able to control myself."

Jane's first long-term relationship was with an alcoholic man who repeatedly expressed a desire to die. Jane now believes that this man was what she called "emotionally dead," yet she felt safe being his girlfriend: "I knew I could not hurt him. He had already done so much damage to himself." Jane's current boyfriend is a manipulative womanizer who prides himself on dating several women simultaneously. He never worries about being hurt by the rejection of one of his many girlfriends; there are always several others from whom he can easily choose. Despite the fact that Jane is not treated well by this current boyfriend, Jane feels safe in his company. Regardless of what she does or how she behaves, Jane is secure in knowing that she cannot harm her boyfriend. Considering herself to be toxic like the black widow spider, Jane only allows herself to have relationships with men who are either already dead or who are so well defended that they are not in danger of being harmed by her presumably deadly sting.

Other individuals make sense of their loss by using the language and metaphor of fairy tales, a language appropriate to childhood but less healthy and functional as one becomes an adult. "Let's pretend and make believe" becomes the lifelong legacy of loss for these individuals. The line between what is real and what is not real never seems quite clear. Actor James Dean and his mother used to play a game every night called the "wishing game."[24] Young Dean would write a wish on a piece of paper and put it under his pillow. Sometime during the night, his mother would come into his bedroom, retrieve the wish, and try to grant it before morning. After his mother died, Dean took a wisp of her hair and attempted to use it as a stand-in for his mother when he played the wishing game by himself. In the world of magic and make-believe, all things should be possible, and a dead mother should be able to play fairy godmother just as well as a living one.

Throughout his life, James Dean was known for often confusing reality with fantasy. Observers commented that he always seemed to be re-creating himself, acting as if he could become a different person at will. Magic and make-believe continued to be part of Dean's life, not merely part of his craft as an actor.

Another woman began telling stories to herself as a child as a way to soothe herself and put herself to sleep. After a while, the stories seemed more real than her everyday life. Her stories ceased to be private and she began sharing them with friends as if they were real memories and real events that had happened to her. As an adult woman, she is always a little nervous when she meets someone from the past. She is not sure what story she might have told to that individual. The reunion begins somewhat tentatively as she tests to see what version of herself this person holds to be true.

"Let's pretend" can be a dangerous game, and although it is comforting to a child to believe that magic and make-believe can control the trauma of childhood, it is dangerous for an adult to continue to live in the world of fantasy.

When we think of an inheritance or a legacy, we often think of something quite positive. A parent leaves behind a treasured memento, a volume of collected wisdom, or years of accumulated wealth. Occasionally, a parent, by his or her premature death, leaves behind a legacy of pain, anger, and emptiness—an unwanted legacy, but a legacy nonetheless.

One woman who had difficulty recovering from her early

loss complained at one point during the interview that she felt doubly cheated. When her father died young, she not only missed out on all the things he could have given her during girlhood, but she was also cheated out of having a rich and successful father who might have bequeathed her an inheritance later in life. She lamented, "I have gotten absolutely nothing from him." Sadly, she could not have been more wrong in that assessment. Her father's death did indeed bequeath her an inheritance. It was, however, an unwanted legacy that burdened her for the rest of her life.

CHAPTER 11

~

Staying in Touch

DURING ONE INTERVIEW, A MAN who had lost his mother remembered a line from a movie he thought might be important in explaining some of his continuing feelings for the woman who had died almost forty years ago: "Let's always stay in touch even though death will come between us."

Sometimes what we mean by staying in touch is simply that we remember. We use pictures, treasured objects, or special places to help us remember a parent who is no longer present. Most survivors of early loss mean something more, however, when they talk about their private rituals for staying connected to a parent they may have known for only a short time. For survivors of early loss, staying in touch often means finding a way to commune with the dead, to reach out in a deeply emotional way and feel touched by the spirit of a long dead mother or father. When a survivor looks at a picture or caresses a favorite necklace, he or she not only remembers the parent, but actually feels his or her presence.

Sometimes these rituals take the form of a continuing conversation, which begins immediately after the death itself. The young child continues a dialogue in his or her mind with a parent who becomes both Father Confessor and fairy godmother, a dialogue that can no longer occur in everyday life. As the child grows, the dialogue does not cease; it matures. The conversation with the deceased parent becomes a source of secret strength and comfort as one confides one's worries, one's plans, and one's dreams.

Occasionally, the connection is formed only in later life at a time of some important decision or transition. The individual feels a need for a special relationship with a parent who will listen without judgment or criticism, a relationship that has long been missing. In these cases, the dialogue may begin accidentally while one is lying in bed thinking, or purposefully with a trip to the cemetery. Once started, this inner conversation may become an ongoing and important part of one's life.

While these silent conversations may seem like the self-talk and internal problem solving in which we all engage, they are something more. The presence of the dead parent is deeply felt at these times, and the survivor uses the ongoing conversation as an essential way of "staying in touch" with the parent who is no longer alive.

Despite the prevalence of these connecting rituals, most people told them to me with some anxiety and not a small amount of shame. Repeatedly, people prefaced their remarks with, "I hope you won't think that I'm strange," or "I know this sounds crazy, but . . . ," or "I've never really told this to anyone before, so I hope it doesn't sound too weird." These ways of maintaining connection, which clearly seemed a source of strength and comfort for an individual, were felt to be unnatural and a bit odd.

As I heard these stories from many, many of the people with whom I spoke, I realized that what was odd was not that people stay in connection, but rather that they feel so ashamed of their continuing relationship with a dead parent that they must keep their ways of "staying in touch" private, not even sharing them with their closest companions.

In Western culture, several factors work against our sharing rituals of remembrance and ongoing connection. For years, conventional wisdom has said that the right way to mourn fully is to move on. As long as one continues to invest emotional energy in the past or in past relationships, so the theory goes, one is not free or able to enter into new relationships in an open and complete way.

The power of this belief persists, despite the fact that counselors who work with the bereaved tell us that rituals to honor the connection to a deceased loved one are a normal part of mourning. Our failure to understand truly the continuing presence the dead play in the lives of the living has led to a tendency to overpathologize normal mourning.[1]

The cause of our reluctance to acknowledge publicly the power of the past can be found in our language, in the everyday metaphors we use to understand human growth and development. We talk about life as a journey, a path, or a road we must travel. If we seem unable to move from one point on the road to the next, we are told that we are "stuck." If we take too much with us from one point in the journey to the next, we label what we carry as "baggage," heavy weight that makes it harder to move along more swiftly. Applied to loss and mourning, this metaphor suggests that if we are to move easily and freely down the road, we must leave our connections to the past behind.

In another metaphor, we see the strings or bonds that attach us to another person as encumbrances. As we grow up we are told that we must "cut the cord," and "stop holding on to Mom's apron strings." A deal with "no strings attached" seems to be a good offer. Rather than feeling enriching and important, our connections often feel like the "ties that bind." It is no wonder, given how reluctant we are to acknowledge ties in general, that we are especially wary of admitting an ongoing tie to one who is long dead.

When Robert Lifton finished his interviews with the survivors of the Hiroshima disaster, he concluded that in order to move beyond the horror of Holocaust, survivors needed a way to establish a continuing connection to those who had died.[2] They also, however, needed to find a way to separate enough from the past so that they were free to make new connections in the present. Both too much and too little connection to the relationships of the past may make it difficult to move forward. A continuing connection to the relationships of the past, when it exists in a balance with the present, may be a necessary condition for establishing connections in the future. Rather than preventing one from moving on, as many have suggested for so long, these connections may actually enable future growth.

As I was preparing to begin writing *The Loss That Is Forever,* I had a dream about the role of ongoing connection. In the dream, I was watching a documentary about the boyhood of President Clinton. Part one of the film ended with the young Clinton preparing to leave home and drive his car to Washington, D.C., where he would attend college. As he was finishing his preparations, his mother noticed that he had printed the lines from an old country-western song around the perimeter of his license plate. The song, she knew, had been the favorite of Clinton's father, a man the young boy had never known. Virginia Kelley asked her son why he wanted that old song around his license plate. He turned to her and said, "That was my father's favorite song. He was a part of me too and I don't want to forget him." While this incident was merely the product of my own active imagination, it is the kind of personal ritual that many of the people with whom I spoke designed for themselves as a way of staying connected to a long gone parent.

Some of the strategies for staying in touch are easy to identify. People use pictures, special objects, and places, as ways to maintain their connection to a deceased parent. Some engage in culturally sanctioned rituals that bring them in contact with a wide community of mourners. And still others continue an ongoing inner dialogue with a lost parent who assumes the role of a personal guardian angel.

Pictures

Rock star Madonna has only one good luck charm she takes with her from place to place, always displaying it on the bureau of her hotel room.[3] It is a picture of her mother. Not of her mother as Madonna knew her, but rather a picture of Madonna's mother when she herself was a young girl. With the picture of her mother in her room, Madonna feels as if she has brought part of home with her wherever she goes.

One woman I interviewed has constructed what she calls a

family wall. It is a special place in her home where pictures of
her, her mother, and her family are arrayed. After her mother
died, her father quickly remarried and her mother was rarely
spoken of in the home. The wall of remembrance reminds this
woman of the life she had when her mother was alive. There
are several pictures of her and her mother together, so that the
wall reminds her not only of her mother but of the relationship
they shared: "I just figured I wouldn't have this stuff in my life
unless I could see it. I have nobody else to share it with." She
does not spend hours staring at the wall of pictures. Rather, it
forms part of the backdrop of her everyday life, something that
is always there every time she walks down the hall, much the
way a parent might have been.

For years, another woman captured the feeling that her father was an everyday presence in her life by placing a picture
of him in a drawer in her dresser. Whenever she opened the
drawer, her father's picture would be there. It was almost as if
she was greeting him for the day. She would close the drawer
and not open it again until the next day. When she went off to
college, her father's picture went along. Years later when she
married, her father's picture once again took up residence in a
drawer in her bureau. At one point in her adult life, she sought
counseling for a matter unrelated to the early death of her father. The therapist asked her about her past and about her
father, and she told him of her habit of having her father's picture sit in the drawer just to remind her of him and to maintain
her connection. The therapist asked her in which drawer her
father's picture had been placed. "Why, my underwear drawer,
of course," she replied. The therapist concluded that there
were unresolved Oedipal issues between her and her father. To
her credit, this woman recognized that the therapist was mistaken, terminated the therapy, and found another counselor
who was better able to understand the role her father's picture
has served. "The picture was in my underwear drawer," she
says, "because that's the only drawer I opened every day. It
was always there. First thing in the morning, I would take a
look and close the drawer again. There was something very ordinary and routine about it all."

Another man, whose mother died when he was only four,

had a portrait of her painted from the only photograph that remained. The portrait of his young mother now hangs prominently in his home. "This is my memory. I want her on my wall. I want her in my life." Once again, this painting is just there, part of the decor, something he glances at in an almost unconscious way several times a day, not unlike the way a child glances at his mother as he goes about his routine. There is something very comforting for this man about having his mother's portrait on his wall.

Another woman has used pictures of her father to introduce her children to the grandfather they will never know. As soon as her sons were old enough to recognize the pictures on the mantel, she began to tell them stories about "Poppa." The pictures are for her sons, but they are also for her father. She wants to bring him into her home as a vital presence, and the pictures are her way of connecting her father to the next generation. She says, "They know my father. He is definitely in our house."

Objects

When she won the 1994 Olympic Gold Medal for figure skating, Russian skater Oksana Baiul carried as her lucky charm the key to the home that she and her deceased mother had occupied together. For this talented orphan, this token key was her connection to her mother. The house they had shared together was gone, but the key could still open the door to memory and her mother's presence.

Many of the interviews I conducted for this book took place in the home of the interviewee. People frequently chose to show me objects in their home that had belonged to their dead parent, objects which now held a place of honor and were important not only as furnishings or decorations, but as very literal connections to the parent who had died. One man commented, "I actually surround myself with the things that will remind me of him." His father's coin collection and a beautiful piece of crystal were proudly displayed. One woman recalls that she carried her father's lucky stone all through her wedding ceremony. "I felt he was there with me. We dedicated a hallelujah chorus to him; it was really neat. I could feel his presence all day." The stone her father had carried in his pocket for years as his lucky charm served as a substitute for the father who could not be there himself to walk her down the aisle.

For one man whose name is the same as his father's, his signature serves as a literal connection between his father and him. "I always go by Junior; that's who I am; that's who I will always be. I sign my name that way." He recalls one time dating a woman who thought it was ridiculous that he, a man in his thirties, continued to sign his name with the *Junior* affixed to the end. She insisted, "There is only one person with that name, and that's you. There isn't a senior anymore." He recalls correcting her and resenting her intrusion into the symbolic connection that he maintained with his father: "My father is Senior and I am Junior, and that's how it's going to be." From such a statement, one might wonder if this man has been able to assume the responsibilities of adulthood. Does he think of himself as a boy still connected to a more powerful father? I spent only three hours with him, but I saw no evidence that he was stuck in childhood. He was married, had a responsible job, a wide circle of friends, and seemed secure and confident. He maintained an emotional bond to the father he had only known for a few years of his young life, a bond that seemed important to him and that linked him to a past and a heritage of which he was proud. Rather than reflecting a kernel of immaturity, his desire to stay in touch via his name seemed a sign of personal integrity and mature adult presence.

Places

Places have special significance for many of us. A return to a childhood home or a college campus triggers remembrance and reminiscence. Sometimes the power of a place can be so strong that we almost feel as if we are transported back in time, reconnecting for a moment with the person we were when we lived in that place. A particular place may provide special comfort. We go there when we want to be alone, when we want to feel secure, when we want enough space to be able to feel our own feelings. For some survivors of early loss, places become an important vehicle for staying in touch with a dead parent.

Jack has made several visits to the town and the street where he last lived with his father and his family. On his most recent visit, he felt a strong desire once again to go inside the home he had last shared with his father. It was a captivating, beautiful country house. "I just wanted to be alone to remember things." On that particular trip, he was with his fiancée and had intentionally brought her back to share in some of his memories. Once he was there, though, he realized that bringing a companion, even someone he loved, was a mistake. This was his special place, a place where he allowed himself to feel connected with his father and with the past. "I wanted to go back in time and just let my imagination run free." He was quite sure that at some point in the future he would once again return to the town and the street where he had grown up. This next time, however, he would go alone and spend the hours remembering and re-creating a time long past.

For Rachel, whose father's early death left her with a neglectful mother, the attic of her family home became for years a place of comfort and safety. "Our house had an attic that was as big as the whole floor of the house. It was a thirteen-room Victorian house, and up in the attic nothing had been thrown out from the time our family had lived there. My father's first schoolbook from first grade was there, the toys he played with as a boy. His saddle was on the rafter. Everything. It was a complete history in that attic. I have two bags with correspondence from the early nineteen hundreds that I haven't opened yet. My father didn't throw anything out, so I loved that attic. It even smelled good."

When she was a girl, Rachel remembers, she spent hours in the attic. It was as if she were visiting with her father when she would go up there to play. "I would always find something I hadn't found before. One day I picked up his diary and turned to the page with the day of my birth. There I was—weight, time of birth—that was the beginning of me."

For years, Rachel's relationship with her father existed only in the attic, which was her special place, her emotional playground. "I always felt that his spirit was there. Being there filled the void you have when you miss a parent. It was such a rich experience for me. It sort of made a connection to who I was." In the attic Rachel discovered the father she never knew. By coming to know his things, she came to know who he was. Each new discovery brought her closer not only to her missing father, but to her past and her family history. Part of Rachel's identity was stored in the attic, and she came to know herself as she discovered the remnants of the past. Even after she left home, married, and had a family of her own, Rachel would return to the attic from time to time. Her last visit occurred when she herself was already sixty years old. "I was ready to let it all go. I have my memories. They are secure now."

For Jerome, returning to the country of his father's birth was a way of connecting to his father as well as discovering his own roots. Jerome had never known his father, who had died when Jerome was only an infant. He always pledged to himself, however, that one day he would return to the island home where his father had been born. When he was forty, Jerome finally fulfilled his boyhood pledge. He says, "Going back to his home was one of the best things that has ever happened to me. It was important to realize this was his hometown, this was where he was from, this was where he was born and raised. It gave me a kinship that I had been looking for, putting me in touch with him and with my own roots." Jerome remembers his own joy at seeing street signs labeled with his family name, a foreign-sounding name that only belonged to him as he was growing up. At last he could see that there were others from his same clan. "As I walked around I kept saying, 'These are my roots. This is my daddy's home. This is part of my blood line right here.' Being there put me in touch with a part of him that I had never had. Something I had always sought and finally obtained."

When a parent dies very young, a child loses not only the connection to that particular parent, but also a connection to the past, to the generations who have gone before. The parent who might have served as a link between past and present is not there. There is no one to tell stories about generations and times long gone. Often other members of that side of the family retreat over time so there are even fewer sources of connection to the past. Jerome needed to reconnect with his father in order to reconnect to his own heritage. For Jerome, staying in touch with his father meant discovering who he himself was.

A number of people with whom I spoke who had lost parents when they were young embarked on personal quests to discover their family genealogy. They wanted to trace their roots into the distant past. These attempts at connection seemed especially important and linked to their more personal feelings of not being connected to the parent who had died. As we get older and begin to contemplate our own mortality, many of us want to understand our origins. Where did we come from? Who were our ancestors? If we are lucky and they are still living, we can answer these questions by simply turning to our parents and asking. We do not need to call distant relatives or make a trip to the town hall. Our parents are our resident historians. If they have died young, our search for roots, more important because we know so little, is also more difficult.

Culturally Sanctioned Rituals

It is always easier to feel comfortable with rituals of connection when they are sanctioned by one's culture and shared by one's community. In the United States, periodic visits to the cemetery to honor the dead are as close as we come to culturally sanctioned rituals for maintaining connection. Regrettably for many, cemetery visits are awkward, brief, and perfunctory with the family going for only a few minutes, saying a prayer, dropping off flowers, and quickly returning home.

Child expert Eda LeShan describes a cemetery ritual in which she participated one year after the death of a father.[4] The family went to the cemetery together and read a letter they had composed to their dad. The letter updated him on what had happened in the past year. It also included declarations of how much the family missed him. The ritual concluded with one of the daughters doing a cartwheel on her father's grave. Her father had always loved watching her do cartwheels, and she did one for him on this day of remembrance. Her ability to do the cartwheel was also a way for her and her family to let their dad know that they were still able to feel joy in their lives.

One of the women with whom I spoke also found a way to make the cemetery ritual more personal and meaningful: "I sat on the ground and I talked to my father, then I left one of my business cards with him. I found a place where the stones met, a place where I could squeeze the card in. I just wanted to tell him who I was."

Other cultures have more sanctioned and established rituals for staying connected to the dead than we do in the United States. In Mexico, All Saints' Day is a recognized time for honoring the deceased.[5] It is also a time for gift exchange and family reunions. When family members gather, they bring food to symbolically feed and honor the dead. The day becomes a way of staying in connection with those who are gone and also a way of reaffirming the continuity of the community.

Bhuddist and Shinto traditions in the Far East provide a wonderful example of a culturally sanctioned way to honor and maintain connection with the dead.[6] Homes often contain an altar honoring a deceased family member. There may be a photo of the deceased along with an urn that contains funeral ashes. At any time, not only on a holiday or anniversary, family members may make offerings to the dead ancestor and go to the altar asking advice and counsel. The dead relative may be cherished, idealized, or even berated, but the connection is never broken with the past.

In his research, Robert Lifton was especially impressed with the concept of *chinkon,* which means "consolation of souls" and is derived from Shinto religious practices in Japan. *Chinkon* refers to a ceremony designed to bring repose to a soul that is hovering in limbo, between life and death. It requires an atmosphere of respect and love toward the dead, a gentle presence that combines continued connection with peaceful separation.[7] Lifton tells the story of a writer who survived the bombings and who used his writing about the tragedy as a way of maintaining a connection with the dead. Writing became a perfect metaphor for involvement at a distance. The writer must be connected to his material, but he cannot become lost in that material. The craft of writing allowed this one mourner to "stay in touch" while keeping a respectful distance.

One woman with whom I spoke who came from a Caribbean culture could not understand the discomfort Westerners felt about acknowledging their continuing communion with the dead. She grew up on a small island that had only one cemetery, so anyone who was buried on the island was buried there and every living islander had a relative who rested there. Every year, the community celebrated All Saints' and All Souls' Day, a day and evening that began with a candlelight procession to the cemetery. Islanders marched together to the graves of their ancestors. The candles were then placed around the gravestones and family members sat together for hours chatting and visiting. Everyone in the community was there. It was a great socializing event. Community members took a ritual food with them, made with corn and sugar, the only food permitted on this occasion. This was a day reserved for celebrating the dead. You could go to the cemetery on your own at any time throughout the year, but this was the one day the whole island went as a community.

Many years after the death of both her father and mother, this woman returned once again to her home to visit relatives both living and dead. "When I went home I went to my mother's grave. I sat on her gravestone and I mourned her death. I took photographs of her headstone and of my father's headstone and I said, 'Yes she is dead, but I'm able to mourn and grieve and miss her.' My parents are still a part of me. They are a part of my experience. I go to the cemetery with my sisters and sit there and take photographs, and chat, and laugh and look at my parents' headstones. It's like going home for a visit. It's part of what makes me whole." Her community and her culture have given her permission to maintain the connection with her dead mother and father. She looks forward to the day when she will have children of her own and when they will be introduced to the ritual of visiting with the dead and staying in touch with the past.

JASON'S STORY

Jason was an infant when his father died in Vietnam. He never knew the man after whom he had been named. As he was growing up, Jason would often ask people about his father but was rarely told more than that his father was a hero. Jason's father was in his early twenties when he died, and he left behind little more than his army medals and his high school yearbook. Jason remembers looking at the medals and reading the inscriptions in the yearbook, all of which referred to his father as a "great guy." Jason was searching for some clue as to just who his father had been. Because there were so few actual memories of his father, Jason had little on to which he might grasp in his search for information.

When he himself was in his early twenties, Jason was introduced to a group called Sons and Daughters. The group formed after the dedication of the Vietnam War Memorial in Washington, D.C., and it consisted of young men and women who had lost parents during the Vietnam War. Jason felt an instant bond with many of these people. "I feel like I have known them my whole life. It's amazing how much we can share." At last Jason had found a community of mourners, other young men and women who knew as little about their fathers as he knew about his own; young men and women who had grown up with the same longing and the same questions. "The common bond that we all seemed to share was that we didn't talk about the death. It was a relief for me to hear from other people that my family wasn't odd. Nobody's family talked about the war or the deaths." In the Sons and Daughters movement, Jason found a culture of mourners who not only allowed him to feel his grief, but also allowed him to begin talking about his father and actively try to understand the war that had taken his father's life.

Over the last several years Jason has made many trips to the Vietnam War Memorial. "I almost enjoy being at the Wall. It allows me to feel a little bit closer than I would if I were just trying to think about my father at home. I've been there under so many different situations, at three in the morning, with the group Sons and Daughters, laughing and crying. I definitely like being there."

Recently, Jason had the opportunity to participate in a national effort to bring the Vietnam memorial called "The Moving Wall" to people around the country. Separate segments of the wall were reproduced and taken to various cities. Jason decided to be a volunteer when the Moving Wall came to his hometown. He made contact with the organizers of the event that was to take place in the town where both he and his father had grown up. He participated in a ritual of twenty-four-hour name reading and was allowed to read the name of his father. He remembers one man in particular who came up to greet him with tears in his eyes. Jason looked so much like his own father, who had been a friend of this man's. Many people came up to Jason during the ceremony to tell him stories about his father. He learned things about his father that he had not known and had a sense of the world in which his father had grown up. During his visit home, his mother also shared with him the over two hundred letters his father had written home from his tour in Vietnam. Jason used these letters to acquaint himself further with the man who had been his father.

Although he has spent many hours volunteering to help families at the Wall, Jason remembers one ritual in particular that was especially moving for him and that made him feel as if he was in touch with the spirit of his father. A group of young men and women had gathered at the Wall for a holiday name-reading ceremony. Jason remembers one man who introduced himself as being from out of town. This man knew that his father's name would not be read until the middle of the night, and he suggested that the group go out for dinner. They all agreed that they would like to go and eat Vietnamese food, and as they sat around the table eating food from far away and drinking the Vietnamese beer their fathers must have enjoyed, they felt closer to the men who had died long ago and far away. After their meal, which felt as much like a ceremony as a dinner, they went back to the monument and waited for this man's father's name to be read. The group decided they would like to make something they could leave behind, something that symbolized the way they had all felt growing up. They stopped in a store and bought a box of toy logs that could be used to construct a small cabin. The group of men and women sat in a circle and built a little house. "It was the house that we were always waiting for our fathers to come back to. We carried it down to the monument and left it there. It stayed at the Basin for almost a week before they took it away. I took a photo of it and sent it to everyone in the group at Christmastime. It was really wonderful."

The Sons and Daughters group has given Jason an opportunity to build connections to his father and feel a sense of community and connection to others as he does so. When he goes to the Wall now, Jason feels that he shares a special communication with his father. "I know exactly where his name is. Put me in front of his panel and his name just pops out at me. When I'm there now, there is always some kind of communication going on. I think that's why I enjoy it. It gives me time to put everything else aside and just kind of say hello. I let him know what I'm doing or what I'm thinking. Sometimes I tell him about something that I might need help with. It's just nice to be there."

Jason has had the opportunity to build in death a relationship that never existed in life. In life he did not know his father. He had only scraps of information left behind by a man who died while he himself was still a boy. In his own adulthood, however, Jason has evolved a relationship with the spirit of his father, a relationship he now finds comforting and enriching, and a relationship that has allowed him to move into his own adulthood a stronger and more secure man.

Guardian Angels

I was at a funeral several years ago of a young woman whose death left behind two small children. The minister who had counseled the woman in the final days of her life told the congregation and her children in particular that she would be watching them from heaven throughout their lives. Ministers frequently talk about the watchful gaze of the departed as part of the funeral ritual. Yet I often wonder how much they actually intend that the family of the deceased will really come to believe they have an angel in heaven.

Several of the people with whom I spoke did indeed believe that the watchful eye of a long gone mother or father continued to oversee the events of their lives. Yet each person who told me of such a belief did so with an apology and some shyness. Adults are not really supposed to believe in guardian angels. Or are they? For many survivors of early loss, a continuing dialogue with one who has died becomes not only a way to stay in touch with a lost parent, but also an important part of one's adjustment to loss.

In the play *I Never Sang for My Father* by Robert Anderson, one of the characters says, "Death ends a life, but not a relationship."[8] A relationship with a dead parent may go on in some form or another for as long as the survivor continues to live. Often the dead parent is imagined to be a protector, a special spirit who looks out for the child throughout his or her life.

In the fairy tale *Cinderella,* Cinderella's mother tells her on her deathbed that she will be there to protect her daughter: "Dear child, be good and pious, and then the good God will always protect you, and I will look down on you from heaven and be near you."[9] When Cinderella needs help later in her life, she goes to the tree that has been planted on her mother's grave and asks for intervention. It is the spirit of her mother that not only protects her, but rescues her from her life of drudgery.

When Scott's mother died, she was elevated to a place of sainthood in the minds of her children. "We were so young when she died that she was perfect in our memory. We never got to the point of growing up and seeing her as a real woman." Throughout his childhood and after, Scott has felt the presence of his mother in his life. "I know she watches over me. I feel strongly that she picked out my wife for me; that it was my mother who led me to her and that my mother watches over me almost like a guardian angel. I just feel that.

I don't want to get too mystical about this, but I definitely feel that my mother is watching my life."

Once, several years after he was married, Scott lost his wedding ring. At first he was panicked. The ring was not only valuable but held great sentimental meaning for him. He sat down and thought about his mother. He conjured her image in his mind and then he retraced his steps during the day, taking himself back to a bus he had ridden earlier in the afternoon. He then located the bus and found the seat on which he had sat, and sure enough, under the chair lay the wedding ring. Scott was convinced that had it not been for the watchful eye of his mother, he never would have found the missing ring.

Often people feel the need to reconnect with the spirit of a lost parent at a time of important transition, a time when one might well feel the need for the support and encouragement of a living father or mother. One woman who still feels that she can sense her father's presence in almost everything she does remembers the night before she took her final graduate oral exams. "I remember the night before the exam. I was taking it in Michigan where I had grown up. I took a jog right by our old house; the house with the swimming pool where we used to live when my father was alive, and I had a conversation with my father. I remember thinking, Gee, I hope no one is looking out their window looking at this crazy woman, but it made me feel better to be able to talk to my father and to feel his support."

Another woman only resumed the dialogue with her father in adolescence after she had an important dream. She was a wild sixteen-year-old who had just received her driver's license. One night she dreamed of her father, who had died six years earlier. Her father's image appeared to her and he looked at her and said, "Take it easy, kid!" She remembers feeling that her father was reaching out to her, giving her the guidance and advice she needed as she entered the rebellious years of adolescence. She is now a woman in her forties with children of her own, but the dialogue begun in a dream has continued to this day.

After the dream, she began going to the cemetery by herself every Sunday. The cemetery visit was a time when she would sit down and talk to her father. She used him as daughters often use their parents, as an outer limit. If what she was doing was acceptable to tell her father, then it could not be something that was very bad. "I'd tell him about my latest boyfriend. If I broke curfew I would tell him that. I had no secrets from my father." She used this dialogue as a way to help her contain her own behavior. Just as Arthur Ashe had said about his mother, she never did anything that she would be ashamed to tell her father.

As the years went on, her relationship to her father changed. He became her confidant. She remembers telling him things before she would tell them to anyone else. "I even told him I was pregnant before I told my own husband." Her worries and fears for her children as well as her own anxieties as she tried to balance the many responsibilities of raising children were things she shared with her father. When each of her children was born, she took the child to the cemetery so that she could introduce them to the grandfather they would never know. At times she would lose her sense of self-consciousness and chat in an animated way, laughing, sometimes crying. "I remember thinking people driving by must think I'm a real nutcase. I don't mean that to be flip, but I'd be laughing or crying or talking and I guess it must have looked really weird."

Now that it is more difficult for her to make the trips to the cemetery, she continues the dialogue with her father inside her head. It's not something that happens every day, just once in a while when she feels the need to talk with him. Although the communication only goes in one direction, her conversations with her father are not unlike those of many adult daughters. She keeps in touch, maybe once a week or twice a month, just letting him know how her life is going and asking for advice when she feels she needs it.

Jack believes that he has changed his relationship with his father as the years have passed. His father died when Jack was a teenager. "I have brought him forward into my life. When I picture the two of us now, I'm an adult and he is an adult and I am talking to him as an adult. My father is the only person with whom I share my insecurities. I tell him about the things that trouble me and the doubts that I have for my future. I feel like I hold a spiritual conversation with my father, asking for his advice and his guidance. I do that with him and with no one else."

Several times a year, Jack drives to the cemetery where his father is buried. "I just sit there. It's good to know that he's there, but it is a very personal thing. I always feel better after leaving. But I don't tell anyone because I'm afraid people will think I'm neurotic or something." Jack, like the others who feel an ongoing bond with a parent who functions as a guardian angel or a spiritual confidant, does not do so as a substitute for having close and intimate relationships in the here and now. His connection to his father serves to enrich his life and gives him a connecting link to the past.

One woman said to me, "You bury a body, not a relationship, not your own sense of loss." Our relationships to the dead continue throughout our lives and are an important source of support and comfort. Several people said, "Why should I give up my connection to my mother or father? After all, you only have one mother; you only have one father."

Long life holds the promise of many meaningful relationships. Yet new relationships do not replace past ones. People, unlike objects, are not interchangeable. If we relinquish our attachment to a particular relationship, it is gone forever; another can not come in and assume its place. Our important relationships are to be treasured. A love that is brief may be no less meaningful than one that lasts a lifetime. We are enriched when we find some way to stay in touch with those we have loved deeply no matter how long ago they passed from our lives. As one woman said to me, "To lose touch with the past is to lose touch with yourself."

CHAPTER 12

~

Owning One's Destiny

THE FINAL STORY THE WISE bear tells to the grieving king in the fairy tale *Through the Mickle Woods* involves a weaver and an owl.[1] The owl comes to the weaver and asks her to weave his story into a beautiful cloth. At first he brings her clouds as beautiful as pearls. To these he adds moonbeams that shimmer like jewels. The weaver begins to work with these objects of great beauty, but she is unable to weave the cloth the owl desires. At first the owl is puzzled. He does not understand why she is unable to take all of these beautiful things and weave his story. The weaver tells him, "Sometimes the cloth will pattern itself, whether we will or no. You must bring everything; things chosen and things not."[2]

The owl sets off on a journey and returns to the weaver with all the things he has found. He brings back objects that are rich in color, some that are somber in mood, objects taken from places where peace reigned, others that he found at the site of tragedy. With these new elements, the weaver takes up her task and brings together the good and the bad, the beautiful and the ugly, all of the pieces of a life woven into a single cloth. When the owl finally wraps his story around him, it is filled with both joy and woe. It mixes together the light and the dark. It is the owl's own and true story, and when he wears it and spreads his wings, he looks like an angel.

For each of us, our life's story consists not only of the happiness and joys, but also of the traumas and tragedies. To be able to accept and own all of the parts of one's story is to embrace life fully. Friedrich Nietzsche, who sustained the early loss of his father, evolved a philosophy that was based on the premise that one must embrace one's fate in its entirety if one is to live a happy and successful life: "My formula for greatness for a human being is amor fati: that one wants nothing to be different, not forward, not backward, not in all eternity."[3]

Nietzsche was concerned that trauma and tragedy would lead to bitterness and anger. When a man or woman feels always deprived and cheated, resentment builds. Life is not appreciated for what it is, but despised for what it is not. Nietzsche feared that such resentment would act like a cancer on the core of one's spirit, destroying all that was good. He saw only one antidote to the danger of resentment: one must love one's fate. Not only must joys and pleasures be embraced, but trauma and pain as well.

A life consists of many parts, and each part, regardless of how important or trivial it may seem, contributes to who one becomes. It is not uncommon to hear people say, "Well, if I could do it over again (my life), I would only change one thing. . . ." When we make such a statement, we often fail to appreciate the complete interdependence of events. We imagine that we could have gone to a different college, married someone else, or lived in a different city and yet somehow still become the person we are today. Nietzsche believed that in order to own one's destiny and to affirm one's life, one needs not merely to accept every aspect of one's past and every part of the present, but also to embrace them.

Nietzsche saw the fundamental connection among all events. "Have you ever said Yes to a single joy? O my friends then you have said Yes too to all woe. All things are entangled, ensnared, enamored. . . ."[4] For Nietzsche to have changed the circumstances of his early childhood and erased the tragic death of his father would have been to change the circumstances that allowed him to become who he was. Nietzsche believed that one cannot say, "I love my life except for the untimely death of my father." If Nietzsche's father had lived, Nietzsche would not have been the Nietzsche he was, instead he would have been someone else. The man he became grew from soil that combined early triumphs with early losses. If the early loss had not been present, the soil would have been different; the plant that grew would have grown differently.

Some of the people with whom I spoke were quite aware that the early death of a parent was key to the very formation of the person they had become. Although they could feel compassion for the parent whose life had been snatched away so young, they also felt a sense of gratitude for the experiences that made them who they were.

The ability to embrace the entirety of one's fate may take a variety of different forms. For some, the acceptance of who one is comes after a period of struggle. These individuals reclaim a destiny they once felt was lost. For others, there is an ongoing tension between personal control and fate. Still others seem to be survivor proud, possessing a sense of personal accomplishment at having survived tragedy. Some others openly acknowledge that they like the person they have become as a result of early loss. And still others are passionate about the intense personal will that has allowed them not only to own but also to create their destiny.

Reclaiming One's Destiny

Some people clearly recall going through a phase during which they felt cheated and deprived because of the early loss of a parent. Their loss seemed to set them apart from others and make the task of becoming a person all the more difficult. For these individuals, several factors contributed to their ultimately reclaiming their own destiny. In some cases, age was an important marker. Once past the age of a parent's death, they felt freed to live their own lives. In other cases, a period of floundering and disorganization was followed by a time during which an individual took him- or herself to task. One man recalls, "I said to myself, 'You've got to get it together because no one else is going to do it for you.' At that point, I began to say, 'I am in control of my own destiny and ultimately I am re-

sponsible for myself. I do not have to be dependent on someone else.' " A life that felt disorganized and in the hands of
some unknown fate suddenly came together, and this man felt
that he was in charge of his own future.

For most individuals, however, destiny is reclaimed through
success. One man who recalled feeling deprived as a child said,
"No one could look at my life and say that I have been disad-
vantaged. I have a great job. I am happily married. I live in a
wonderful house. I am healthy. I feel as if I have succeeded
against all odds." Another man commented, "Nothing ever
fills the void, but it is easier when you have had successes and
been able to achieve some of your dreams." It is harder to continue to believe that one has been cheated and deprived when
one sees the obvious signs of a successful and fulfilled life.

Another man said, "I felt cheated and very much disadvan-
taged when I was younger. Now I feel like I was cheated but I
am not at a disadvantage anymore." Through hard work, perseverance, and accomplishment, one balances the scales. The
heavy weight of early loss is counterbalanced by the success
and accomplishment of midlife. One man commented, "Even
without a father, I have demonstrated that I can win by the
standards and rules of the world. My sense now is that the responsibility for my life is completely my own. It's my choice;
how I spend my time, what I do. Sometimes I have problems
making the right choices, but they are my choices to make. It
all comes from the inside now."

The Tension between Personal Control and Fate

A Chinese proverb reads, "You cannot prevent the birds of
sorrow from flying overhead, but you can prevent them from
building nests in your hair."[5] Eleanor Roosevelt believed that
the true measure of a person was not his or her achievements,
but rather the way in which he or she adapted to life's changes.[6]
Fate presents each of us with a set of circumstances, cards dealt
at the beginning of the game over which we have no control.

One does have control, however, in how one chooses to play the hand. As any seasoned card player knows, it is easy to play a hand when one has been dealt good cards. In fact, it takes special effort to lose when one's cards are certain winners. It is much more difficult to play wisely and skillfully when one has been dealt bad cards.

Some survivors of early loss felt that they had created themselves in the face of adversity. They did not deny that fate had dealt them a bad hand, but they did not linger long with self-pity. Rather, they focused on the ways they had lived their lives despite adverse circumstance. Jean-Paul Sartre is known to have especially liked a quote from Karl Marx: "Men make their own history, but not in any way they please; they make it under circumstances not chosen by themselves. . . ."[7] We do not choose the circumstances under which we must create ourselves. Yet it is our task to create ourselves nonetheless.

Shawna, whose single mother died when Shawna was only two, wonders about the origin of her own intense desire to survive. "I don't even know what was inside of me. I just knew I was going to survive. I knew I had to. I had to keep going. I wanted a different life for myself." As she looked around her at young boys and girls becoming involved in drugs and criminal activities, she knew that she had a choice to make her life different. She also knew that anger and resentment would lead only to self-destruction. "There was no point in feeling sorry for myself. I knew it would only put me in a worse situation. I would fall back on things that could not help me at all: drugs, alcohol, whatever. There was no point. It was only going to hinder my progress and I knew I wanted more. I just wanted more."

By the time she was a teenager, Shawna had already evolved her own philosophy of life: "As I see it, you have two choices. You can think the world owes you something: 'I've been cheated, I've been neglected,' and you can go off in a corner somewhere and feel sorry for yourself. Or you can say to yourself, 'This is it. These are the cards that life has dealt me. I had no control over it but now I can do something about my future.' "

Shawna's intense personal will allowed her to find a surrogate mother who helped in her reparenting during early adulthood. It also has allowed her to be the only member of her family ever to attend and graduate from college and to achieve a level of professional success and accomplishment in the world. Shawna feels that she is responsible for her own destiny and her own future. When she meets someone she tells them, "I come with no baggage. This is who I am. If you want a relationship with me, you have me. That's it. There is no one else you need to look around to or to report to. The only person you have to report to in our relationship is me." Shawna firmly believes that she will rise or fall on the power of her own will.

Ever since his father was killed in a car accident, Luke has assumed responsibility for his life and his decisions. Luke never recalls feeling sorry for himself. He was different from the other boys in his neighborhood, all of whom had fathers, but he always tried to make the most of his experiences and to get the most from the many mentors who guided his early development and later growth. Rather than feeling envious or resentful about what he did not have, Luke assumed responsibility for getting what he could from the opportunities that came along. "I take responsibility for myself. That's the way I've led my life. Taking responsibility doesn't mean taking blame for anything. It just means you take responsibility for where you are, what you are, and what you are doing, whatever that may be. If you don't have a father, you don't have a father. You just take responsibility for what you're doing in your life at that time. That's not something that has ever been a problem for me." Luke has little tolerance for people who assume a victim mentality. "At times, life serves up adversity, but one does not need to be defeated by bad circumstances. One must pick oneself up and fight on." Luke did that in his own life, and he expects nothing less from others.

Many of the people with whom I spoke had a similar sense of intolerance for weakness and self-pity. It was not that they denied that certain circumstances were unfortunate or even tragic, but they appreciated their own will to fight on and they expected the same level of passionate commitment to life on the part of others. They also knew the difference between real adversity and trauma and everyday trials and tribulations. One man recalled with much disdain a friend who complained of being unable to balance her checkbook after the untimely death of her husband. Her complaint may just have been a way of expressing her loss and her sense of being overwhelmed. Yet, this survivor of early loss had no tolerance for her problem. Of course it was sad and unfortunate that her husband had died, but it was now her responsibility to take charge of her life and to become a self-sufficient woman.

Patrick was dealt a bad hand when his father died when he was only three, but the dealer took another of Patrick's cards away when four years later his stepfather also died. Before he was eight years old, Patrick had lost two fathers. By the time he was twelve, his mother had remarried for the third time and Patrick changed his name once again as he prepared to become the son of yet another man. Patrick remembers thinking that it would be easy to feel angry; easy to be resentful. Occasionally his grandmother would tell him what a "poor sad boy" he was and remind him of how he was not treated like a true son by his adoptive father. As his grandmother would talk, Patrick remembers thinking, I don't want to hear this. These words will take me down a road I do not want to go. The path of resentment was a dead end, and although he was only thirteen, Patrick knew that. Patrick thought about his life with his new stepfather and his newly acquired extended family, and he decided that he could find a good life for himself within this new family. Like the boy who comes downstairs on Christmas morning and sees a pile of manure under the Christmas tree only to declare happily, "Where's the pony? Where's the pony?" Patrick looked at his life, a young life marked by two serious losses, and always asked himself in every new situation, regardless of how promising it did or did not seem, "What good can I find here?"

Unlike his younger brother, who became angry and resentful, Patrick found a way not only to learn from his new father but to love him as well. Patrick's affection was returned and he developed a relationship with his third father that mentored him into adulthood. When he looks back on his life, Patrick refuses to label his losses as tragedies. "Life has been good to me.

Things work out for the best. My whole life has been an affirmation of that."

Charlotte Brontë, whose life was filled with loss, came to believe that what could not be helped "imperatively must be borne."[8] Yet one has a choice in how one bears the traumas of childhood. Some ignore their scars, others bare them proudly as badges of honor and triumph. Brontë said of a character in her final novel, *Vilette,* "Before calamity she is a tigress . . . on sickness, on death itself, she looks with the eye of a rebel."[9] A determined and confident card player can play even a bad hand with dignity, and if he or she is just a bit lucky, he or she may even win the game.

Survivor Pride

Much has been written about survivor guilt, the sense that survivors of tragedy have that they survive at the expense of those who died.[10] Survivor guilt often leaves one unable to enjoy the pleasures of a healthy life. Rather than feeling guilty, however, some survivors of early loss felt proud at their own accomplishment and their own triumph over adversity. One man felt quite clear that he had survived in spite of his abusive family. His mother had died when he was a young boy, leaving him with a critical and cruel father and eventually a passive stepmother. Survival was the only issue growing up, and he now feels that he has made it, almost as if he beat the odds and survived not because of his family but in spite of them. "It is now my target to live longer than my father. I feel that I have earned the right to a long life. My life is good. Sure my knees click when I walk up and down the stairs but I'm still here and kicking." He feels proud of his accomplishments and determined to embrace life fully.

At the end of our interview, he told me a story of sitting with some friends and talking about a relative who had recently died. The room was heavy with gloom as the group reminisced about this lost friend. He remembers turning to the window and opening the curtains, revealing a beautiful sunset. His decision has always been to turn toward life, to refuse to be mired either in the past or in the despair of loss.

Another woman felt similarly when she boasted, "I see myself as a survivor. People have said I have an incredibly high threshold for pain. I have come through major losses and I have survived completely." Throughout her career, she has been actively involved in the women's movement and she talked candidly about what she believed to be an overemphasis on female victimization. Like many recent feminist writers, she wanted to see a woman's strength and accomplishments recognized. She was tired of the focus on the abuse and victimization that women have endured. "You rarely see images of strong, self-sufficient, happy women. Mothers and their children just growing and getting along fine and healthy, but I know it's really possible." She speculated that it would be nice to see women's organizations give awards that recognize women who have survived adversity. She laughed as she said, "What we need is some positive reinforcement for those of us who have made it." She is proud of herself for having survived and created a successful life for herself.

Another woman who is equally proud of her ability to triumph over adversity was almost affronted when a friend worried that she might be having a difficult time following the breakup of a new romance. She thought to herself, Do you know who you're talking to? Of course I will survive. What do you expect me to do? I have been down this road before. I can survive anything.

In the final stage of successful mourning, children come to see loss and their ability to survive as part of the same tapestry. Rather than feeling overwhelmed by grief and despair, they are aware of their own strength to manage adversity. Family therapist Claudia Jewett comments, "The child reorganizes herself to get on with life. It is as if she says, 'The worst possible thing that could happen did happen, and I survived it. Now I'm ready to get back to the business of living and growing.' "[11] This sense of survivor pride fortifies and strengthens those who are fortunate enough to have it throughout their entire lives.

Liking One's Life

Toward the end of their interviews, a number of people commented spontaneously that they liked the person they had become as a result of having sustained an early loss. Often individuals pointed to particular traits or qualities: an ability to be sensitive to the needs and longings of others, a sense of independence and self-reliance, a determination to persevere despite difficult times. Each of these survivors believed that these personal qualities were born and nurtured through the adversity of early loss. Since they now valued and affirmed the person they had become, they felt uneasy damning the tragic circumstances that had helped them to grow into the men and women they now were. "How can I rail against fate when fate has made me who I am?"

One woman who had been the adored daughter of a loving father commented about the kind of woman she might have become if her father had lived. "I probably would have been a snooty little rich girl. When I see women like that now I really don't like them. I'm sure I would have been a lot more spoiled if my father had lived. My life would have been easier, but perhaps I would not have appreciated things as much. The loss of my father made me a more complete person. In order to have a full character, you have to have bad things happen to you. Going through my father's death made me a deep and caring person. I think it also made me a better person." She loved her father dearly, and his loss caused her and her family great pain, yet she has become a woman of deep compassion, and part of what she loves about herself is her ability to give unselfishly and to empathize with the pain of others.

FRANK'S STORY

Frank was only three years old when his father died in an industrial accident. He was the youngest child and the only son of a large and close-knit Greek family. Because Frank had three older sisters who ranged from ten to eighteen years older than he, Frank remembers growing up feeling as if he had four mothers instead of one. His mother and his older sisters made him feel loved, adored, and special.

While he was growing up, Frank's family occupied the top floor of a large apartment building. Everyone in the building was a cousin, aunt, or uncle of Frank's, and the members of this large extended family eagerly opened their doors to the little boy who had no father. Frank remembers being loved and welcomed, but most importantly, he remembers feeling secure.

Frank has often thought that if his father had lived, his childhood and his life would have been quite different. As his father's only son, Frank would have been expected to follow in his father's footsteps. He would have been pushed to enter his father's profession and he would have learned how to be a man from his "macho and patriarchal father." Frank is quite sure that he would have been a very different man if his father had survived to help raise him.

When he looks at his contemporaries, young men who grew up in the neighborhood where Frank was raised, Frank sees many men he does not like. These are men who drink hard, gamble, beat their wives, and insist on their right to rule their families. "I'm glad I'm not like that and I don't know how I would have escaped if my father had lived." Instead, Frank was raised in a household of women. His mother and sisters taught him to be nurturing and family oriented. Frank remembers "hanging out" with his mother in the kitchen, talking and chatting and learning to cook just the way his sisters did and the way girls often do with their mothers. His mother would gossip and tell stories about people in the neighborhood. Frank remembers listening intently and learning about life from his mother's stories. Instead of cruising the neighborhood with his father, Frank was in the kitchen with his mother, learning how relationships work, developing empathy for people's feelings, and becoming what he jokingly calls "that sensitive man that women are always looking for."

Frank's mother was a gentle woman who was known as a caretaker within her community. Frank believes that he learned to be gentle from his mother. His gentleness is something he loves about himself. When he asks people about his father, he hears no stories of tenderness or softness. His father is described as flamboyant, loud, fun-loving, charismatic, but never as soft. Frank wonders what this very masculine father would have done with a gentle son, and whether or not it would have been possible for Frank to become a sensitive man if his father had lived.

Frank also believes that the absence of a father gave him a sense that he could accomplish anything. There was no father to rebel against. There was also no father to set limits. His mother adored him and she nurtured him in the belief that he could accomplish anything he set out to do. Because in his mother's eyes he could do no wrong, Frank also believes that he learned that he could get away with anything. When he did not want to go to school he would ask his mother to write a note to the teachers. He could always charm his mother into complying with his wishes. He can even remember now the note that she would write explaining why her son needed to stay home.

Like Sartre, who grew up fatherless with an adoring mother, Frank grew up without a sense of his own limitations. Frank seemed to know that his father's death freed him from certain inevitable constraints. There was no king to honor. There were no dragons that needed to be slayed. Sartre said of himself, "A father would have weighted me with a certain stable obstinacy. Making his moods my principles, his ignorance my knowledge, his disappointments my pride, his quirks my law, he would have inhabited me. . . . My begetter would have determined my future."[12]

Because there was no father to teach him how to be a man, Frank treasured the few lessons he was taught, and he turned some of the stories of his childhood into a personal philosophy for living. When he was nine years old, Frank remembers, he wanted to play softball with some friends. The boys discovered, however, that they did not have the right ball for their game. Frank remembers going to one of his uncles and asking for some money. Frank did not realize that his uncle had just recently been dismissed from his job and was now unemployed, needing all of his limited resources to take care of his own family. Frank's uncle reached into his pocket and gave him the two dollars needed to buy the ball. When he went home that evening, Frank told his mother about the wonderful day he had had and about his uncle's generosity. Frank's mother was appalled. "Don't you know that Uncle Jimmie doesn't have a job? He must have given you his last two dollars to buy that softball." Frank remembers sitting down and thinking to himself, "No matter how little you have, you must always share it with family. Family comes first. You literally give those related by blood the shirt from your back. That tied me closer than anything to my family."

Throughout his life, Frank has not only been a good son to his mother, but a responsive and caring brother to his sisters. He has supported each of his sisters in times of crisis, not only emotionally but financially as well. He remembers once when one of his sisters was in financial trouble, he took a check from his savings account and signed it. He handed his sister the blank check and said to her, "Just use it if you need it for as much as you need." His sister never cashed the check, but she carries it with her still, a sign of Frank's commitment and loyalty to his family.

Frank remembers going hunting at the age of twelve with another one of his uncles. He grew up in a family where boys learned to shoot guns early and hunting was a part of family life and male camaraderie. Frank remembers sighting a deer with his rifle. He had his finger on the trigger, but he could not shoot. Frank put his gun down, ashamed at his failure "to be a man." He remembers his uncle putting his arm around him and saying, "Frankie, that's okay. Not everyone has to be a hunter." His uncle was giving him permission to be the boy he was, permission that allowed him to honor his own gentle side. Frank is certain that if his father had lived, his father would not have responded similarly. His father would have insisted that he learn how to shoot, that he learn how to hunt, and that he become a certain kind of man. Frank is confident and successful: "I live my life as if I am going to get what I want and I usually do." As he approaches his fortieth birthday, Frank is pleased with the man he has become and he is quite certain that he would have been a very different man, a man he might have liked less, if he had been raised by his father.

Personal Will

One needs passion, courage, and determination to assume responsibility for one's destiny. In some cases, however, an almost defiant refusal to be thwarted becomes the driving force behind the creation of the self. For these individuals, no is never an acceptable answer.

When Iosif Dzugashvili lost his father, a shoemaker, in boyhood, he lost a brutal oppressor, a man who beat him and spent what little money the family had on drunken binges. When his father died, the boy wanted revenge for the pain he had endured. He became fiercely determined to re-create the world in his own image and to let nothing stand in his way. He renamed himself Stalin, "man of steel."[13] When his father died, Stalin was freed of the shoemaker's legacy. He was no longer to follow in his father's footsteps, adhering to his father's limited ambitions. Stalin was free to create his own destiny and to inflict his vision of the world on an entire country.

Fierce will does not always manifest itself as evil. For some, it is tenacious determination and an unwillingness to accept no for an answer.

KEITH'S STORY

Before his father's death when Keith was twelve, Keith's boyhood was uneventful. He had been adopted by a middle-aged couple who had no sense of play or adventure, and Keith spent many hours amusing himself with books and fantasies. When his father died, he felt little sadness because he believed that he had never received much love or guidance from him. In the years after his father's death, Keith convinced himself that if there were any effects from losing a father, they were all positive. Before he finally left home at age sixteen to join the military, Keith spent four years running wild. His aging mother had little experience with a growing boy and no idea of how to tame or nurture her son.

Once Keith left home, he returned only five times to visit his mother before her own death ten years later. As he was going through his mother's papers, Keith discovered his birth certificate. He had always known that he was adopted, but now he had proof, a birth certificate that had a name on it he had never seen before. Keith began asking people about his birth parents. Who were they? Where had they come from? His relatives gave him a number of stories: "Oh, your father was a professor at the local college and your mother was one of his students." "No, your father was a doctor and your mother was one of his nurses." None of these was true, and Keith knew from the way his relatives told the stories that they were inventing information for their curious nephew. Keith was determined to find out who he was. For the next ten years, Keith embarked on an off-and-on search to learn the story of his birth. He was tenacious in his determination to know his roots and to own his destiny fully.

Knowing the year and city of his birth, Keith first went to the hall of records to obtain a listing of all births occurring in that year, in that particular town. The list was long but Keith held on to it nonetheless, determined to find out who his mother and father had been. For five years he tracked down every woman who might possibly have been his mother. Many times he said to himself, "Why am I doing this? Do I really want to do this? Why do I care, anyway?" And finally he just said, "I want to know. I am willing to face whatever the truth is. I just want to know." When he finally made the call that led to his birth mother, Keith picked up the phone and said in a matter-of-fact voice, "I have reason to believe that you are my mother. I know you could lie to me and tell me you are not, but I believe you are and I am asking you to tell me the truth." Keith assured the woman on the other end of the line, as he had done so many times before, that he had no desire to disrupt her life. He only wanted to know who he was. Keith's biological mother finally told him her story, the circumstances of his birth, and a few details about her family. Keith discovered that he had brothers, sisters, and cousins with whom he might be able to build a relationship. Several years after his search began, it had ended, but not quite.

Keith had only answered half of the story for himself. He still needed to know who his father had been and something about the other side of his heritage. Keith asked his biological mother for information. When she refused, he began his investigation once again. She had told him enough so that this time his search was more manageable. Keith discovered that his father had died many years ago, killed in a hunting accident when he himself was a young man. There was no father Keith could meet and get to know, but his father was survived by a mother and an older brother. Once again, Keith was determined to meet these missing members of his family. He prepared himself emotionally, mustered his courage, and went to find the remaining members of his father's family.

Keith recalls one Saturday morning knocking on the door of an old house in a small town. When the gentle woman with graying hair answered the door, he responded once again in a matter-of-fact voice, saying, "I have reason to believe that I am your grandson." His resemblance to his long dead father was sufficient to convince the old woman within a matter of minutes. Keith spent the afternoon with a grandmother he had never known, hearing stories about a father whose name he had only recently learned. As an adult, Keith has maintained connections to the families of his biological mother and father.

Fierce determination and an overriding belief in personal will and power have been hallmarks of Keith's life. He has brought determination and passion to raising his children and achieving worldly success. His professional résumé is several pages long and boasts multiple awards and honors. Keith has been determined to create his own destiny and has been unyielding in his search for the truth. Many would have abandoned the hunt that took Keith deep into the past. Few would have persevered for as long as the search demanded. Keith wanted and needed nothing from his relatives. For himself, however, he needed to know who he was.

In Chinese culture, the symbol for crisis combines danger with opportunity. For some, the trauma of early loss provided the opportunity to create the self. Some people became strong, more self-reliant, and more compassionate as a result of having sustained the early death of a parent. Nietzsche said once,

"That which does not kill me, makes me stronger."[14] Some survivors clearly felt strengthened by their triumph over adversity.

After his interviews with the survivors of Hiroshima, Robert Lifton concluded that resolution of the trauma required that one accept an essential human paradox.[15] One must be both passive and active in the face of disaster. A child, and then an adult, needs to accept the reality of loss. One may rail against heaven for a time, but cursing the fates cannot become a lifelong preoccupation. Acceptance must be followed by action and a determination to create one's own life and to continue living in the face of death.

As I was concluding the interview with one woman who was in her midsixties, she turned to me and asked, "Is this loss something you ever get over?" "No," I replied, "the pain may go away, but the loss is forever." "I thought so," she said.

The experience of loss is woven into the fabric of one's very being. Even for survivors who insisted that "they never even think of the deceased parent anymore" the experience of early loss was indelibly written across their life experience. At the conclusion of his autobiography, Sartre wrote, "One gets rid of a neurosis, one doesn't get cured of one's self."[16] When a parent dies young, the experience of loss and the creation of the self are forever merged.

Epilogue

When I first set out to write *The Loss That Is Forever*, I was clear that I did not want to write an advice book. If people took advice from what I wrote, fine, but that was not my intent.

After many hours of interviews and much soul-searching, I decided to add this brief epilogue. So many people left the interview urging me to write something that would be useful to a young person who was just beginning to deal with loss. These men and women wanted their experiences to reach out and help others. These final remarks are dedicated, with my deepest gratitude, to the sixty-six men and women who shared their stories with me.

Remember. Your memories are all you have of the mother or father who is no longer there. Do not let those memories slip away. At times it will be hard. You will want to forget in order to drive the pain away. But forgetting is a voracious beast—it gobbles up everything in sight. Soon the good times are lost and forgotten along with the bad. One woman, who remembers very little of her mother, told me that even now she has to work hard not to let forgetfulness blank out her recollections of things that happened even just a few weeks ago.

If you were too young to have any memories of your own, then you must ask others. Someone remembers your mother;

someone knew who your father was. These borrowed memories can help you construct an image of the parent you never knew. And you'd be surprised: that image, alive only in your mind and in your heart, can bring you comfort.

Talk about your loss. In our very open society, there are only a few things we will not discuss easily with one another—unfortunately death is one of them. People feel awkward talking about their loss, especially if it happened a long time ago. And others—even close friends—feel awkward listening. Don't let that awkwardness stop you. Talking about the death and the feelings you have often brings a sense of relief. These are normal feelings and it's okay to be public about them. Once you are out of the closet yourself, you will discover that there are many many others like you, others who can understand exactly how you feel because they have been there themselves. It feels wonderful to find another survivor who knows what you are going through firsthand. Pain is miraculously halved when it is shared.

One woman told me of her feelings while marching in a Gay and Lesbian Pride parade. She held her banner high and felt a part of a community as she marched openly with other lesbians. Yet on the inside, she still felt separate and alone. You see, she had another secret she never shared with anyone. Her father had died when she was seven, and she still cried like a little girl when she remembered him. She longed for a fellowship of mourners, others who had known death at too early an age and could understand her longings and her dreams. She was comfortable being out of the closet about her sexuality—she felt more uneasy being public about her loss.

Don't give up hope. C. S. Lewis remarked that grief feels like fear—the sensations are the same.[1] When death first happens you may find yourself unable to breathe, much less think or even feel. Some survivors doubt they will be able to go on living. Everything feels so changed, so unknown, so awful. Yet all sixty-six of the men and women who have told their stories here did survive. They struggled; they hurt; they cried; and (not *but*) they went on to become courageous and strong adults.

Richard Rhodes tells a story of one summer at camp when the scout leader drove the troop into the woods and instructed the boys to search for a personal totem from the spirit world. Each boy was told to build a fire and meditate until the right totem revealed itself. The boy could then retrieve his talisman and store it for safekeeping in a soft leather medicine pouch. Rhodes waited for a long time but no sign came. It began to rain, and Rhodes despaired of ever finding his totem. As he looked at his fast fading fire, he noticed one small ember that refused to be doused by the rain. Rhodes knew he had found his spirit magic—his true totem—"a burning center that held back the dark."[2]

It may be hard to believe when a mother or father first dies that you too have an unquenchable life force inside you. It was kindled by the mother or father you loved, and if nurtured, it can grow into a mighty blaze.

None of this means that you won't continue to hurt from time to time. Some ache will be there forever—that's just the way it is. But you can survive and, like so many of those who speak out here, you may come to feel stronger for what you have endured.

Endnotes

CHAPTER ONE

1. Virginia Woolf, "A Sketch of the Past," in *Moments of Being* (San Diego: Harcourt Brace Jovanovich, 1985), p. 81.

2. Ibid., p. 84.

3. Robert Bruce, "Lincoln and the Riddle of Death," *The Fourth Annual R. Gerald McMurtry Lecture* (Ft. Wayne, Indiana, 1981), pp. 6–7.

4. George Steiner, "The Long Life of Metaphor: An Approach to the Shoah," in *Writing and the Holocaust*, ed. Berel Lang, (New York: Holmes & Meier, 1988), pp. 154–171; Robert Lifton, *Death in Life* (Chapel Hill: University of North Carolina Press, 1991).

5. Berel Lang, "Introduction," in *Writing and the Holocaust*, ed. Berel Lang, (New York: Holmes & Meier, 1988), pp. 1–15.

6. *American Heritage Dictionary* (Boston: Houghton Mifflin Co., 1969).

7. Robert Lifton, *Death in Life*, p. 30.

8. Virginia Woolf, "A Sketch of the Past," in *Moments of Being,* p. 84.

9. Alexandre Dumas, *My Memoirs,* translated by A. Craig Bell, (Westport, Conn.: Greenwood Press, 1961).

10. Virginia Woolf, "Reminiscences," in *Moments of Being,* p. 40.

11. Tove Ditlevsen, "Self Portrait 2," in *The Other Voice,* ed. Joanna Bankier et al., (New York: W. W. Norton, 1976), p. 28.

12. Russell Baker, *Growing Up* (New York: Signet, 1982), p. 81.

13. Ibid., p. 79.

14. John Berryman, "Poem 101," in *The Dream Songs* (New York: Farrar, Straus & Giroux, 1959), p. 118.

15. C. S. Lewis, *Surprised by Joy* (San Diego: Harcourt Brace, 1956), p. 21.

16. Liv Ullmann, *Changing* (New York: Alfred A. Knopf, 1977), p. 12.

17. Arthur Ashe, *Days of Grace* (New York: Alfred A. Knopf, 1993), p. 50.

18. Richard Rhodes, *A Hole in the World* (New York: Simon & Schuster, 1990).

19. Ibid., p. 15.

20. Ibid.

21. Ibid., p. 21.

22. Ellen Fine, "The Absent Memory," in *Writing and the Holocaust,* ed. Berel Lang, (New York: Holmes & Meier, 1988), p. 49.

23. Ibid., p. 45.

24. Ibid., p. 45.

CHAPTER TWO

1. Emily Dickinson, "The Bustle in a House," in *The Oxford Book of Death,* ed. D. J. Enright, (Oxford University Press, 1987), p. 103.

2. Sandra Bertman, *Facing Death* (Washington, D.C.: Hemisphere Publishing, 1991), p. 16.

3. Ibid.

4. C. S. Lewis, *Surprised by Joy* (San Diego: Harcourt Brace, 1956), p. 19.

5. Arthur Ashe, *Days of Grace* (New York: Alfred A. Knopf, 1993), p. 304.

6. John Berryman, "Poem 107," in *The Dream Songs* (New York: Farrar, Straus & Giroux, 1959), p. 144.

7. D. J. Enright, *The Oxford Book of Death* (Oxford: Oxford University Press, 1987), p. 88.

8. Raymond Carver, "What We Talk about When We Talk about Love," in *What We Talk about When We Talk about Love* (New York: Vintage Books, 1989), p. 142.

9. Russell Baker, *Growing Up* (New York: Signet, 1982), p. 79.

10. Robert Lifton, *The Broken Connection: On Death and the Continuity of Life* (New York: Basic Books, 1983), p. 244.

11. John-Paul Sartre, *The Words* (New York: Vintage Books, 1981), p. 94.

CHAPTER THREE

1. Richard Rhodes, *A Hole in the World* (New York: Simon & Schuster, 1990), p. 61.

2. Froma Walsh & Monica McGoldrick, "Loss and the Family: A Systematic Perspective," in *Living Beyond*

Loss, eds. Froma Walsh and Monica McGoldrick, (New York: W. W. Norton, 1991), pp. 1–29.

3. Virginia Woolf, "A Sketch of the Past," in *Moments of Being* (San Diego: Harcourt Brace Jovanovich, 1985), p. 94.

4. C. S. Lewis, *Surprised by Joy* (San Diego: Harcourt Brace, 1956), p. 19.

5. Howard Kushner, *Self-Destruction in the Promised Land* (New Brunswick: Rutgers University Press, 1989), p. 134.

6. David Dalton, *James Dean: The Mutant King* (New York: St. Martin's Press, 1974).

7. Rebecca Fraser, *The Brontës* (New York: Fawcett Columbine, 1988), p. 22.

8. Helene Moglen, *Charlotte Brontë: The Self Conceived* (Madison, Wisconsin: The University of Wisconsin Press, 1984), p. 20.

9. Richard Rhodes, *A Hole in the World* (New York: Simon & Schuster, 1990), p. 222.

10. Maxine Harris, *Down from the Pedestal* (New York: Doubleday, 1994).

CHAPTER FOUR

1. Russell Baker, *Growing Up* (New York: Signet, 1982).

2. Carl Pletsch, *Young Nietzsche* (New York: The Free Press, 1991).

3. Ibid.

4. Virginia Woolf, "Reminiscences," in *Moments of Being* (San Diego: Harcourt Brace Jovanovich, 1985), p. 32.

5. Virginia Woolf, "A Sketch of the Past," in *Moments of Being,* p. 89.

6. Bruce Duffy, "Feeling Something: When a Father Dies," *Harper's Magazine,* June 1990, p. 71.

7. Eleanor Roosevelt, *The Autobiography of Eleanor Roosevelt* (New York: Harper & Bros., 1937), p. 5.

8. Joseph Lash, *"Life Was Meant to Be Lived": A Centenary Portrait of Eleanor Roosevelt* (New York: W. W. Norton, 1984), p. 35.

9. Joseph Lash, *Eleanor and Franklin* (New York: W. W. Norton, 1971), p. 58.

10. Helene Moglen, *Charlotte Brontë: The Self Conceived* (Madison, Wisconsin: University of Wisconsin Press, 1984), p. 191.

11. Ibid., p. 194.

12. Gloria Vanderbilt, *Once Upon a Time* (New York: Ballantine, 1985), p. 31.

13. Duffy, "Feeling Something: When a Father Dies," p. 72.

14. Shelly Taylor, *Positive Illusions* (New York: Basic Books, 1989).

CHAPTER FIVE

1. Rebecca Fraser, *The Brontës* (New York: Fawcett Columbine, 1988), p. 66.

2. Ibid., p. 138.

3. Helene Moglen, *Charlotte Brontë: The Self Conceived* (Madison, Wisconsin: University of Wisconsin Press, 1984), p. 26.

4. Arthur Ashe, *Days of Grace* (New York: Alfred A. Knopf, 1993), p. 4.

5. Joseph Lash, *Eleanor and Franklin* (New York: W. W. Norton, 1971), p. 3.

6. Ibid., p. 46.

7. Carl Pletsch, *Young Nietzsche* (New York: The Free Press, 1991), p. 45.

8. Friedrich Nietzsche, "Schopenhauer as Educator," in *Untimely Meditations* (Cambridge: Cambridge University Press, 1983), p. 130.

9. Pletsch, *Young Nietzsche*, p. 74.

10. Ibid., p. 174.

11. Adrienne Rich, "Jane Eyre: The Temptations of a Motherless Woman," *Ms. Magazine*, October 1973, pp. 68ff.

12. Jean-Paul Sartre, *The Words* (New York: Vintage Books, 1981), p. 19.

13. Ibid., p. 32.

14. Ibid., p. 23.

15. Ronald Hayman, *Sartre: A Biography* (New York: Carroll & Graf Publishers, 1987), p. 394.

16. Ibid., p. 61.

17. Sartre, *The Words*, p. 172.

18. Hayman, *Sartre*, p. 308.

19. Ibid., p. 394.

20. Sartre, *The Words*, p. 206.

21. Ibid., p. 172.

22. David Dalton, *James Dean: The Mutant King* (New York: St. Martin's Press, 1974), p. 248.

23. Ibid.

24. Ibid., p. 122.

25. Lash, *Eleanor and Franklin*, p. 58.

26. Karita Hummer and Arnold Samuels, "The Influence of the Recent Death of a Spouse on the Parenting Function of the Surviving Parent," in *Childhood Bereavement and*

Its Aftermath, ed. Sol Altschul, (Madison, Conn.: International Universities Press, 1988), pp. 37–63.

27. Mark Bego, *Madonna: Blonde Ambition* (New York: Harmony Books, 1992), p. 10.

28. Richard Rhodes, *A Hole in the World* (New York: Simon & Schuster, 1990).

CHAPTER SIX

1. C. S. Lewis, *Surprised by Joy* (San Diego: Harcourt Brace, 1956), p. 228.

2. Ibid.

3. David Dalton, *James Dean: The Mutant King* (New York: St. Martin's Press, 1974), p. 171.

CHAPTER EIGHT

1. D. J. Enright, *The Oxford Book of Death* (New York: Oxford University Press, 1987), p. 39.

2. Kenneth Silverman, *Edgar A. Poe: Mournful and Never-Ending Remembrance* (New York: HarperCollins, 1991).

3. Ibid., p. 78.

4. Robert Lifton, *The Broken Connection: On Death and the Continuity of Life* (New York: Basic Books, 1983).

5. David Dalton, *James Dean: The Mutant King* (New York: St. Martin's Press, 1974).

6. Jean-Paul Sartre, *The Words* (New York: Vintage Books, 1981), p. 249.

7. Robert G. L. Waite, *The Psychopathic God: Adolf Hitler* (New York: Da Capo Press, 1993), p. 192.

8. Ibid., p. 20.

9. Howard Kushner, *Self-Destruction in the Promised Land* (New Brunswick: Rutgers University Press, 1989), p. 135.

10. Ibid., p. 140.

11. Ibid., p. 142.

12. Ibid.

13. Robert Bruce, "Lincoln and the Riddle of Death," *The Fourth Annual R. Gerald McMurtry Lecture,* (Ft. Wayne, Indiana, 1981).

14. Robert Kastenbaum, *The Psychology of Death* (New York: Springer Publishing, 1992), p. 83.

15. Robert Lifton, *Death in Life* (Chapel Hill: University of North Carolina Press, 1991), p. 130.

16. Ibid., p. 489.

17. Sartre, *The Words*.

18. Ronald Hayman, *Sartre: A Biography* (New York: Carroll & Graf, 1987), p. 272.

19. Lifton, *Death in Life*.

20. Russell Baker, *Growing Up* (New York: Signet, 1982), p. 83.

21. Lifton, *Death in Life,* p. 492.

22. William Helmreich, *Against All Odds* (New York: Simon & Schuster, 1992), p. 225.

23. Ibid.

24. C. S. Lewis, *Surprised by Joy* (San Diego: Harcourt Brace, 1956).

25. Valiska Gregory, *Through the Mickle Woods* (Boston: Little, Brown, 1992).

26. Ibid.

27. Enright, *The Oxford Book of Death,* p. 4.

28. A. N. Wilson, *C. S. Lewis: A Biography* (New York: Fawcett Columbine, 1990), p. 109.

29. Eleanor Roosevelt, *The Autobiography of Eleanor Roosevelt* (New York: Harper & Bros., 1937), p. xix.

30. Mark Bego, *Madonna: Blonde Ambition* (New York: Harmony Books, 1992), p. 189.

31. Hayman, *Sartre,* p. 212.

32. Erik Erikson, "Identity and the Life Cycle," *Psychological Issues,* vol. 1, no. 1, 1959.

CHAPTER NINE

1. C. S. Lewis, *A Grief Observed* (New York: Bantam Books, 1976).

2. William Niederland, "Trauma, Loss, Restoration, and Creativity," in *The Problem of Loss and Mourning,* eds. David Dietrich and Peter Shabad, (Madison, Conn.: International Universities Press, 1989), pp. 61–82.

3. George Pollack, "The Mourning Process, the Creative Process and the Creation," in *The Problem of Loss and Mourning,* eds. David Dietrich and Peter Shabad, pp. 27–59.

4. Ibid., p. 35.

5. Virginia Woolf, "A Sketch of the Past," in *Moments of Being* (San Diego: Harcourt Brace Jovanovich, 1985), p. 72.

6. Ibid.

7. Ibid., p. 80.

8. Ibid., p. 81.

9. Virginia Woolf, *To the Lighthouse* (San Diego: Harcourt Brace, 1927), p. 170.

10. Ibid., p. 206.

11. Ibid., p. 221.

12. Ibid., p. 224.

13. Ibid., p. 309.

14. Lois Akner, *How to Survive the Loss of a Parent* (New York: William Morrow, 1993), p. 8.

15. Judith Wallerstein and Sandra Blakeslee, *Second Chances* (New York: Ticknor & Fields, 1989), p. xiii.

16. A. N. Wilson, *C. S. Lewis: A Biography* (New York: Fawcett Columbine, 1990).

17. Ibid., p. 72.

18. Woolf, *To the Lighthouse,* p. 208.

19. Richard Rhodes, *A Hole in the World* (New York: Simon & Schuster, 1990).

20. Ibid., p. 267.

CHAPTER TEN

1. Tove Ditlevsen, "Self Portrait I," in *The Other Voice,* ed. Joanna Bankier et al., (New York: W. W. Norton, 1976), p. 27.

2. Virginia Woolf, "A Sketch of the Past," in *Moments of Being* (San Diego: Harcourt Brace Jovanovich, 1985), p. 92.

3. John Bowlby, *Charles Darwin: A New Life* (New York: Fawcett Columbine, 1990).

4. Ibid., p. 58.

5. Ibid., p. 245.

6. Ibid., p. 71.

7. Ibid., p. 225.

8. Ibid.

9. A. N. Wilson, *C. S. Lewis: A Biography* (New York: Fawcett Columbine, 1990), p. 110.

10. John Bowlby, *Loss: Sadness and Depression* (New York: Basic Books, 1980), p. 300.

11. David Dalton, *James Dean: The Mutant King* (New York: St. Martin's Press, 1974), p. 160.

12. Howard Kushner, *Self-Destruction in the Promised Land* (New Brunswick: Rutgers University Press, 1989), p. 136.

13. William Styron, *Darkness Visible* (New York: Random House, 1990), p. 56.

14. Ibid., p. 56.

15. Ibid., p. 78.

16. Ibid., p. 84.

17. Ibid., p. 81.

18. Michael Simpson, "Death and Modern Poetry," in *New Meanings of Death*, ed. Herman Feifel, (New York: McGraw-Hill, 1977), p. 327.

19. John Berryman, *The Dream Songs* (New York: Farrar, Straus & Giroux, 1959), p. 81.

20. Ibid., p. 138.

21. Ibid., p. 260.

22. Ibid., p. 332.

23. Bowlby, *Loss*, p. 28.

24. Dalton, *James Dean*, p. 4.

CHAPTER ELEVEN

1. John Bowlby, *Loss: Sadness and Separation* (New York: Basic Books, 1980).

2. Robert Lifton, *The Broken Connection: On Death and the Continuity of Life* (New York: Basic Books, 1983).

3. Mark Bego, *Madonna: Blonde Ambition* (New York: Harmony Books, 1992).

4. Eda LeShan, *Learning to Say Goodbye* (New York: Avon Books, 1976).

5. David Meltzer, ed., *Death: An Anthology of Ancient Texts, Songs, Prayers, and Stories* (San Francisco: North Point Press, 1984), p. 28.

6. Bowlby, *Loss*, p. 134.

7. Robert Lifton, *Death in Life* (Chapel Hill: University of North Carolina Press, 1991), p. 409.

8. Monica McGoldrick, "Echoes from the Past: Helping Families Mourn Their Losses," in *Living Beyond Loss*, eds. Froma Walsh and Monica McGoldrick, (New York: W. W. Norton, 1991), p. 50.

9. *The Complete Grimm's Fairy Tales* (New York: Pantheon Books, 1944), p. 121.

CHAPTER TWELVE

1. Valiska, Gregory, *Through the Mickle Woods* (Boston: Little, Brown, 1992).

2. Ibid.

3. Alexander Nehamas, *Nietzsche: Life as Literature* (Cambridge, Mass.: Harvard University Press, 1985), p. 145.

4. Ibid., p. 155.

5. Sandra Bertman, *Facing Death: Images, Insights, and Interventions* (Washington, D.C.: Hemisphere Publishing Corp., 1991), p. 88.

6. Joseph Lash, *"Life Was Meant to Be Lived": A Centenary Portrait of Eleanor Roosevelt* (New York: W. W. Norton, 1984), p. 49.

7. Ronald Hayman, *Sartre: A Biography* (New York: Carroll & Graf, 1987), p. 353.

8. Helen Moglen, *Charlotte Brontë: The Self Conceived* (Madison, Wisconsin: University of Wisconsin Press, 1984), p. 194.

9. Rebecca Fraser, *The Brontës* (New York: Fawcett Columbine, 1988), p. 405.

10. Robert Lifton, *Death in Life* (Chapel Hill: University of North Carolina Press, 1991).

11. Claudia Jewett, *Helping Children Cope with Separation and Loss* (Boston: The Harvard Common Press, 1982), p. 48.

12. Jean-Paul Sartre, *The Words* (New York: Vintage Books, 1981), p. 87.

13. Robert Tucker, *Stalin as Revolutionary* (New York: W. W. Norton, 1973).

14. Lawrence Langer, "Interpreting Survivor Testimony," in *Writing and the Holocaust,* ed. Berel Lang, (New York: Holmes & Meier, 1988), p. 28.

15. Lifton, *Death in Life.*

16. Sartre, *The Words,* p. 254.

EPILOGUE

1. C. S. Lewis, *A Grief Observed* (New York: Bantam Books, 1963), p. 1.

2. Richard Rhodes, *A Hole in the World* (New York: Simon & Schuster, 1990), p. 226.

References

Adam, Kenneth S. "Loss, Suicide, and Attachment." In *The Place of Attachment in Human Behavior,* edited by Colin Murray Parkes and Joan Stevenson-Hinde, 269–93. New York: Basic Books, 1982.

Adam, Kenneth S., Anthony Bouckoms, and David Streiner. "Parental Loss and Family Stability in Attempted Suicide." *Archives of General Psychiatry,* vol. 39, Sept.: 1081–85, 1982.

Agee, James. *A Death in the Family.* New York: Grosset & Dunlap, 1967.

Akner, Lois F. *How to Survive the Loss of a Parent.* New York: William Morrow, 1993.

Altschul, Sol (ed.). *Childhood Bereavement and Its Aftermath.* Madison, Conn.: International Universities Press, 1988.

———. "Denial and Ego Arrest." *American Psychoanalytic Association Journal,* vol. 16, no. 2: 301–18, 1968.

Altschul, Sol, and Helen Beiser. "The Effect of Early Parent Loss on Future Parenthood." In *Parenthood: A Psychodynamic Perspective,* edited by Rebecca S. Cohen, Betram J. Cohler, and Sidney Weissman, 173–82. New York: Guilford Press, 1980.

Anthony, Sylvia. *The Discovery of Death in Childhood and After*. New York: Basic Books, 1972.

Archibald, Herbert C., Dorothy Bell, Christine Miller, and Read D. Tuddenham. "Bereavement in Childhood and Adult Psychiatric Disturbance." *Psychosomatic Medicine,* vol. 24, no. 4: 343–51, 1962.

Aries, Philippe. *The Hour of Our Death*. New York: Oxford University Press, 1981.

Ashe, Arthur. *Days of Grace*. New York: Alfred A. Knopf, 1993.

Baker, Russell. *Growing Up*. New York: Signet, 1982.

Balk, David. "Death and Adolescent Bereavement: Current Research and Future Directions." *Journal of Adolescent Research,* vol. 6, no. 1: 7–27, 1991.

Bankier, Joanna (ed.). *The Other Voice*. New York: W. W. Norton, 1976.

Barnes, Marion J. "Reactions to the Death of a Mother." In *The Psychoanalytic Study of the Child,* vol. XIX, edited by Ruth S. Eissler, Anna Freud, Heinz Hartmann, and Marianne Kris, 334–57. New York: International Universities Press, 1964.

Barry, Jr., Herbert, Herbert Barry III, and Erich Lindemann. "Dependency in Adult Patients Following Early Maternal Bereavement." *Journal of Nervous and Mental Disease,* 140: 196–206, 1965.

Beck, Aaron, Brij Sethi, and Robert Tuthill. "Childhood Bereavement and Adult Depression." *Archives of General Psychiatry,* vol. 9: 295–302, 1963.

Becker, Diane, and Faith Margolin. "How Surviving Parents Handled Their Young Children's Adaptation to the Crisis of Loss." *American Journal of Orthopsychiatry,* 37: 753–57, 1967.

Becker, Ernest. *The Denial of Death*. New York: The Free Press, 1973.

Bego, Mark. *Madonna: Blonde Ambition*. New York: Harmony Books, 1992.

Benedek, Elissa D. "Children and Disaster: Emerging Issues." *Psychiatric Annals*, vol. 15(1): 168–72, 1985.

Berryman, John. *The Dream Songs*. New York: Farrar, Straus & Giroux, 1959.

Bertman, Sandra. *Facing Death: Images, Insights, and Interventions*. Washington, D.C.: Hemisphere Publishing Corporation, 1991.

Birtchnell, John. "The Possible Consequences of Early Parent Death." *British Journal of Medical Psychology*, 42: 1–12, 1969.

———. "Women Whose Mothers Died in Childhood: An Outcome Study." *Psychological Medicine*, 10: 699–713, 1980.

Bowlby, John. *Charles Darwin: A New Life*. New York: W. W. Norton, 1990.

———. *Loss: Sadness and Depression*. New York: Basic Books, 1980.

———. "The Adolf Meyer Lecture: Childhood Mourning and Its Implications for Psychiatry." *American Journal of Psychiatry*, vol. 118: 481–98, 1961.

Brown, Felix. "Depression and Childhood Bereavement." *Journal of Mental Science*, vol. 107: 754–77, 1961.

Brown, Fredda Herz. "The Impact of Death and Serious Illness on the Family Life Cycle." In *The Changing Family Life Cycle: A Framework for Family Therapy* (2nd edition), edited by Betty Carter and Monica McGoldrick, 457–82. New York: Gardner Press, 1988.

Brown, George W. "Early Loss and Depression." In *The Place of Attachment in Human Behavior*, edited by Colin Murray

Parkes and Joan Stevenson-Hinde, 232–68. New York: Basic Books, 1982.

Brown, G. W., T. O. Harris, and A. Bifulco. "Long-Term Effects of Early Loss of Parent." In *Depression in Young People: Developmental and Clinical Perspectives,* edited by M. Rutter, C. E. Izald, and P. B. Read, 251–96. New York: Guilford Press, 1985.

Bruce, Robert V. "Lincoln and the Riddle of Death." *The Fourth Annual R. Gerald McMurtry Lecture,* Fort Wayne, Indiana, 1981.

Carver, Raymond. *What We Talk about When We Talk about Love.* New York: Vintage Books, 1989.

Cohen, Theodore B., Helen R. Beiser, Henry Seidenberg, Benjamin Garber, and Henry Peter Coppolillo. "The Effects of Parent Loss on the Development of Psychic Structure." *Journal of Preventive Psychiatry,* vol. 2, no. 1: 33–44, 1984.

The Complete Grimm's Fairy Tales. New York: Pantheon Books, 1944.

Cook, Alice Skinner, and Dworkin, Daniel S. *Helping the Bereaved.* New York: Basic Books, 1992.

Crenshaw, David A. *Bereavement.* New York: Continuum Publishing Co., 1990.

Crook, Nora. *Kipling's Myths of Love and Death.* New York: St. Martin's Press, 1989.

Crook, Thomas, and John Eliot. "Parental Death During Childhood and Adult Depression: A Critical Review of the Literature." *Psychological Bulletin,* vol. 87, no. 2: 252–59, 1980.

Dalton, David. *James Dean: The Mutant King.* New York: St. Martin's Press, 1974.

Desmond, Adrian, and James Moore. *Darwin: The Life of a Tormented Evolutionist.* New York: Time Warner Books, 1991.

Deutsch, Helene. "Absence of Grief." *Psychoanalytic Quarterly,* vol. 6: 12–22, 1937.

Dietrich, David R., and Peter C. Shabad. *The Problem of Loss and Mourning.* Madison, Conn.: International Universities Press, 1989.

Duffy, Bruce. "Feeling Something: When a Father Dies." *Harper's Magazine,* 70–78, June 1990.

Dumas, Alexandre. *My Memoirs,* translated by A. Craig Bell. Westport, Conn.: Greenwood Press, 1961.

Dunn, Robert, and Donna Morrish-Vidners. "The Psychological and Social Experience of Suicide Survivors." *Omega,* vol. 18(3): 175–215, 1987–88.

Eisenstadt, Marvin, Andre Haynal, Pierre Rentchnick, and Pierre Senarclens. *Parental Loss and Achievement.* Madison, Conn.: International Universities Press, 1989.

Enright, D. J. (ed.). *The Oxford Book of Death.* Oxford: Oxford University Press, 1987.

Esman, Aaron. "Fathers and Adolescent Sons." In *Father and Child: Development and Clinical Perspectives,* edited by Stanley H. Cath, Alan R. Gurwitt, and John Munder Ross. Boston: Little, Brown and Company, 1982.

Feifel, Herman. *New Meanings of Death.* New York: McGraw-Hill, 1977.

Feinstein, David, and Peg Elliott May. *Mortal Acts.* San Francisco: HarperCollins, 1993.

Formanek, Ruth. "When Children Ask about Death." *Elementary School Journal,* vol. 75, no. 2: 92–97, 1974.

Fraser, Rebecca. *The Brontës.* New York: Fawcett Columbine, 1988.

Furman, Erna. *A Child's Parent Dies.* New Haven: Yale University Press, 1974.

———. "Children's Patterns in Mourning the Death of a

Loved One." In *Issues in Comprehensive Pediatric Nursing: Childhood and Death*, edited by Hannelore Wass and Charles A. Corr, 185–203. Washington, D.C.: Hemisphere Publishing Corporation, 1985.

Gregory, Valiska. *Through the Mickle Woods*. Boston: Little, Brown, 1992.

Grollman, Earl A. *Talking About Death*. Boston: Beacon Press, 1990.

Grudin, Robert. *Time and the Art of Living*. New York: Ticknor & Fields, 1982.

Harris, Maxine. *Down from the Pedestal*. New York: Doubleday, 1994.

Harris, Tirril O., George W. Brown, and Antonia T. Bifulco. "Depression and Situational Helplessness/Mastery in a Sample Selected to Study Childhood Parental Loss." *Journal of Affective Disorders*, vol. 20(1): 27–41, 1990.

———. "Loss of Parent in Childhood and Adult Psychiatric Disorder: The Role of Adequate Parental Care." *Psychological Medicine*, 16: 641–59, 1986.

———. "Loss of Parent in Childhood and Adult Psychiatric Disorder: The Role of Social Class Position and Premarital Pregnancy." *Psychological Medicine*, 17: 163–83, 1987.

Hayman, Ronald. *Sartre: A Biography*. New York: Carroll & Graf, 1987.

Helmreich, William B. *Against All Odds*. New York: Simon & Schuster, 1992.

Henderson, Joseph L., and Maud Oakes. *The Wisdom of the Serpent*. Princeton, New Jersey: Princeton University Press, 1990.

Hilgard, Josephine R., Martha F. Newman, and Fern Fisk. "Strength of Adult Ego Following Childhood Bereavement." *American Journal of Orthopsychiatry*, 30 Oct. 788–98, 1960.

Jacobson, Edith. "The Return of the Lost Parent." In *Drives*,

Affects, Behavior, edited by Max Schur, 193–211. New York: International Universities Press, Inc., 1965.

Jewett, Claudia. *Helping Children Cope With Separation and Loss.* Harvard, Mass.: Harvard Common Press, 1982.

Kastenbaum, Robert. *The Psychology of Death.* New York: Springer Publishing Co., 1992.

Kestenberg, Judith S. "Notes on Parenthood as a Developmental Phase, With Special Consideration of the Roots of Fatherhood." In *Clinical Psychoanalysis,* vol. III, edited by Shelley Orgel and Bernard D. Fine, 199–234. New York: Jason Aronson, 1981.

Krementz, Jill. *How It Feels When a Parent Dies.* New York: Alfred A. Knopf, 1993.

Krueger, David W. "Childhood Parent Loss: Developmental Impact and Adult Psychopathology." *American Journal of Psychotherapy,* vol. XXXVII, no. 4: 582–93, 1983.

Kushner, Howard I. *Self-Destruction in the Promised Land.* New Brunswick: Rutgers University Press, 1989.

Lang, Berel (ed.). *Writing and the Holocaust.* New York: Holmes & Meier, 1988.

Lash, Joseph P. *Eleanor and Franklin.* New York: W. W. Norton, 1971.

———. *"Life Was Meant to Be Lived": A Centenary Portrait of Eleanor Roosevelt.* New York: W. W. Norton, 1984.

LeShan, Eda. *Learning to Say Goodbye.* New York: Avon Books, 1976.

Lewis, C. S. *A Grief Observed.* New York: Bantam Books, 1976.

———. *The Last Battle.* New York: Collier Books, 1956.

———. *Surprised by Joy.* San Diego: Harcourt Brace, 1956.

Lifton, Robert Jay. *The Broken Connection: On Death and the Continuity of Life.* New York: Basic Books, 1983.

————. *Death in Life.* Chapel Hill: University of North Carolina Press, 1991.

————. *History and Human Survival.* New York: Random House, 1970.

Masterman, Sharon Hale, and Redmond Reams. "Support Groups for Bereaved Preschool and School-Aged Children." *American Journal of Orthopsychiatry,* vol. 58(4): 562–70, 1988.

Meltzer, David, (ed.). *Death: An Anthology of Ancient Texts, Songs, Prayers, and Stories.* San Francisco: North Point Press, 1984.

Miller, Alice. *The Untouched Key.* New York: Anchor Books, 1990.

Moglen, Helene. *Charlotte Brontë: The Self Conceived.* Madison, Wisconsin: University of Wisconsin Press, 1984.

Nehamas, Alexander. *Nietzsche: Life as Literature.* Cambridge, Mass.: Harvard University Press, 1985.

Nietzsche, Friedrich. *Untimely Meditations.* Cambridge: Cambridge University Press, 1983.

Osterweis, Marian, Frederic Solomon, and Morris Green, (eds.). *Bereavement: Reactions, Consequences, and Care.* Washington, D.C.: National Academy Press, 1984.

Palombo, Joseph. "Parent Loss and Childhood Bereavement: Some Theoretical Considerations." *Clinical Social Work Training,* vol. 9, no. 1: 3–33, 1981.

Parkes, Colin Murray. *Bereavement: Studies of Grief in Adult Life.* Middlesex, England: Penguin Books, Ltd., 1975.

————. "The First Year of Bereavement: A Longitudinal Study of the Reaction of London Widows to the Death of Their Husbands." *Psychiatry,* vol. 33: 444–67, 1970.

Pletsch, Carl. *Young Nietzsche.* New York: The Free Press, 1991.

Pollock, George H. "Childhood Parent and Sibling Loss in Adult Patients." *Archives of General Psychiatry*, 7: 295–305, 1962.

———. "Mourning and Adaptation." *International Journal of Psycho-Analysis*, vol. 42: 341–61, 1961.

———. "Mourning and Memorialization Through Music." In *The Annual of Psychoanalysis*, vol. III, edited by John E. Gedo et al., 423–36. New York: International Universities Press, Inc. 1976.

———. "Process and Affect: Mourning and Grief." *International Journal of Psycho-Analysis*, vol. 59: 255–76, 1978.

Raphael, Beverly. *The Anatomy of Bereavement*. New York: Basic Books, 1983.

———. "The Young Child and the Death of a Parent." In *The Place of Attachment in Human Behavior*, edited by Colin Murray Parkes and Joan Stevenson-Hinde, 131–50. New York: Basic Books, 1982.

Rhodes, Richard. *A Hole in the World*. New York: Simon & Schuster, 1990.

Rich, Adrienne. "Jane Eyre: The Temptations of a Motherless Woman." *Ms. Magazine*, October 1973: 68ff.

Rioch, Margaret. "Personal Perspective." In *Models of Achievement: Reflections of Eminent Women in Psychology*, edited by Agnes N. O'Connell and Nancy Felipe Russo, 173–86. New York: Columbia University Press, 1983.

Roosevelt, Eleanor. *The Autobiography of Eleanor Roosevelt*. New York: Harper & Brothers, 1937.

Rosenblatt, Paul, and Carol Elde. "Shared Reminiscence About a Deceased Parent: Implications for Grief Education and Grief Counseling." *Family Relations*, vol. 39: 206–10, 1990.

Rutler, Michael. *Maternal Deprivation Reassessed*. Middlesex, England: Penguin Books, Ltd., 1981.

Sameroff, Arnold J., and Robert N. Emde, (eds.). *Relationship*

Disturbances in Early Childhood. New York: Basic Books, 1989.

Sartre, Jean-Paul. *The Words.* New York: Vintage Books, 1981.

Scharl, Adele E. "Regression and Restitution in Object Loss: Clinical Observations." In *The Psychoanalytic Study of the Child,* vol. XVI: 471–80, 1961.

Schowalter, John E., Paul R. Patterson, Margot Tallmer, Austin H. Kutscher, Stephen V. Gullo, and David Peretz, (eds.). *The Child and Death.* New York: Columbia University Press, 1983.

Sekaer, Christina, and Sheri Katz. "On the Concept of Mourning in Childhood." *Psychoanalytic Study of the Child,* vol. XII: 287–92, 1986.

Siggins, Lorraine D. "Mourning: A Critical Survey of the Literature." *International Journal of Psycho-Analysis,* 47, no. 1: 14–25, 1966.

Silverman, Kenneth. *Edgar A. Poe: Mournful and Never-Ending Remembrance.* New York: HarperCollins, 1991.

Stastny, Peter, Deborah Perlick, Lynne Zeavin, Maureen Empfield, and Meredith Mayer. "Early Parental Absence as an Indicator of Course and Outcome in Chronic Schizophrenia." *American Journal of Psychiatry,* 141(2): 294–96, 1984.

Styron, William. *Darkness Visible.* New York: Random House, 1990.

Taylor, Shelley E. *Positive Illusions.* New York: Basic Books, 1989.

Tennant, Christopher, Paul Bebbington, and Jane Hurry. "Parental Death in Childhood and Risk of Adult Depressive Disorders: A Review." *Psychological Medicine,* 10: 289–299, 1980.

Tucker, Robert G. *Stalin as Revolutionary.* New York: W. W. Norton, 1973.

Ullmann, Liv. *Changing.* New York: Alfred A. Knopf, 1977.

Vanderbilt, Gloria. *Once Upon a Time.* New York: Ballantine Books, 1985.

Viorst, Judith. *Necessary Losses.* New York: Ballantine Books, 1986.

Volkan, Vamik D., and Elizabeth Zintl. *Life After Loss.* New York: Charles Scribner's Sons, 1993.

Waelder, Robert. "Trauma and the Variety of Extraordinary Challenges." In *Psychic Trauma,* edited by Sidney S. Furst, 221–34. New York: Basic Books, 1967.

Waite, Robert G. L. *The Psychopathic God: Adolf Hitler.* New York: Da Capo Press, 1993.

Wallerstein, Judith S., and Sandra Blakeslee. *Second Chances.* New York: Ticknor & Fields, 1989.

Walsh, Froma, and Monica McGoldrick, (eds.). *Living Beyond Loss.* New York: W. W. Norton, 1991.

Webb, Nancy Boyd (ed.). *Helping Bereaved Children.* New York: The Guilford Press, 1993.

Wilson, A. N. *C. S. Lewis: A Biography.* New York: Fawcett Columbine, 1990.

Winnicott, D. W. *Deprivation and Delinquency.* London: Tavistock/Routledge, 1990.

Wolfenstein, Martha. "Effects on Adults of Object Loss in the First Five Years." *Journal of the American Psychoanalytic Association,* vol. 24, no. 3: 659–68, 1976.

———. "How Is Mourning Possible?" *Psychoanalytic Study of the Child,* vol. XXI: 93–122, 1966.

———. "The Image of the Lost Parent." *Psychoanalytic Study of the Child,* vol. XXVIII: 433–56, 1973.

———. "Loss, Rage, and Repetition." *Psychoanalytic Study of the Child,* vol. XXIV: 432–60, 1969.

Woolf, Virginia. *Moments of Being.* San Diego: Harcourt Brace Jovanovich, 1985.

————. *To the Lighthouse.* San Diego: Harcourt Brace, 1927.

Wortman, Camille, and Roxane Cohen Silver. "The Myths of Coping With Loss." *Journal of Consulting and Clinical Psychology,* vol. 57, no. 3: 349–57, 1989.

INDEX

seeing only love side of, 151–59

M

Madonna, 124–25, 210, 273
Mantle, Mickey, 198
Marriage
  and anxiety, 261–62
  of child, 183–85
  and creating self, 137–38
  and repair, 240
  and tension between love and loss, 143–44, 148–49, 153–55, 156–57, 158–59, 161–62, 167
Marx, Karl, 293
Medical crisis, unexpected, 22, 24
Memories, 306–7
Mentors, 112–13, 116, 133–34, 176, 177
Models
  creating self without, 114–15
  parenting without, 173–78
  search for, 110–13
Moore, Mrs., 234–35
Mortality, 197–201
"Mortality" (poem), 196
Mother/daughter companionship, 72–73
Motherless Daughters, xviii
Mother loss, xviii, xix
"Moving Wall, The," 283
Murder, 22
Mythologies, 82–106
  destructive, 245, 262–69

idiosyncratic, 103–6
  about lost parent, 84–90
  about relationship that might have been, 96–106
  about self, 90–96

N

Neglectful surviving parent, 51
Negligent surviving parent, 58–64
Nietzsche, Friedrich, 83, 112–14, 290–91, 304–5

O

Objects for connection, 275–76
On the Waterfront (movie), 94
Order, loss of, 7, 8
Out of control response, 114, 136–39
Overwhelmed and panicked response, 114, 128–36
Owens, Mary, 257

P

Panic
  and creating self, 128–36
  and relationships, 165–67
Parenting problems, 169–89
  applying lessons learned in past, 185–87
  and childlessness by choice, 170–73